THE ART OF PHOTOSHOP
CS2 Edition

by Daniel Giordan

Sams Publishing, 800 East 96th Street, Indianapolis, Indiana 46240 USA

THE ART OF PHOTOSHOP
CS2 Edition

International Standard Book Number: 0-672-32810-0

Library of Congress Catalog Card Number: 2005902138

Printed in the United States of America

First Printing: September 2005

08   07   06   05   4   3   2   1

Trademarks

Warning and Disclaimer

Acquisitions Editor
Betsy Brown

Development Editor
Alice Martina Smith

Technical Editor
Alan Hamill
Lisa Lee
Mara Zebest

Indexer
Lisa Wilson

Interior Design
David Giordan
Cindy Lounsbery

Interior Layout
Eric S. Miller

Cover Design
David Giordan
Cindy Lounsbery

CONTENTS AT A GLANCE

Preface		xiv
Introduction		xvii
It's Not What It Is, It's How It Feels		1
Gallery of Images		5

Part One   Image Handling

Chapter 1   Making Complex Selections: *Tomb of the Capulets*   46

Chapter 2   Using Quickmask to Make Selections: *Sanguine Expectations*   58

Chapter 3   Transforming Layers: *Absence of Voice*   70

Part Two   Image Editing

Chapter 4   Optimizing Images: *Impedance*   84

Chapter 5   Enhancing Image Focus: *Requiem*   96

Chapter 6   Mastering Curves: *Numerical Uncertainty*   108

Chapter 7   Mastering Color Correction Techniques: *Oblique Ascension*   122

Chapter 8   Making Hue and Saturation Adjustments: *Gesture*   134

Chapter 9   Working with Adjustment Layers: *The Mystery of Folded Sleep*   146

Part Three   Montage

Chapter 10   Silhouetting with the Extract Filter: *Occupation*   160

Chapter 11   Working with Layer Masks: *Dark with Excessive Bright*   170

Chapter 12   Using the Clone Stamp Tool: *The Space Between*   182

Chapter 13   Understanding the Blending Modes: *Ominous Botanicus*   192

Part Four   Special Effects

Chapter 14   Painting and Custom Brushes: *Trilogy*   210

Chapter 15   Mastering the Distort Filters: *Tree House*   232

Chapter 16   Making Photoshop Patterns: *Earthly Delights*   250

Chapter 17   Using Gradients and Gradient Maps: *FreeFall*   260

Chapter 18   Using the Liquify Filter: *Birch Trees*   270

Chapter 19   Working with Lighting Effects: *On the Edge*   282

Index   292

TABLE OF CONTENTS

Preface   xiv

Introduction   xvii

It's Not What It Is, It's How It Feels   1

Gallery of Images   5

Part One   **Image Handling**

Chapter 1   Building Complex Selections
            Tomb of the Capulets   46

            Making Complex Selections   48
            Selecting with Color Range   50
            Fine-Tuning Selections   52
            Building the Image: *Tomb of the Capulets*   54
            Image Design Log   56

Chapter 2   Using Quick Mask Mode to Make Selections
            Sanguine Expectations   58

            Making Selections with Quick Mask   60
            Advanced Quick Mask   62
            Using Filters to Add Patterns and Distortion 64
            Building the Image: *Sanguine Expectations*   66
            Image Design Log   68

Chapter 3   Transforming Layers
            Absence of Voice   70

            Transforming Layers And Selections   72
            Breaking Down the Transform Options   74
            Transform Options and Shortcuts   76
            Building the Image: *Absence of Voice*   78
            Image Design Log   80

Part Two   **Image Editing**

Chapter 4   Optimizing Images
            Impedence   84

            Optimizing the Tonal Range   86
            The Info Palette   88
            Tracking Multiple Pixel Values   90
            Building the Image: *Impedance*   92
            Image Design Log   94

Chapter 5   Enhancing Image Focus
            Requiem   96

            Enhancing Image Focus   98
            Image Focus Strategies   100
            It's About Focus, Not Sharpness   102
            Building the Image: *Requiem*   104
            Image Design Log   106

Chapter 6　Mastering Curves
　　　　　　Numerical Uncertainty　108
　Anatomy of a Curve　110
　Basic Curve Techniques　112
　Other Curve Shapes　114
　Color Correcting with Curves　116
　Building the Image: *Numerical Uncertainty*　118
　Image Design Log　120

Chapter 7　Mastering Color Correction Techniques
　　　　　　Oblique Ascension　122
　Correcting Image Color　124
　Correcting Color Casts　126
　Using Color Controls to Optimize Grayscale　128
　Building the Image: *Oblique Ascension*　130
　Image Design Log　132

Chapter 8　Making Hue and Saturation Adjustments
　　　　　　Gesture　134
　Hue/Saturation and HSB Color　136
　Localized Hue/Saturation Techniques　138
　Hue/Saturation Strategies　140
　Building the Image: *Gesture*　142
　Image Design Log　144

Chapter 9　Working with Adjustment Layers
　　　　　　The Mystery of Folded Sleep　146
　Using Adjustment Layers　148
　Adjustment Layer Strategies　150

　Building the Image: *The Mystery of Folded Sleep*　154
　Image Design Log　156

Part Three　Montage

Chapter 10　Silhouetting with the Extract Filter
　　　　　　Occupation　160
　Silhouetting Objects　162
　Advanced Extraction Techniques　164
　Building the Image: *Occupation*　166
　Image Design Log　168

Chapter 11　Working with Layer Masks
　　　　　　Dark with Excessive Bright　170
　Mastering Layer Masks　172
　Advanced Layer Masking and Related Techniques　174
　Exploring the Apply Image and Calculations Commands　176
　Building the Image: *Dark with Excessive Bright*　178
　Image Design Log　180

Chapter 12　Using the Clone Stamp Tool
　　　　　　The Space Between　182
　The Clone Stamp Tool　184
　Clone Stamp Techniques　186
　Building the Image: *The Space Between*　188
　Image Design Log　190

Chapter 13　Understanding the Blending Modes
　　　　　　Ominous Botanicus　192
　Blending Modes　194

Understanding the Blending Mode Categories   196
Working with Blending Modes   202
Building the Image: *Ominous Botanicus*   204
Image Design Log   206

Part Four   Special Effects

Chapter 14   Painting and Custom Brushes
               Trilogy   210
Photoshop Painting Basics   212
Building a Custom Brush   214
Why Build a Custom Brush?   218
Painting Strategies: Tinting a B&W image   220
Painting Strategies: Painting a Textured Mask   222
Painting Strategies: Making Brushes from Photos   224
Painting Strategies: Cloning with Scatter   226
Building the Image: *Trilogy*   228
Image Design Log   230

Chapter 15   Mastering the Distort Filters
               Tree House   232
Understanding the Distort Filters   234
The Texture and Warp Filters   236
The Shear and Wave Filters   240
Mastering the Displace Filter   242
Building the Image: *Tree House*   246
Image Design Log   248

Chapter 16   Making Photoshop Patterns
               Earthly Delights   250
Introduction to Photoshop Patterns   252
Pattern Strategies   254
Building the Image: *Earthly Delights*   256
Image Design Log   258

Chapter 17   Using Gradients and Gradient Maps
               FreeFall   260
Creating and Using Gradients   262
Gradient Special Effects   264
Building the Image: *FreeFall*   266
Image Design Log   268

Chapter 18   Using the Liquify Filter
               Birch Trees   270
Introduction to Liquify   272
Using Channels as Liquify Masks   274
Working with the Liquify Mesh   276
Building the Image: *Birch Trees*   278
Image Design Log   280

Chapter 19   Working with Lighting Effects
               On the Edge   282
Introduction to Lighting Effects   284
Lighting Effects Strategies   286
Building the Image: *On the Edge*   288
Image Design Log   290

Index   292

LIST OF STEP-BY-STEP INSTRUCTIONS

Making Color Range Selections	**51**	Using Extract to Delete a Background	**164**
Creating a Basic Quickmask Selection	**62**	Creating a Type-Based Layer Mask	**174**
Optimizing Tonal Range	**91**	Using the Clone Stamp Tool	**186**
Controlling Image Focus with Multiple Layers	**101**	Saving Custom Brushes	**217**
Creating an "S" Curve	**113**	Creating a Custom Texture for the Glass Filter	**237**
Using Color Balance	**126**	Creating a Seamless Tile with the Shear Filter	**239**
Using Replace Color	**128**	Creating a Pattern	**254**
Adjusting Hue and Saturation	**138**	Creating a Custom Gradient	**264**
Editing A Color Range With Hue/Saturation	**141**	Reusing the Liquify Mesh	**276**
Creating Adjustment Layer Clipping Masks	**153**	Creating Embossed Text with Lighting Effects	**286**

ABOUT THE AUTHOR

Daniel Giordan is an artist and author who has shown his work in galleries and museums throughout the United States. He began his career as a painter, gradually transitioning to photography and digital imaging as the technology matured. As computers became more powerful, and digital photography advanced, Giordan fully embraced the new medium.

He has been awarded fellowships and awards from prominent institutions such as Yale University and The Museum of Fine Arts in Boston. In addition, his work resides in numerous private collections.

Giordan holds a masters degree in Fine Arts from The Milton Avery Graduate School of the Arts at Bard College, and an undergraduate degree in Fine Arts from the Museum School in Boston.

He began writing computer books in 1994 with the publication of *Kai's Magic Toolbox* (published by Hayden Books). Other releases have included *Using Photoshop* 5 (published by Que), *How to Use Photoshop 5.5, 6.0, 7.0, and CS* (all published by Sams Publishing), and *Dynamic Photoshop* (published by MIS Press/M&T Books). *The Art of Photoshop* is his ninth book.

Giordan has also written for the leading magazines in his field; he is a regular contributor to *Adobe Magazine*, *Publish*, *Digital Camera Magazine*, and *Dynamic Graphics Magazine*. He currently works as the Design Director for AOL Web Properties, coordinating the design for Netscape.com, AIM Today, and other Time-Warner endeavors.

Dan welcomes email from readers; write to him at dgiordan@mac.com.

DEDICATION

This book is for my father.

ACKNOWLEDGEMENTS

As you hold this book, it's very difficult if not impossible to understand the thousands of hours that went into its creation. Dozens of people must work to bring a book into existence, and they all are extremely important. I assure you that the best efforts of author and designer can be derailed by sloppy development, an unreasonable schedule, or indiscriminate budget reductions. Coming into this project, these were the primary fears that kept me up nights.

To my absolute delight, everyone involved with this book has shown an incredible level of commitment and dedication. We have all extended ourselves in some way, through time, budget, attention to families, and perhaps even justification to superiors in our efforts to bring this book in for a landing. It was a team effort, and I'm proud of what we've accomplished. As a result, this book stands out in a crowded field of Adobe Photoshop books as a unique product and a labor of love.

The first order of thanks go to Mark Taber, the Associate Publisher at Sams, who has shown a high level of commitment in making this happen. Mark approached me through Betsy Brown with the idea of doing an advanced Photoshop book, and has consistently been receptive to new ideas and concepts where others in similar positions were preemptive in their thought process. He understood early on what we were trying to accomplish and has cleared the necessary obstacles to make it happen.

Betsy Brown and Alice Martina Smith were central to the production team as the book's acquisition and development editors. This is my fourth project with them, and my respect and admiration continues to grow with each project. While putting this book together, I was continually amazed and grateful for their individual and collective dedication, focus, and patience in dealing with a bunch of philosophical artsy types like Dave, Cindy, and myself.

Even though Betsy didn't completely understand why contract proofing was essential for each gallery image, or why a 175-line screen made a difference, she respected our skills and the high standards we set, working hard to ensure that we did things the right way. This was true day in and day out; throughout the life of the project she worked in the trenches to maintain overall project integrity.

While Betsy worked behind the scenes, Alice worked directly with author and designers to encourage creativity while maintaining editorial consistency and professional publishing standards. The duration of our three-way conference calls is the stuff of legend, as we all came together to copyfit, design, and polish the final result. She held her ground editorially when she had to, but indulged the ideas and brainstorming that swirled about her head each time we got together.

Thanks also go to the rest of the Sams Publishing team: to Dan Uhrig for making our printing dreams come true, to Alan Hamill, Lisa Lee, and Mara Zebest for their technical editing expertise, and anyone else I may have missed. Sams did an outstanding job supporting this project, and I'm grateful.

On the creative side, I don't know where to start in thanking my brother, Dave Giordan, and his wife, Cindy Lounsbery, for their collaboration and support. Dave and Cindy led the layout and graphic design efforts in this project and seem to have made every decision flawlessly, crafting a layout that is distinctive and supportive of the text and images. We worked as a team, listened to each other, and collectively raised the bar on what this project would eventually become. Someday in the distant future, I hope we can do this again (please don't hit me).

As always, my final and most heartfelt thanks go to my wife and son. Yes, the editors and designers made sacrifices along the way, but no one sacrificed more than Barb and Josh, who had to occupy themselves for eight-plus months while Dad was working. Even when I was there, I was often tired or distracted as I obsessed on this or that detail. I'm grateful for your patience, and thank God for you both.

Thanks Josh, for letting Dad work, even though it was hard sometimes. If I could, I'd buy you a pony.

Thank you Barb, for holding things together while I was busy and distracted. For pushing me to sleep and take care of myself (which I did perhaps half the time). Thank you for patiently waiting for me to finish and for understanding how important this project was to me. Kiss you, Angel.

WE WANT TO HEAR FROM YOU!

As the reader of this book, you are our most important critic and commentator. We value your opinion and want to know what we're doing right, what we could do better, what areas you'd like to see us publish in, and any other words of wisdom you're willing to pass our way.

You can email or write me directly to let me know what you did or didn't like about this book—as well as what we can do to make our books stronger.

Please note that I cannot help you with technical problems related to the topic of this book, and that due to the high volume of mail I receive, I might not be able to reply to every message.

When you write, please be sure to include this book's title and author as well as your name and phone or fax number. I will carefully review your comments and share them with the author and editors who worked on the book.

Email: graphics@samspublishing.com
Mail: Mark Taber
        Sams Publishing
        800 East 96th Street
        Indianapolis, IN 46240 USA

PREFACE

Welcome to a book that has been a labor of love for all who have worked on it. To explain what this book is about, I felt that it was important to elaborate a bit on how it came together and why it stands out from the dozens of other Photoshop books currently on the market.

From Dream to Reality

When I started writing computer books in 1994, I had always wanted to write a book like the one you're holding now—one that is artistic, visual, and produced with the highest possible production values.

When I would approach publishers with my ideas, they would nod that such a product would be nice but was impractical to produce; it didn't fit in with their business model of fast turnaround and straightforward information. Publishers would tell me that it was too much work, that their in-house design teams were built for speed rather than nuance, that the market just wanted how-to books, that readers didn't care about design quality. As a result of this input, I wrote "how-to" books, "tips and tricks," and commentary, all with a decidedly technical twist. But in the back of my head, I knew that an artistic computer book would do well if given the chance.

The problem in bringing this book to reality went far beyond simply overcoming an established business model. Had publishers been receptive, I would have still been faced with the task of lining up resources for book layout and design, doing the organization and writing, and getting the editors on the publisher's side to establish a level of commitment that would hold up to the efforts of the design and writing.

Things began to move forward when I started discussing book projects with my brother, David, and his wife, Cindy, a husband/wife design team with over 40 combined years of experience in art, design, and graphics. They had done other book design projects, and we began talking about how we could put together a Photoshop book for designers—one that would resonate on a visual and artistic level while still delivering valuable information about image design and Photoshop techniques.

We floated various project ideas up to a few publishers, but we were never able to line up the right constellation of subject, resources, and budget approval. Three years went by, and still we collaborated and exchanged ideas on how to create a book that would bridge the gap between technical information and an aesthetic approach.

In the meantime (and in addition to maintaining my career as an artist and Web designer), I began an outstanding business relationship with Sams Publishing, a division of Pearson Education. I worked on the *How to Use* series, producing books on Photoshop 5.5, 6, 7, CS, and CS2. Although these books were series-based and very rigid in their parameters, their visual approach to the subject did allow me to select some sample images that contributed substantially to the overall aesthetic of the book.

In the fall of 2000, Betsy Brown, the Acquisitions Editor at Sams, called to say that her publisher, Mark Taber, was looking for a high-end

Photoshop book that would target an advanced audience. She wanted me to provide a project outline that she could submit for board approval.

To be honest, I took the inquiry with a grain of salt. I'd been approached like this at least a dozen times by companies such as Adobe Press and New Riders, who were well established in graphic design publishing. I had had numerous meetings at trade shows, over dinner, and on the phone. We would spin ideas and options, laying out creative book projects that would stand out and resonate with a design audience. In each case, I found myself a few months older and a bit more jaded as budgets, negotiations, or publishing reorgs derailed the proposed project.

It just so happened that a week or so after Betsy's inquiry, I got together with my brother to go to the U.S. Open tennis championships in New York. Alone in the car as we drove the two hours from Connecticut, we began to lay the foundation for this book. As the ideas bounced back and forth, the old excitement returned about what was possible if we were given the chance. I also knew that the resources were falling into place: With Dave and Cindy on board, I had a talented and experienced design team; I also had a solid relationship with Sams, who appeared to be behind the project.

To me, that was the big question: How dedicated was Sams to the project? It's one thing to ask for a designer-targeted book. It's another to allocate budget to high-end printing costs and materials, not to mention the longer development times and resource requirements. Thus, as I submitted the proposal and sample table of contents to Betsy, I discussed these factors, emphasizing that if we were going to do this, we needed to do it right.

A few months later, we had all the necessary approvals, and Mark Taber had demonstrated a solid commitment to the project. A workable budget was in place, we lined up a top-notch development editor, and the book outline was refined and polished. It was March 2001, and we were off to the races. The project was born.

Why This Book Is Different

Anyone can throw a big budget at a project and produce a beautiful product. The difference between this book and the numerous other Photoshop books on the market is that it considers the creative process at the same time it outlines how to use a brush or specific technique.

To move from tools to aesthetics, this book features a suite of images that stand on their own as photographic works of art. They're not samples, stock photography, or an amalgam of other people's work. The suite of images is presented in the first section of the book, independent of the instructional text or other commentary.

The second section is composed of 19 chapters, each of which features a single image from the suite. Early on, I knew that I wanted to build the majority of the book around two-page spreads rather than single pages or even chapters. Each spread would be a self-contained capsule or subset of information. To accomplish this design goal, we had to construct a format that would be repeatable across these 19 chapters. After a ton of back-and-forth collaboration, we settled on the format you see in this book: We begin with an overview of the feature image, outline the basic characteristics of the tool being profiled, discuss advanced techniques and ideas, and present an overview of how each image was constructed, along with a detailed design log.

Each chapter comments on the image aesthetics, explains how to use a specific Photoshop tool or technique, and describes the exact process used to create the image. The layout takes full advantage of the high-quality printing and larger page size by featuring tons of image examples, decorative designs, and a creative use of color.

Another difference is that this book is written for an intermediate to advanced user. It does not attempt to cover every nook and cranny of the Photoshop software, and it assumes a certain familiarity with the application. It does not stop in midsentence to explain how to copy and paste or duplicate a layer. Again, this book does not attempt to replace the manual or a 600-page Photoshop supermanual; it simply documents how Photoshop plays a central role in the creation of a series of images.

INTRODUCTION TO
THE ART OF PHOTOSHOP

The Art of Photoshop chronicles Photoshop's role in the creative development of a suite of images.

Why do we buy books on computer design? What are our expectations and what do we think these books will do for us? Do we think that the book will make us a better designer? Do we just want to know how to set the preferences for a particular tool or feature? Perhaps we just want to know how to achieve a certain effect, such as making a drop shadow or a texture. Do we want to be inspired, informed, or entertained—and in what order?

I considered all these questions as we laid the groundwork for the *Art of Photoshop.* What did we want to achieve and communicate? (Okay, okay, I'll stop with the questions and start giving you some answers.) The goal in producing the *Art of Photoshop* was to show how Photoshop facilitates the creative process, creating a more expressive approach to photography and digital imaging.

It was also important to emphasize that art is not a step-by-step instructional process, in which you go through the steps and create a special effect. Although I do not want to engage in a debate about what art is or is not, I'm pretty confident in stating that art is the concise expression of a particular idea, emotion, or subject. If the image is good and the message is focused, the creative process may be brief. Art history is full of examples in which someone found an object or executed a few brush strokes, and the work was done. It's not the time invested or the complexity that makes the art....

I wanted to convey some of this truth in the *Art of Photoshop.* Thus, I started with my own photography, which ranged from solid and competent to somewhat marginal. I gathered a finite set of images that would serve as the raw material for 19 final designs. The result is a book in which the image quality is of the highest caliber, and every image and example was captured by the author/artist. *The Art of Photoshop* maintains a consistency of vision and approach to create a visually cohesive presentation.

The presentation is important because it gives rise to the next logical question: How did you do that? In explaining how the designs were completed, I give you a glimpse of the process and personal aesthetic of the artist. This information is presented for illustration and encouragement, not for emulation. The works in this book are a personal vision; I don't expect that other artists will rush to copy it. In this respect, the spotlight is on the myriad of decisions the author made throughout the creative process.

Last but not least, this book provides concise instruction on how Photoshop works. It assumes an intermediate-to-advanced skill level as it delves into the specific features and controls used in the design process. The expectation is that you know the basics and want to push things further. Thus I left the basic instruction to the manual-based books and jumped right to the interesting and obscure.

This book will certainly teach you how to open up some of Photoshop's complexities, making you a better technician and craftsperson. If that is all you desire, you will find it here. If you're also looking to develop a personal aesthetic and artistic approach, you will find that here as well. All wrapped up in a beautiful package that is as delightful to look at as it is to read.

Daniel Giordan
Author | Artist

xx

IT'S NOT WHAT IT IS, IT'S HOW IT FEELS

THOUGHTS ON DIGITAL IMAGING

When you look at a picture, your mind instantly scrambles to organize the shapes, colors, and linear elements into recognizable objects. What is it? Is it a face, a horse, a landscape? This basic cognitive effort starts at birth, with a baby's ability to recognize the faces of those around him, especially his mother. By the time we're just a few years old, we can quickly read and categorize a vast inventory of visual objects.

This ability to inventory, store, and retrieve an object is an amazing feat of organization. Each object or scene is not only recognized, it is placed within a category with a host of subcategories and descriptors that convey various positive or negative associations. Is this thing safe, fun, scary, or did it make me sick once? Some of these associations are universal: smiles are pleasant, wild animals are threatening, snow is cold. We are especially sensitive to faces and their expressions because it is extremely important to anticipate the disposition of those we encounter, especially in a society that is less civilized. In fact, many of these shared experiences and associations are what define us as a society and a culture.

The series of images created for this book is not interested in shared experiences and common interpretations. Rather, the images seek to explore the unique and subtle inter-

pretations found in metaphor and aesthetic correlation. These associations stand outside of clichéd classifications, taking on a nuance and subtlety of meaning that moves from the realm of the archetypal into the dark musty sitting room of the personal.

The metaphorical practice of imposing the characteristics of one object onto another is an effective way to get at the elusive meaning that cowers between the lines and evades the reach of language. One could argue that this expressive practice is the role of art in general (although in this postmodern age, that could be challenged as being too narrow a definition). Thus, through surreal juxtaposition and abstract incongruity, objects are imbued with meaning and significance beyond what our normal associations assign to them. Why is there a ten-foot lily in the living room? Why is the pear glowing?

The reference to "aesthetic correlation" refers to the common associations we have with various aesthetic components. Bright colors carry one association, while dark and somber colors convey the opposite. This goes for compositional placement, sharp and soft focus, light and dark tones, and various font designs. Each of these variables has the ability to reference a specific emotion or mood, whether they appear in a minor musical chord, a somber sky, or the bright face of a sunflower.

I began with a limited set of raw materials for this book because I was less concerned with finding the archetypal example of a various object or scene. In addition, it was not my intention to convey specific information about the object, which might necessitate a specific photograph. I did make sure that there were enough images to provide adequate expressive range, but I had no concern about running out to capture more images for the "perfect" specimen to be placed in a design.

In this same respect, the image did not have to exhibit perfect photographic technique. Although some of the images do show a solid technique, others are noticeably average. The objective was not to present a photographic aesthetic, but rather to show a digital aesthetic that bore the marks of the digital processes of copy/paste, multiple undos, and an almost limitless array of Photoshop choices and options.

Early in his career, the artist Robert Rauschenberg created a series of paintings that began with sheets of the daily newspaper. In many cases, areas of the paper remained visible in the final product, which elicited various positive and negative reactions. Rauschenberg commented that he used the grid and predefined structure of the newspaper as a springboard to get him into the act of painting. It allowed him to jump in and react intuitively, engaging the paint and the surface.

In the same way, the images in this series begin with photos as a way of engaging the digital process and the controls within Photoshop. The photos provide object information for the viewer to embrace or react to, but this object info is sometimes affiliated more with a painting than a photo. The object in the image may be grainy, obscured, or hard to see, but in most cases we can read it and understand its connotations. All of this underscores the fact that the primary tool in all these designs is the software, not the camera.

As a result, an image may be repeated several times in the course of this series, appearing in multiple compositions. Initially, this had my editors worried that the designs would be repetitive and redundant. As the designs evolved and came together, the editorial team could see that the metaphorical and aesthetic variations of the images created a new context within each design, which in turn presented the images in a unique perspective. Thus, the occasional repetition of an image emphasizes the digital nature of the work rather than the photographic perfection of the original images. In the end, the series of images represents a range of emotions and ideas while maintaining an interpretive thread that resonates throughout. In graduate school, I had a mentor who said that it's not what it is, it's how it feels. He was referring to the notion that anything could be emotive, provocative, and emphatic if it was created and presented in the right way. The designs that follow are patterned after this basic premise; they seek to imbue the ordinary and commonplace with personal significance and meaning.

THE ART OF PHOTOSHOP
GALLERY OF IMAGES

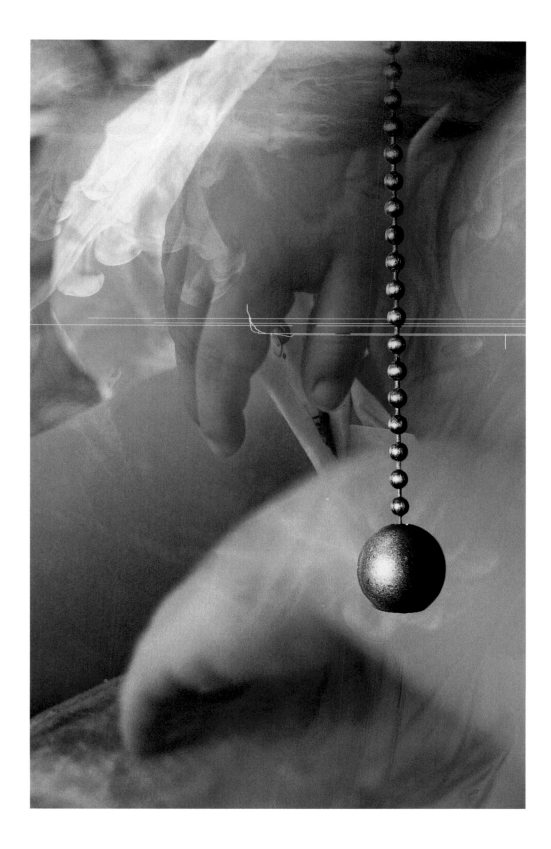

Occupation

© *2002 Daniel Giordan*

Chapter 10, "Silhouetting with the Extract Filter"

The Mystery of Folded Sleep

Chapter 9, "Working with Adjustment Layers"

Tomb of the Capulets

©*2002 Daniel Giordan*

Chapter 1, "Making Complex Selections"

S a n g u i n e   E x p e c t a t i o n s

Chapter 2, "Using Quick Mask Mode to Make Selections"

Impedance

Chapter 4, "Optimizing Images"

Birch Trees

©*2002 Daniel Giordan*

Chapter 18, "Using the Liquify Filter"

Gesture

Chapter 8, "Making Hue and Saturation Adjustments"

Ominous Botanicus

Chapter 13, "Understanding the Blending Modes"

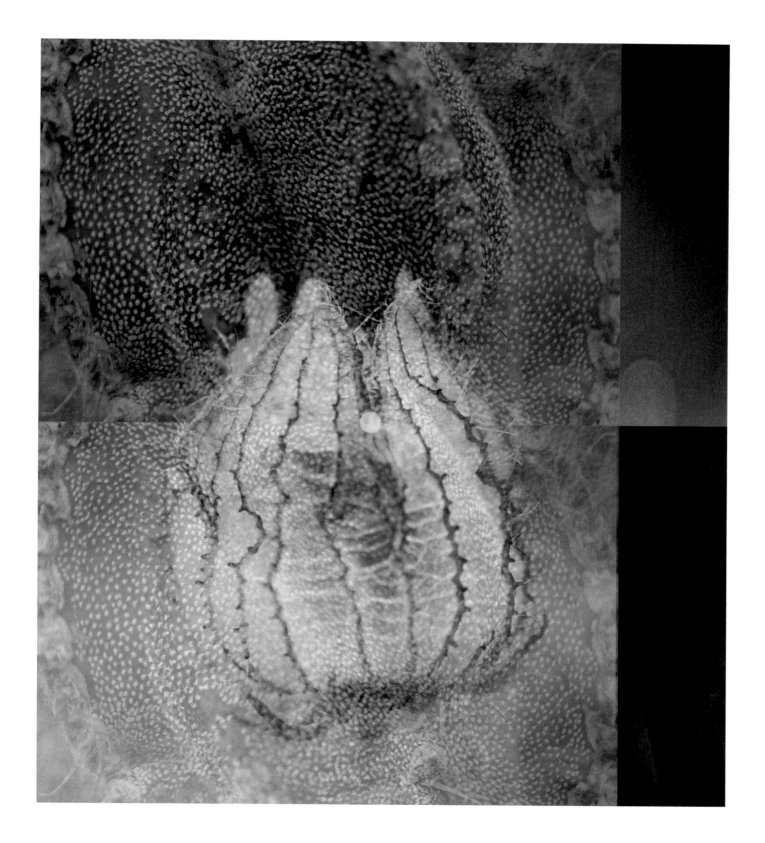

Tree House

©*2002 Daniel Giordan*

Chapter 15, "Mastering the Distort Filters"

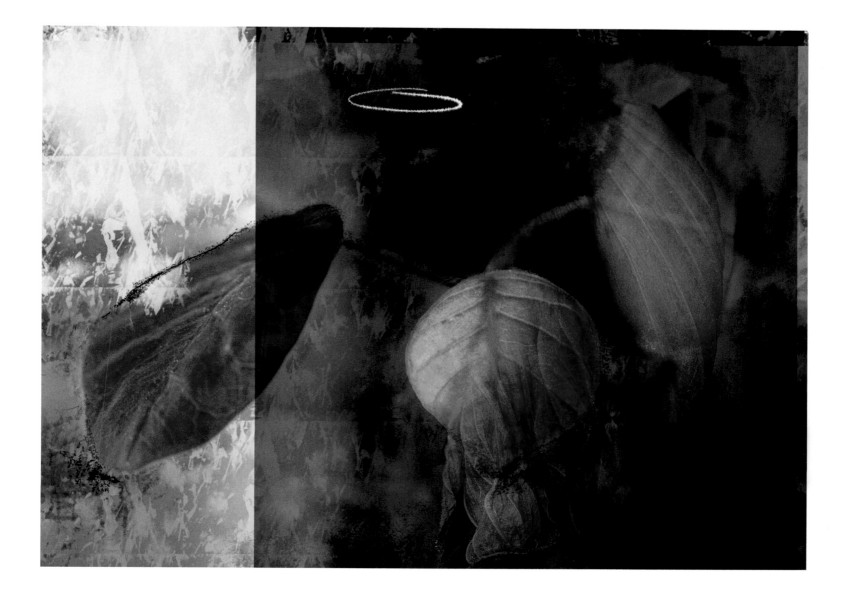

FreeFall

©*2002 Daniel Giordan*

Chapter 17, "Using Gradients and Gradient Maps"

Dark with Excessive Bright

Chapter 11, "Working with Layer Masks"

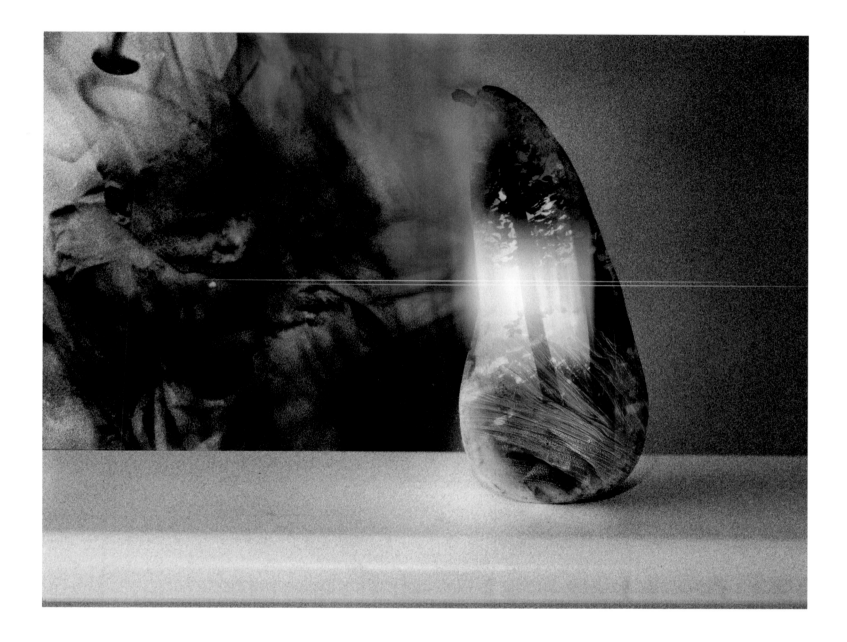

Absence of Voice

©*2002 Daniel Giordan*

Chapter 3, "Transforming Layers"

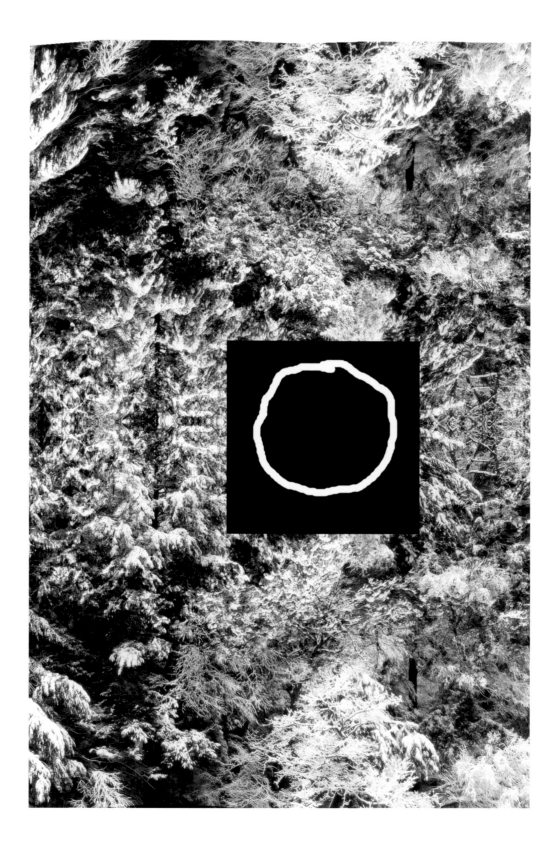

Oblique Ascension

Chapter 7, "Mastering Color Correction Techniques"

The Space Between

Chapter 12, "Using the Clone Stamp Tool"

Earthly Delights

©*2002 Daniel Giordan*

Chapter 16, "Making Photoshop Patterns"

Requiem

©*2002 Daniel Giordan*

Chapter 5, "Enhancing Image Focus"

On the Edge

Chapter 19, "Working with Lighting Effects"

CONTENTS

Chapter 1
Making Complex Selections:
Tomb of the Capulets
46

Chapter 2
Using Quick Mask Mode to Make Selections:
Sanguine Expectations
58

Chapter 3
Transforming Layers:
Absence of Voice
70

PART ONE

IMAGE HANDLING

Image 1
Tomb of the Capulets | ©2002 Daniel Giordan

CHAPTER 1

MAKING COMPLEX SELECTIONS

Tomb of the Capulets considers the fragile nature of thought, memory, and the mysterious act of remembering itself. It's about the gradual yet impulsive process of holding on and letting go. We single out, collect, and cultivate certain memories, embellishing some and editing others; sometimes we use our memories to establish and defend our perception of reality. The title of this image is a reference to the process of forgetting, which is sometimes referred to as "being consigned to the tomb of the Capulets."

What makes us cling to certain memories and disregard others? How is it that so many of the things we once regarded as crucial become transparent to our conscious thought? Thoughts, dreams, and memories are more than just a collection of data randomly preserved in our minds. They define us, even as we edit and shape them.

The image is anchored by a complex network of branches and leaves, woven across the full expanse of the work. These synaptic elements create an organic grid for the main image of the faded and dying rose. The horizontal division at the top of the image calls our attention to the relationship between clear conscious thought and the vague and elusive realm of subliminal thought. The line represents a point of demarcation between recollection and the gradual decay of memory.

Although the flower in the original White Rose image is sharp and symmetrical, the image takes on a soft, fading quality in *Tomb of the Capulets.* The rose is nested in the tangle of branches, yet it feels as if it could dematerialize and slip through the cracks at any moment. Once it does, it seems certain that it will drift into space, vanish, and be gone forever.

MAKING COMPLEX SELECTIONS

Photoshop selections involve isolating and defining specific areas of an image for edits and modifications. A good selection is clean and precise, allowing you to isolate portions of an image for editing, leaving unselected areas unaffected. With good selection skills, you can seamlessly integrate a person into a background, explore object-based collage, and add transparency and directional light effects. The criterion defining a good selection varies from image to image, depending on your intentions.

In a naturalistic photograph, a good selection has edges that smoothly transition into the nonselected areas. Such selections enable you to place an object convincingly into a landscape. They allow for light and color changes and have smooth shadow transitions.

Hard-edged geometric selections exclude any discolored edges that can halo the object against the background. Collage effects feature selections that are clean and precise, even if they do succeed in giving a cut-out appearance.

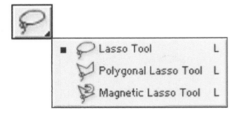

The Basic Tools

Adobe provides for a wide variety of selection options, acknowledging that each image is unique and may require its own combination of selection techniques. The proper approach to mastering selections is to understand the basic options and then to focus on combining techniques to arrive at the desired result. Acquiring a good hand for making selections is important: The most amazing techniques are often the result of amazing selections.

The basic selection options are geometric, organic, and color based.

Geometric Selections

Geometric selections are made using the Marquee tools (rectangle, oval, pixel column, and pixel rows), the Polygonal Lasso tool, and sometimes the Magnetic Lasso and Paths tools. Geometric selections usually have a hard-edged, linear shape. The most basic geometric selections are symmetrical, describing basic rectangles or ovals.

More complex geometric selections can have more irregular angles, but still tend to be made up of straight line segments.

The Path tool is the most powerful and flexible of the geometric selection options. It can select almost any object with straight lines and curves, and the resulting paths can be saved without adding much to the overall file size. For more on paths, see Chapter 4, "Using Paths."

Geometric Tools

These tools can be defined and controlled from the Photoshop Options bar. The Options bar allows you to define height/width ratios, selection sensitivity, and other functional parameters.

Organic Selection Tools

Organic Selections

Organic selections refer to naturalistic shapes found in nature. These kinds of selections can range from the irregular shape of a tree against the sky to the smooth drape of fabric on a sleeve or to the splash of a wave against a rocky shore. These objects do not lend themselves to geometric selections. Effective organic selection tools include the Magic Wand, Lasso, and Magnetic Lasso.

Color-Based Selections

Color-based selections are some of the most interesting and powerful of the basic selection options. Color selections allow you to select a blue crayon out of a pile of other crayons and change it to a green one. When you use color selections, an ethereal sky can become overcast and gray, the light can change from morning yellow to midday white, and a tree can change from the green of June to the rusty orange of September. Color selection options are the Color Range and Select Similar commands, both of which are located in the Select menu.

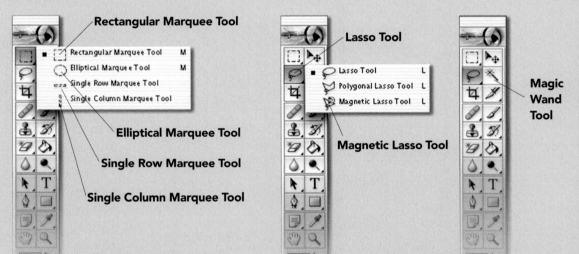

Rectangular Marquee Tool
Elliptical Marquee Tool
Single Row Marquee Tool
Single Column Marquee Tool

Lasso Tool
Magnetic Lasso Tool
Magic Wand Tool

Color Selection Options in the Select Menu

The Color Range command in the Select menu launches a dialog box that allows you to select specific color ranges within an image. Refer to the following section for more information on the commands in the Select menu.

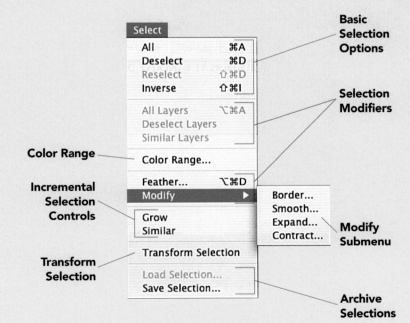

Basic Selection Options
Selection Modifiers
Color Range
Incremental Selection Controls
Modify Submenu
Transform Selection
Archive Selections

SELECTING WITH COLOR RANGE

Although most selections are based on objects or areas, there are times when you should think of selecting things by color. This could involve selecting just the red pixels in an image, or perhaps all the red and green ones. Photoshop allows you to define a single color value, multiple values, or a range of tones, so that selecting by color has a new level of control when you're making complex selections.

The Color Range command is the main command for making color-based selections and modifications. You can sample specific colors or select by colors or tones; you also have full control over the overall tolerance. You can also use the Color Range command to get a good look at the color distribution in your image.

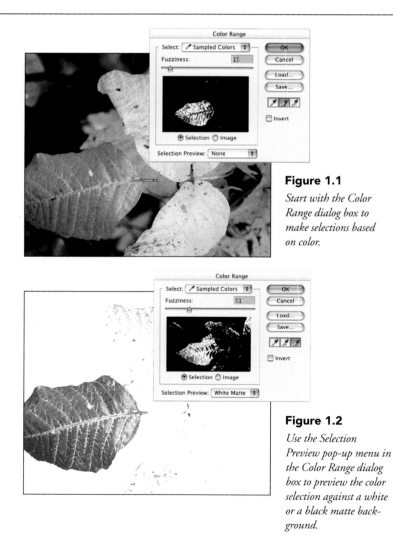

Figure 1.1
Start with the Color Range dialog box to make selections based on color.

Figure 1.2
Use the Selection Preview pop-up menu in the Color Range dialog box to preview the color selection against a white or a black matte background.

Selecting Specific Colors

Choose Select, Color Range to open the Color Range dialog box (see Figure 1.1). You are presented with a preview window, a Select pop-up menu, and a Select Preview option. If the Sampled Colors option is active in the Select pop-up menu, the Fuzziness slider is also active. The Fuzziness slider acts like a tolerance setting for the colors sampled in the image.

The most common use for Color Range selections is to select specific color areas. Selecting a tree on a foggy day could be difficult using area-based selections. However, if the tree's color is distinct from the mist around it, the Color Range command can be an effective selection approach. The basic technique involves using the dialog box's Select pop-up menu to

enable the Sampled Color option; then you use the eyedropper to select specific colors in the image or preview window. See the step-by-step instructions on the next page for specific details.

Using the Select Menu

The Select pop-up menu provides even more control over the color selection process because it allows you to select specific sampled colors or to select color sets (such as reds or greens). The Sample option is the most powerful of the commands because it allows you to sample color areas and add colors to an overall selection set. The Sample option provides access to the Fuzziness slider, which allows you to increase the sample sensitivity. With an initial sample active, you can increase the Fuzziness value to grow the selection.

MAKING COLOR RANGE SELECTIONS

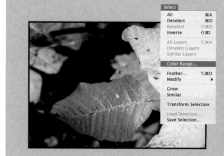

1. Choose Select, Color Range to launch the Color Range dialog box.

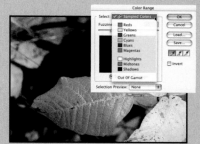

2. From the Select pop-up menu, choose the Sampled Colors option.

3. Click the Eyedropper tool icon, located under the Save button.

4. In the image, click the color you want to select.

5. Adjust the Fuzziness slider to isolate the exact range of color desired. Watch the preview window in the dialog box to see how adjustments to the slider affect the selection.

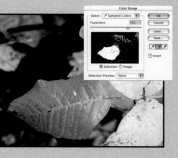

6. Click the Eyedropper + tool or the Eyedropper – tool icon to add colors to or subtract colors from the selected range. Click OK to close the dialog box and activate the selection in the image.

This effect is similar to increasing the Tolerance setting for the Magic Wand tool.

Selecting specific colors using the Select menu is much more direct. If you select the Reds option, for example, all the reds in the image are selected. The Fuzziness slider becomes gray and inactive when you choose any of these options, forcing the selection to include all the colored pixels.

Color Proofing

You can also use the Color Range command to check color balance and distribution within an image. To do this, open the Color Range dialog box; from the Selection Preview pop-up menu at the bottom of the dialog box, enable the White Matte option. This option makes everything in the image window turn white, except for the color being evaluated (see Figure 1.2). With White Matte selected, click and hold on the Select pop-up menu, and drag down to Reds. This will show you all of the reds in your image. You can go down the line, looking at red, green, blue, as well as cyan, magenta, and yellow. This approach is effective in that you can see how color is distributed, regardless of what color model you're using. In addition, Color Range shows the results as the actual color or value being evaluated, rather than the grayscale image you see when you evaluate channel information.

FINE-TUNING SELECTIONS

One of the prerequisites for making complex selections is patience. Certain selections must be approached with the mindset that things might take a while. Although patience is key, it is also important to understand how to combine the various selection tools to save time and make things easier.

The basic trick for combining selections is knowing that you can hold down the Shift key to add to a selection; you hold down the Option key (on the Mac) or the Alt key (in Windows) to subtract from the selection. With that basic infor-

mation, you can start a selection by using the Magic Wand tool to select a general area, switch to the Lasso tool, press and hold the Shift key, and drag around the smaller noise segments not initially selected by the Magic Wand tool.

In addition to these basic selection techniques, Photoshop offers selection modifiers that allow you to fine-tune an existing selection. The following sections describe the selection modifiers and how they operate.

Feather

The Select, Feather command softens the edges of the current selection, fading them into the unselected area. This command allows you to create a soft fade-out of a selection or to anti-alias a selection to hide any mistakes or rough edges.
You can also use the Feather command to vignette a selection for soft edge treatments.

After making an initial selection, access the Feather dialog box by choosing Select, Feather. In the

dialog box, specify the amount of the feather in pixels. You should have some idea about the dimensions of your image in pixels, so that you can specify an accurate and relevant feather value. Type the number of pixels you want to feather the selection and click OK to apply the feather.

Select Similar and Grow

The Select, Similar command activates all unselected pixels that have the same values as those currently selected. This command allows you to select a green area and then select all the green pixels in the entire image. The tolerance setting in the Magic Wand Options bar controls the variation of colors selected. A low tolerance setting selects only the values originally selected, while a higher setting selects a wider range of similar values.

The Select, Grow command enlarges the current selection area based on the tolerance setting in the Magic Wand Options bar. Just as is true for the Magic Wand tool, the higher the tolerance setting for the Grow command, the more pixels are selected.

Modify Commands

The Modify commands are a subset of the Select menu that allow you to alter the current selection with a high degree of control. The Select, Modify, Border command allows you to transform an area selection into a thin border selection of a specified thickness. The result is similar to creating a selection of just the outer edge, deselecting what was inside.

The Select, Modify, Expand and Contract commands grow or

shrink a selection by a specific number of pixels. The Select, Modify, Smooth command rounds the edges of a selection by a specific pixel value. The Smooth command is especially effective for rounding corners or creating a soft, eroded effect in a selection.

Transforming Selections

You can also distort or scale a selection in a manner similar to the way the Free Transform option works for layers. (See Chapter 3, "Transforming Layers," for details on the Transform and Free Transform tools.) To access the option, choose Select, Transform Selection.

THE TOP 12 SELECTION MODIFIERS

To select complex shapes and areas, you must sometimes combine multiple selection methods. Here are the top 12 shortcuts for working with selections. Combine them as you see fit to select exactly the right area of your image.

Add to Selections

To add to a selection, press and hold the Shift key as you're using any of the Photoshop selection tools. Alternatively, click the Add To Selection button in the Options bar. A plus sign appears next to the cursor to show that you're adding to the current selection.

Subtract from Selections

To subtract from a selection, press and hold the Option key (Mac users) or Alt key (Windows users) as you're using any of the Photoshop selection tools. Alternatively, click the Subtract from Selection button in the Options bar. A minus sign appears next to the cursor to show that you're subtracting from the current selection.

Intersect Selections

With an area selected, it's possible to create a second, overlapping area that leaves only the common, intersecting area selected. First, select an area. Then press Shift+Option (Mac users) or Shift+Alt (Windows users) as you draw a second selection that overlaps the first. An × appears next to the cursor as you do this. After you release the mouse and the keyboard keys, only the intersecting area remains selected.

Nudge a Selection

After you select an area, you can nudge the selection area up, down, left, or right one pixel at a time. Select one of the Marquee tools from the toolbox and press the arrow keys on your keyboard.

Invert Selections

To invert an active selection, choose Select, Inverse. This command selects the exact opposite of the current selection.

Smooth Selections

Smoothing a selection involves a gradual rounding of corners or sharp edges. To smooth an active selection, choose Select, Modify, Smooth. In the Smooth Selection dialog box that appears, type a smoothing value from 1 to 100 pixels.

Expand Selections

To expand an active selection, choose Select, Modify, Expand. In the Expand Selection dialog box that appears, type an expand value from 1 to 100 pixels. Repeat this step as desired to expand the selection even more.

Contract Selections

Contracting a selection makes the overall selection area smaller. To contract an active selection, choose Select, Modify, Contract. In the Contract Selection dialog box that appears, enter a value from 1 to 100 pixels.

Isolate Selection Borders

When you're working with geometric selections, there may be times when you want to apply an effect to only the border of a selected area. Choose Select, Modify, Border. In the Border dialog box that appears, type a value from 1 to 200 pixels for the thickness of the border.

Feather a Selection

Feathering a selection involves vignetting the selection edges, softening any effects that are applied to the selected area. To feather a selection, type a pixel value in the Feather field of the Options bar. Alternatively, choose Select, Feather. In the Feather Selection dialog box that appears, type a feather value from 0.2 to 250 pixels and click OK.

Select Similar Colors

After you select an area, you can select all other pixels in the image that have the same color value. To do this, select a color or range of colors, and then choose Select, Similar. All pixels with similar pixel values are selected.

Selections from Paths

Paths are easily converted to selections. After drawing a path, select Make Selection from the Paths palette menu. A dialog box allows you to make the selection as is, to add to the selection, to subtract from the selection, or to intersect the current selection with an existing selection.

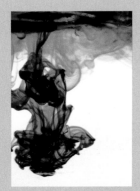

Green Liquid

Vines

Statue Head

White Rose

BUILDING THE IMAGE: *TOMB OF THE CAPULETS*

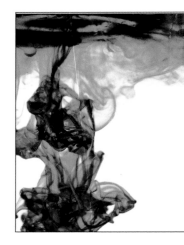

Figure 1.3
The vines are integrated into the green liquid image.

Figure 1.4
The Color Range command is used to add texture and complexity.

Figure 1.5
The Color Range command is used a third time to add even more depth and detail.

Saving Selections as Alpha Channels

Tomb of the Capulets began with the idea of combining abstract images of a green dye dissolving in water with an image of a dense vine pattern The basic intention was to force the vine pattern into the green areas of the billowing liquid, while leaving the other image areas untouched. The plan was to selectively use the complexity of the vine to add texture and depth to the billowing areas of the liquid. This required the creation of a selection that was based on the tonal range in the Green Liquid image.

To do this, the entire Green Liquid image was selected, copied, and then pasted into a new alpha channel (in the Channels palette, select New Channel from the Options menu). When you paste the image into the new channel, the image appears in grayscale. Because alpha channels translate gray tones into transparency, this is a quick way to create a soft, misty selection into which we can push other images.

The Vines image was copied and then pasted into the selection (Edit, Paste Into), achieving the desired depth and complexity. Although this effect did not stay in the final design, it served as a first step in integrating objects into abstract patterns, which was a thematic process for the image as a whole (see Figure 1.3).

Using Color Range

With the Vines image creating such interesting patterns, the next step was to make the vines appear beyond the liquid area. To do this, the entire Vines image was pasted again as a separate layer and the Color Range command was used to select a specific tone in the branches. Inverting the selection and deleting the unwanted parts created an interesting web effect (see Figure 1.4).

Figure 1.6

A fourth application of the Color Range command, using the Vines image, emphasizes the highlights.

Figure 1.7

The image is inverted.

Figure 1.8

A statue's head is added as a focal point.

Figure 1.9

The White Rose image is blended with the background.

The Vines image was pasted a third time, and a different color range was selected, this time emphasizing the shadows of the vine pattern. The two vine layers were combined using layer masks to create the intricate grid that anchors the final image (see Figure 1.5).

A Fourth Vine Layer

A fourth vine layer was pasted into the image and processed with the Color Range command, emphasizing the highlights. This layer provided an additional level of detail, complexity, and depth (see Figure 1.6).

A Dark Ground

With the billowing liquid and the grid of vines in place, the next step was to change the background from white to black. This was achieved easily by selecting the Green Liquid layer and inverting it with the Image, Adjust, Invert command (see Figure 1.7).

Ultimately, the Green Liquid image proved to be too distracting; a ground of flat black was substituted by creating a separate layer and filling it with black.

A Child's Head

In an effort to create a focal point, I added the Statue Head image, which features the head of a child, carved in stone. This layer was superimposed over the vines and blended in with a layer mask (see Figure 1.8).

The Rose

After some consideration, I decided that the Statue Head image was too dramatic and forced; it was replaced with the White Rose image. The layer with the rose and its leaves was blended into the vine grid using the Screen blending mode, and a layer mask was

added to conceal some of the leaves on the outer edge. This created the dissolving effect that drove the thematic focus of the image (see Figure 1.9).

Graphic Effects

After experimenting with circles and colors, I decided to use a simple gray line to divide the area containing the rose and the area at the top of the image.

1

TOMB OF THE
CAPULETS

1. Open the Green Liquid image.

2. Choose Image, Adjustments, Curves and set a white point and a black point to optimize the tonal range for the Green Liquid.

3. Select the entire image (Select, All) and copy it (Edit, Copy).

4. Open the Channels palette (Window, Channels), select New Channel from the Options menu, and paste the image from step 3 (Edit, Paste). Name the new channel and save it.

5. Load the alpha channel selection (Select, Load Selection) and choose the named channel from step 4.

6. Invert the Green Liquid image to create a dark background (Image, Adjustments, Invert).

7. Open the Vines image; copy it (Edit, Copy) and paste it into the active selection in the RGB or alpha channel (Edit, Paste Into).

8. Deselect the selection (Select, Deselect), and paste the Vines image again, positioning it as the top layer in the Layers palette.

9. Use the Color Range command to select the midtone portion of the Vines image (Select, Color Range). Invert the selection and delete the inverted selection to eliminate other areas of the image.

10. Paste the Vines image a third time and use the Color Range command to select only the shadows. Invert the selection and delete these areas.

11. Paste the Vines image a fourth time and use the Color Range command to select only the highlights. Invert the selection and delete these unwanted areas.

12. Create a new layer above the Green Liquid, select black as the foreground color, and fill the new layer with black using the Paint Bucket.

13. Hide the Green Liquid layer (the background layer) and the midtone vine layer you created in steps 8 and 9.

14. Paste the Statue Head image and position it within the vine matrix (Edit, Paste). Position it as the top layer in the Layers palette.

15. Create a layer mask and silhouette the Statue Head image against the vines (Layer, Layer Mask, Reveal All).

16. Paste the White Rose image (Edit, Paste), positioning it as the top layer in the Layers palette.

17. Create a layer mask and silhouette the rose leaves and branches against the vines (Layer, Layer Mask, Reveal All).

18. Hide the Statue Head layer.

19. Create a new layer above the White Rose.

20. Select the Pencil tool with a 3-pixel brush. Hold down the Shift key and draw a straight line across the upper image to complete the design.

1

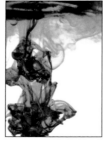

9

10

11

14

17

Image 2
Sanguine Expectations | ©2002 Daniel Giordan

CHAPTER 2

USING QUICK MASK MODE TO MAKE SELECTIONS

The subject in **Sanguine Expectations** is our ability to trust—an obvious fact since the word *trust* is scattered across the image in three different places. And yet the presence of this word is not at all reassuring or hopeful. It is tentative, almost uneasy in the way it is presented. The words are blurred, hidden, or obscured, and the eye bounces from one instance to the next, looking for an anchor where the text and aesthetic join to deliver a consistent message.

The overlapping images create a very spatial effect, with the pattern of tree trunks creating a ground for the flower and the text. The black jumble of lines floats on top of it all, its kinetic quality adding to the tension. Within this scribble is the only piece of text we can clearly read, suggesting that trust and hope resonate most clearly within a sort of suspended tension.

Hoping that our trust will be rewarded, we hold our breath, close our eyes, and jump.

Lying just beneath the tree trunks and the scribble, almost rising up from these other images, is the red flower. Its strong color and position suggests the fulfillment of hope or faith. This juxtaposition symbolizes the relationship between the act of faith and the object of faith. We place our trust in someone or something, and we wait nervously to see whether our faith will be rewarded.

Using overt text in an image can be very risky. If you don't handle it properly, the text can pull the viewer into obvious meanings or place too much emphasis on one particular part of the message.

trust

MAKING SELECTIONS WITH QUICK MASK MODE

The Photoshop Quick Mask mode feature lets you define a selection by painting an area, brushing in the selection using the full gamut of Photoshop's set of tools. If you tend to think in terms of painted areas rather than outlines and paths, you might find that Quick Mask mode selections are a more intuitive way of making selections.

Quick Mask mode gets its name from the fact that, as you define the selection area, Photoshop masks that area off, tinting it with a color to show what has been selected. When the selection is finished, you exit the Quick Mask mode, and Photoshop automatically converts the mask to a standard selection. Quick Mask mode is a visual and painterly way to make a selection. If you handle it correctly, you can make unique selections that are impossible to create in any other way.

Getting Started

The easiest way to get started with Quick Mask mode is to begin a selection with another tool, such as the Magic Wand or Lasso. After the selection is active, click the Quick Mask mode icon to convert the selection to a colored mask that you can further edit.

You can edit the mask with just about any Photoshop tool—from a paintbrush to the eraser and even filters.

Although you can edit the mask using draw and paint tools, the editing process does not allow for the use of color, although you can specify grayscale values. Recall that

Photoshop uses grayscale values to control the relative intensity of the mask you are painting. If black is your active color, the paint tools paint the mask at 100% intensity. If white is the active color, the mask is erased. Any shades of gray cause the paint tools to paint the mask in relative degrees of opacity. In summary, black lays down the mask color, white erases it.

Because black reveals and white conceals, it is possible to use the same brush for both tasks by switching between black and white as background and foreground colors. You can do this quickly by clicking the switch arrows in the toolbox or by pressing the X key.

Set the foreground to black and paint a mask; then switch the foreground to white and erase to clean up the edges.

Painting Translucency

By painting a Quick Mask with a grayscale, you can create a selection that affects an area only partially. For example, if an area is partially selected, painting with black results in a gray stroke that is lighter or darker, depending on how much it is selected. The effect is similar to when a selection edge is feathered, and an effect fades out toward the edges. If you paint a mask with an 80% gray, any edits through that selection are applied at 80%.

The best way to paint a translucent mask is with a feathered Paint Brush tool or the Eraser set to a large brush size. Lightly painting into an area results in a soft, translucent area that has a wide variety of uses.

Toolbox Icons

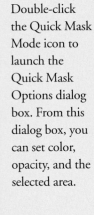

Double-click the Quick Mask Mode icon to launch the Quick Mask Options dialog box. From this dialog box, you can set color, opacity, and the selected area.

Brush Tool

Switch Arrows

Edit in Standard Mode

Edit in Quick Mask Mode

Quickmask Options

Click the color swatch to launch the Color Picker and select a new color for the mask. Enter a percentage value in the Opacity field to control the mask's transparency.

Color Indicates Masked Areas

Color Indicates Selected Areas

Color Swatch

Opacity Field

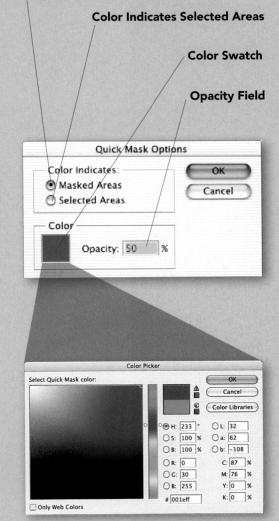

Color Picker

Clicking on the color swatch opens the Color Picker so that you can select a custom color.

CREATING A BASIC QUICK MASK MODE SELECTION

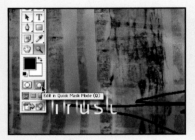

1. Click the Quick Mask Mode icon in the toolbox to enter Quick Mask mode.

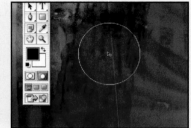

2. Select the Paint Brush tool from the toolbox, choose a brush size appropriate for the area to be selected, and select black as the foreground color.

3. Begin painting the area to be selected. Notice that Photoshop paints the mask over the area as you paint.

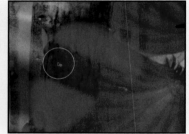

4. To erase any of the mask, select white as the foreground color and paint over the area to be erased. Notice that the mask disappears as you do this.

5. When the mask covers the appropriate area, click the Edit in Standard Mode button in the toolbox to convert the masked area to a selection.

ADVANCED QUICK MASK

Quick Mask mode is a great tool for defining a selection area in an image. As you paint the mask, remember that you can make all or part of it transparent, which will result in the translucent, partial selections mentioned on the preceding page. You achieve transparency with the mask by lowering brush opacity or by selecting a gray foreground tone rather than black in the toolbox. (Remember that gray values in Quick Mask mode create transparency in the selection.) Because the mask is a grayscale channel, it is also possible to push the tonality of the mask using other Photoshop tools. The result can be a complex selection that can create a texture, a blend, or a subtle modification in the main image.

Sharpen/Blur

A Quick Mask can be sharpened or softened using many of Photoshop's tools or filters. You can sharpen a Quick Mask to reduce feathered-edge selections. You can also sharpen the mask to shift the distribution of transparency within an area. In these instances, sharpening tends to make the transition from transparency to opacity less gradual and more pronounced. Blurring a Quick Mask creates softer edges while making transitions more subtle.

Filters such as Unsharp Mask or Gaussian Blur work well with global mask modifications. Consider using the Sharpen and Blur tools to modify a specific area of a mask. These tools allow you to use custom brush shapes and opacity to make specific local corrections.

Dodge and Burn Tools

The Dodge and Burn tools modify a mask by making the mask value darker or lighter. The Burn tool allows you to darken an edge, which sharpens it and eliminates any anti-aliased or feathered effects that may be applied there. Conversely, the Dodge tool lets you soften an edge, creating more of a feathered selection.

The Dodge and Burn tools also let you modify the translucency of a mask, making it more opaque or transparent. You can use the Burn tool to darken and solidify a selection area; use the Dodge tool to lighten and feather an area. You can also create

When making advanced Quick Mask mode selections, it's a good idea to modify the Quick Mask mode options so that the mask color and opacity accurately represent the mask in relationship to the main image—especially if the main image gets in the way when you're working.

While the mask is still active, consider using some of the modifications listed here as a starting point for exploration. You can use any tool or command that works with grayscale, so the possibilities are extensive.

translucency by applying a gradient to the mask; a gradient creates a smooth fade across the entire image or selection.

Curves Controls

After you've started a translucent mask using a gradient, the Dodge and Burn tools, or any of the filters, you can modify the relative translucency of the mask with curves. While in Quick Mask mode, select Image, Adjustments, Curves to launch the Curves dialog box; adjust the curve to modify the "density" of the mask. You can make similar modifications by choosing Image, Adjust, Brightness/Contrast or Image, Adjust Levels.

Edge Effects: Invert/ Equalize/Threshold/ Posterize

You can also modify a mask using the four edge-effect controls found at the bottom of the Image, Adjust submenu. These controls deliver quick shortcuts to various mask-editing requirements:

- **Invert:** Turns the current mask inside out, switching the selected and deselected areas.

- **Equalize:** Sharpens the mask globally, while adding a slight degree of feather, exaggerating any anti-alias effect that may have been present in the original selection.

- **Threshold:** Eliminates all feathered effects, defining an absolute edge between the select

ed and deselected areas. You can control where this break occurs by moving the Threshold slider in the dialog box that appears when you select the command.

- **Posterize:** Divides the mask into distinct levels of opacity, which in turn creates distinct levels of translucent selections. Simply select the Posterize command and enter the number of levels desired in your mask; Photoshop divides the mask into that many distinct sections. Be sure that the Preview check box is enabled so that you can preview the effect from the dialog box.

USING FILTERS TO ADD PATTERNS AND DISTORTION

One of the most exciting ways to modify a Quick Mask is by using filters. Filters affect the grayscale values of an active mask in the same way that they affect any other pixel values (excluding color modifications). This means that you can apply a texture or pattern to a mask; when you turn the mask into a selection, you have a textured selection that you can fill with a color or another image; alternatively, you can simply delete the textured selection to reveal the background or lower layers. The following sections describe the general range of effects you can apply to a mask.

Sharpen/blur filters:

Apply special sharpen/blur effects to a mask, using the Motion Blur or Radial Blur filter. Explore the Filter, Sharpen and Filter, Blur submenus to appreciate the full range of options available (see Figure 2.1).

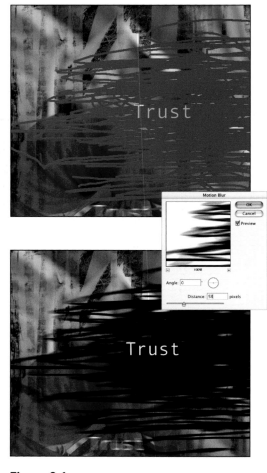

Figure 2.1

This sequence shows the original mask, the application of a Motion Blur, and the resulting selection filled with black.

Texture effects:

Apply textures or patterns with any of the filters found in the Artistic, Brush Strokes, Noise, Sketch, or Texture submenus in the Filter menu (see Figure 2.2).

Figure 2.2

This sequence shows the original mask, the application of the Spatter filter (Filter, Brush Stroke, Spatter), and the resulting selection filled with black.

Distortion effects:
You can apply twirl or wave patterns to a mask using the filters found in the Distort, Render, and Other submenus in the Filter menu (see Figure 2.3).

Liquify: The Liquify command lets you smear an image across the screen as if you were finger-painting. In the same way, you can distort a mask for a unique abstract selection (see Figure 2.4). See Chapter 18, "Using Liquify," for details about the Liquify command.

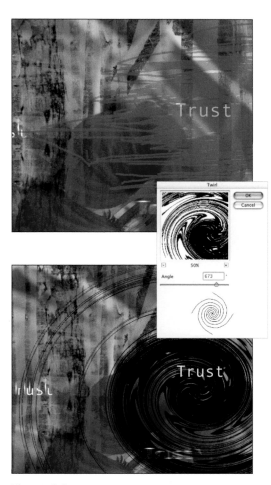

Figure 2.3

This sequence shows the original mask, the application of the Twirl filter (Filter, Distort, Twirl), and the resulting selection filled with black.

Figure 2.4

This sequence shows the original mask, the application of the Liquify command, and the resulting selection filled with black.

Birch Trees

Red Flower

BUILDING THE IMAGE: *SANGUINE EXPECTATIONS*

Figure 2.5

The rotated Quick Mask, based on the grayscale image data.

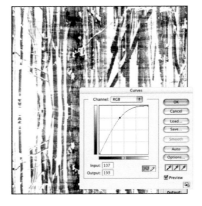

Figure 2.6

Converting the resulting selection to an Adjustment layer, and the associated Curves settings.

Figure 2.7

Adding the Red Flower image, using 70% transparency and the Darken blend mode.

Beginning Images

Quick Mask played a central role in creating the background textures in *Sanguine Expectations.* A cropped image of birch trees was copied, pasted, flipped, and edge-aligned to create a stripped background. The entire image was then selected and copied to the Clipboard using the Copy Merged command (Edit, Copy Merged).

After clicking the Quick Mask Mode icon to enter Quick Mask mode, I pasted the background image as a grayscale mask. The mask was rotated by selecting Edit, Transform, Rotate 90° CCW. Then I selected the Edit in Standard Mode icon to exit Quick Mask mode (see Figure 2.5).

The result was a complex, translucent selection that ran across the vertical tree image. For maximum flexibility, I captured this selection into an adjustment layer: With the complex selection active, click and hold the Adjustment Layer icon in the Layers palette and select Curves from the pop-up menu that appears (see Figure 2.6). This action adds the adjustment layer to the Layers palette. As a result, the adjustment effect was applied only to the active selection so that the curves affected only the active areas. You can apply adjustment layers to masks with varied transparency; the adjustment layers support the full range of blending modes for full creative control—

all without touching the image layers beneath the adjustment layers. In this case, the complex selection created an intricate matrix of birch trees as a background for the rest of the image.

Adding the Flower

After the background pattern was established, the next step was to introduce the Red Flower image. It was pasted as a separate layer with a transparency of 70%. In order to blend the grass detail in the flower image with the trees beneath it, the Darken blending mode was selected from the Blending Mode pop-up menu in the Layers palette (see Figure 2.7). Although the textures of the layers

Figure 2.8

A second red flower layer is added at full intensity and brushed into the image with a layer mask.

Figure 2.9

The Halftone Pattern filter is applied to the scribble layer

Figure 2.10

The word "Trust" is added three times to complete the image.

Figure 2.11

The final image: Sanguine Expectations.

blended well, the flower itself was somewhat washed out. To remedy this, the flower layer was duplicated by selecting Duplicate Layer from the Options menu in the Layers palette. After naming the new layer, a layer mask was added by selecting Layer, Layer Mask, Hide All. After selecting white as a foreground color, I used a large feathered Paintbrush to brush in parts of the flower at full intensity (see Figure 2.8). For details on using layer masks, see Chapter 12, "Working with Layer Masks."

Black Scribble

A host of other options were attempted before the scribble effect was allowed to remain. Fading,

blending, and filtering did not have the desired effect; they did not hold the space and enhance the image.

Ultimately, I created a new layer and used the Pencil tool with a 3-pixel brush. After considerable trial and error, I decided that the scribble effect seemed to work against the stripes of the trees and the background.

To finish the effect, I used the Halftone Pattern filter on the scribble, applying a subtle pattern of horizontal lines. With the scribble layer active, I selected black and a dark gray as foreground and background colors and then launched the filter (Filter, Sketch,

Halftone Pattern). I selected Line as the pattern type and used the default settings of 1 and 5 for Size and Contrast (see Figure 2.9).

"Trust"

Adding the word *trust* involved more than just typing a few letters in a layer. The text was entered and the Andale Mono font selected. The result was placed prominently over the scribble area (see Figure 2.10).

After I set the font and size, I duplicated the layer and converted it from a type layer to a bitmap (Layer, Rasterize, Type). The text was altered with a Motion Blur filter (Filter, Blur, Motion Blur), set in a horizontal 0° axis at a distance

of 6 pixels. The result was placed in the middle of the red flower.

For the third instance of the word trust, I duplicated and rasterized the layer two more times. The first layer cut off the top of the word with the Eraser, using the Block brush type. The second layer was modified using the Motion Blur filter, this time set to a −90° vertical direction at a distance of 5 pixels. The two layers were aligned and offset to complete a text effect that is a combination of sharp and soft: in short, unsettling (see Figure 2.11).

2

SANGUINE
EXPECTATIONS

1. Open the Birch Trees image.

2. Select Image, Adjustments Curves; set a white point and a black point to optimize the tonal range.

3. Select the entire image (Select, All) and copy it (Edit, Copy).

4. Paste the image from step 3 (Edit, Paste), creating a new layer.

5. Select Edit, Transform, Flip Vertical to flip the image upside down.

6. Select Image, Canvas Size; set the anchor at the top-center of the grid and double the height of the image.

7. Select the Move tool from the toolbox and drag the flipped image to align the edges of the two layers, filling the new canvas.

8. Select the entire image (Select, All) and copy it (Edit, Copy).

9. Click the Quick Mask mode icon in the toolbox to enter Quick Mask mode.

10. Select Edit, Paste to paste the image copied in step 8 as a Quick Mask mode effect.

11. Select Edit, Transform, Rotate 90° CCW to rotate the mask.

12. Select the Edit in Standard Mode icon to return to Standard editing mode and to convert the mask to a selection.

13. Click and hold the Adjustment Layer icon in the Layers palette and select Curves from the icon's pop-up menu.

14. In the Curves dialog box, add a single point to the curve with coordinates of Input 91, Output 178; click OK.

15. Paste the Red Flower image as a layer, set to 70% opacity, using the Darken blending mode.

16. Duplicate the flower layer by selecting Duplicate Layer from the Layers palette menu.

17. Select Layer, Layer Mask, Hide All, to add a layer mask to the new flower layer.

18. Select the Brush tool with a 200-pixel brush. Set the foreground color to white and paint in portions of the flower to increase its intensity.

19. Create a new layer; select the Pencil tool with a 3-pixel brush, set the foreground color to black, and draw a scribble pattern.

20. Set the background color to dark gray and apply a Halftone Pattern filter (Filter, Sketch, Halftone Pattern) to the background with a Pattern Type of Line, a Size of 1, and a Contrast of 5.

21. Select the Type tool and type the word *Trust* in 12-point Andale Mono over the black scribble.

22. Duplicate the type layer and select Layer, Rasterize, Type to convert the type layer to a bitmap.

23. Apply a Motion Blur filter (Filter, Blur, Motion Blur), set to a 0° angle and an 8-pixel distance. Position this copy of the text in the center of the red flower.

24. Duplicate the type layer two more times and select Layer, Rasterize, Type.

25. Select the Eraser tool from the toolbox with Block mode. Erase the top 4 pixels from the first rasterized type layer.

26. Apply the Motion Blur filter (Filter, Blur, Motion Blur) to the second rasterized type layer, set to a −90° angle and a 5-pixel distance.

27. Align the final two rasterized type layers at the center-left edge of the image.

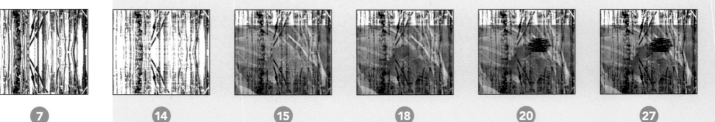

Image 3
Absence of Voice | ©2002 Daniel Giordan

CHAPTER 3

TRANSFORMING LAYERS

There is something unsettling about the silence that occurs after a heavy snow. Sounds hang in the air: oppressive, ominous, distinct, and amplified. Subtleties assert themselves: the sound of breath, muffled footsteps, our own heartbeats. We stand balanced between the transformation of the outside world and the intimate awareness of our own physicality.

Absence of Voice speaks to that suspended balance and fleeting sense of wonder. A dramatic hillside shrouded in snow provided the impetus for the feelings just described. I edited the image to heighten and amplify this sensibility. The composition succeeds in creating a hypnotic, looping rotation that is anchored by the strong black square and the loosely drawn circle.

The pattern of snow on branches is abstract and beautiful, inviting the viewer to indulge and explore the textured detail. The symmetry of the image adds to the sense of visual exploration because the eye rotates though the composition. It looks for a place to rest and anchor, but is denied a suitable point of reference.

Absence of Voice is about more than just the feelings after a snowfall. It is also a cohesive design that hovers between detail and abstraction. The crudely drawn circle acts as a counterpoint to the detailed symmetry of the surrounding branches. The background is an image of a heavy, wet snow that moves in a circle. The foreground is a circle that moves and feels like heavy, wet snow.

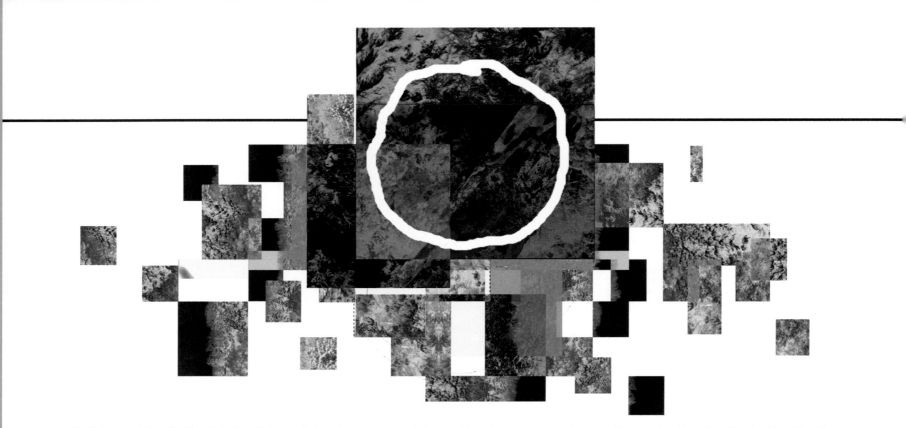

TRANSFORMING LAYERS AND SELECTIONS

By their very nature, Photoshop layers are made to be combined and juxtaposed. At times, they can be maneuvered into specific alignment; other situations call *for scaling, rotating, or other tweaks. These functions are driven by a series of commands nestled in the Transform and Free Transform submenus.*

Layer Transformations

The basic process of transforming a layer involves selecting the layer, choosing the desired command from the menu, and dragging to make the changes. If your image consists of only the background layer, Photoshop does not allow you to transform it. There are two ways to get around this limitation: One is to double-click the background layer in the Layers palette, rename the layer in the dialog box that appears, and click OK. Photoshop looks at this copy as a standard layer and makes available all the transformation potions. The other option is to make a selection on the background layer; you can then distort the selected area with-

out changing the background status of the layer itself.

When you choose a transform command, a bounding box with handles surrounds the layer or selection. The transformation is applied by clicking and dragging the handles to create the various scaling, rotation, or skewing effects. When the effect is complete, apply it by double-clicking inside the bounding box or by selecting any of the tools from the toolbox.

Using the Options Bar

The Options bar at the top of the Photoshop window offers a variety of controls you can use whenever you select a transform command.

These options are available for either the Transform or Free Transform command set.

- **Reference Point Control:** The first field in the Options bar allows you to design and activate a reference point for the bounding box. The reference point is the relative center point on which the transformation is centered. For example, if you scale an image around a centered reference point, the image will expand outward in all directions. If the reference point is in one of the corners or sides, however, that area is anchored, and the remaining areas of the image expand or distort. The control is an icon showing the handles of the

bounding box. Click one of the nine handles to select and activate the reference point in the desired location.

- **Reference Point Placement:** This control consists of entry fields to designate the pixel location of the reference point along the x and y axes. This control is valuable for precise placement of the image layer. For example, you can align the reference point to the upper-left corner of the image layer and then make the reference point location 100 pixels across and 50 pixels down. The reference point (the upper-left corner of the image) automatically moves to the designated pixel coordinates.

- **Relative Reference Point Control:** Click the triangle icon between the x and y input fields to change the location reference from the uppermost left corner of the image to the current reference point location. For example, entering an x value of 500 and clicking the Relative Reference Point triangle icon moves the reference point and bounding box 500 pixels from the current reference point location, rather than 500 pixels from the upper-left corner of the image.

- **Horizontal and Vertical Scale Controls:** The next two fields allow you to enter numeric scaling percentages for vertical or horizontal dimensions. For example, enter 60% in the Horizontal field to reduce the image width to 60% of its original size. Click the link icon between the fields to activate and deactivate the current aspect ratio.

- **Rotation and Skew Controls:** The final three fields in the Options bar allow you to enter numeric degrees of rotation and of horizontal and vertical skew.

- **Commit Transform and Cancel Buttons:** The ∅ button cancels the transformation without changing the layer. The checkmark button applies the transformation to the layer.

Photoshop Transform Commands

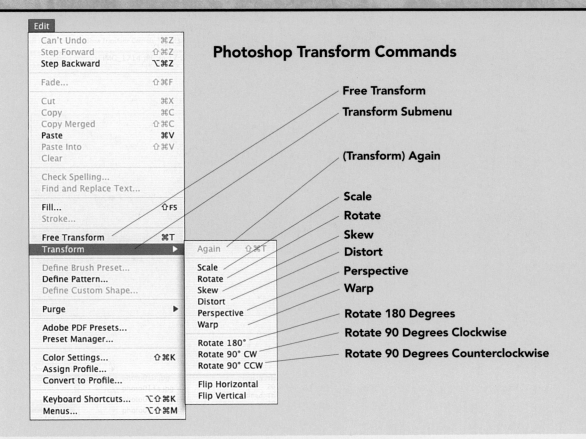

Transform Options Bar Settings

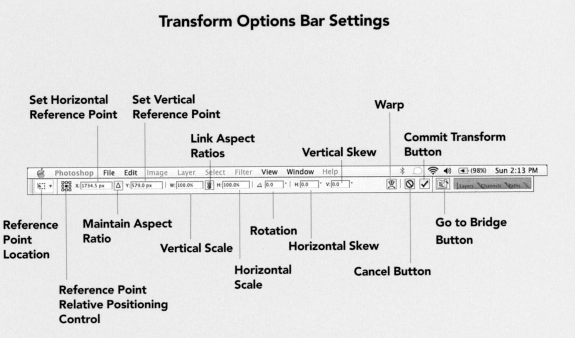

BREAKING DOWN THE TRANSFORM OPTIONS

Figure 3.1
The original image.

Figure 3.2
The result of the Scale command is superimposed over the original.

Figure 3.3
The result of the Rotate command is superimposed over the original.

Figure 3.4
The result of the Skew command is superimposed over the original.

The Edit, Transform submenu offers a range of transformation options. These options are listed here along with brief descriptions of how each option impacts the image. The figures show the result of each transformation, superimposed over a tinted version of the original image (see Figure 3.1).

• **Again:** Reapplies the previous transformation.

• **Scale:** Places corner and center handles around the layer, allowing you to scale the layer up and down around a movable center point. Drag any handle to resize the layer (see Figure 3.2). Click and drag the center point to move it, which will affect the way the layer is modified. Hold down the Shift key while dragging a handle to maintain the height and width proportions as you scale the image. Click any tool in the toolbox to apply the transformation.

• **Rotate:** Places corner and center handles around the layer, allowing you to rotate the layer around a movable center point. Drag any handle to rotate the layer (see Figure 3.3). Click and drag the center point to move it, which will affect the way the layer rotates. Click and drag within the transform object to reposition the layer anywhere on the screen. Click any tool in the toolbox to apply the transformation.

• **Skew:** Places corner and center handles around the layer, allowing you to skew the layer at any angle around a movable center point. Drag any corner handle to create an angled effect for the corresponding corner (see Figure 3.4). Move the segment handles to shift the two connected corner handles in tandem, skewing that side of the image. Click and drag the center point to move it, which will affect the way the skew is applied. Click and drag within the transform object to reposition the layer anywhere on the screen. Click any tool in the toolbox to apply the transformation.

Figure 3.5
The result of the Distort command is superimposed over the original.

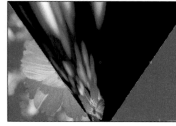

Figure 3.6
The result of the Perspective transformation is superimposed over the original image.

Figure 3.7
The result of the Rotate 90° CCW command is superimposed over the original image.

Figure 3.8
The result of the Flip Horizontal command.

- **Distort:** Places corner and center handles around the layer, allowing you to distort the layer around a movable center point. Drag any corner handle anywhere in the image to distort the layer (see Figure 3.5). Click and drag the center point to move it, which will affect the way the distortion is applied. The main difference between Distort and Skew is that Skew restricts the handles you can use to modify the layer, while Distort allows free placement of any handle in any area. Click and drag within the transform object to reposition the layer anywhere on the screen. Click any tool in the toolbox to apply the transformation.

- **Perspective:** Places corner and center handles around the layer, allowing you to apply basic perspective effects. As you drag any corner handle, the opposite corner handle automatically moves in a mirror image. Click and drag the center point to move it, which will affect the way the distortion is applied (see Figure 3.6). Click and drag within the transform object to reposition the layer anywhere on the screen. Click any tool in the toolbox to apply the transformation.

- **Warp:** Creates a nine-section mesh around the layer or selection, with handles and movable intersection points. Drag any intersection point to distort the mesh, or drag the corner points for a more extreme distortion. There are also Bezier handles attached to each corner point that create more of a global distortion based on the corner radius.

- **Rotate 180°, 90° CW, 90° CCW:** These presets allow you to rotate the image 90 or 180 degrees clockwise or counterclockwise. After you select the command, Photoshop automatically rotates the layer as specified (see Figure 3.7).

- **Flip Horizontal, Flip Vertical:** Rather than rotating the image around a reference point, these commands flip the layer, mirror-image style, around the vertical or horizontal pole (see Figure 3.8).

TRANSFORM OPTIONS AND SHORTCUTS

While working in any transform mode, hold down the Ctrl key and click (Mac users) or right-click (Windows users) to access a pop-up menu of all transform options. The pop-up menu provides access to multiple transform modes without your having to access the main menu or actually applying the transformation. For example, you could make initial modifications in the Rotate transform

mode, access the Perspective mode through the pop-up menu for further changes, and then use the pop-up menu to go to Scale mode for resizing. These change options can be accessed and applied as a single transformation instead of as a sequence of individual transformations.

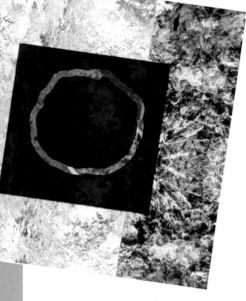

Free Transform

The Free Transform option allows you to intuitively apply a series of multiple transformations. At any given time, you can rotate, scale, and reposition the layer or selection, interactively dragging it into the desired position. This is similar to the pop-up menu approach just described, although the options are somewhat limited in comparison.

Start Free Transform by selecting Edit, Free Transform; Photoshop

places handles around the selection or layer at the corners or in the center of each segment border. Click and drag the center segments to resize in a vertical or horizontal direction. Click and drag the corner points to resize up or down diagonally. In addition, if you move the cursor inside the active shape, the cursor changes to a pointer, and you can drag the shape or layer into any position onscreen. To rotate, position the cursor outside the active shape; the cursor changes to a rotation icon to show you that dragging will now rotate the image.

Numeric Transform Options

If you need more precision or want to repeat your transformations, you'll appreciate Photoshop's ability to make changes based on numeric information. For example, instead of dragging a corner for a random rotation, you can enter a specific value—such as 38 degrees—for an exact position. Selecting any of the Transform commands changes the Options

bar to the subset of Transform options described in the following sections. When in doubt of a tool's function or identity, place the cursor over the tool in the Options bar to activate the ScreenTip pop-up window, which shows the tool name.

Reference Point Controls

The transformation reference point sets a fixed point of reference for the resizing and modifications to come. For example, when you rotate an image, it revolves around a fixed axis point. When you scale an image, it can resize from the center or from one of the corners. The reference point is a circle with crosshairs; its default position is the center of the object. To manually reset the reference point, click the crosshairs and drag it anywhere in or out of the object.

The first set of numeric controls in the Options bar controls the placement of the reference point. The first control is the Reference Point Location icon, which is a grid of small squares that represent the

handles on an object selected for transformation. Click one of the squares to shift the reference point to the corresponding handle in the object.

The next controls in the Options bar allow you to move the object itself by designating the x and y coordinates for the reference point. Enter 100 in the X field, and the entire image moves until the reference point is 100 pixels from the left of the image. Click the Relative Positioning icon (the triangle), and the reference point (and the object) move horizontally 100 pixels from its previous spot.

Scale, Rotate, and Skew Controls

The next set of controls in the Options bar controls the scaling of the object. Enter a width or height percentage in the associated field to scale the image in that direction. To avoid distortion, click the chain icon to link the proportions of the scaling. You can also set the degree of rotation or the degree of horizontal or vertical skew.

Free Transform Keyboard Modifiers

Adobe includes additional keystroke modifiers that deliver even more control to the Free Transform command. The figures that accompany the following explanations show the Free Transform keyboard modification options as applied to a square shape (shown in yellow).

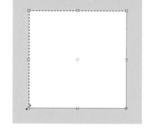

Shift+drag a corner point to resize diagonally, maintaining a proportional aspect ratio.

Shift+drag outside the object to rotate in 15-degree increments.

Shift+drag inside the object to constrain the repositioning to 45-degree increments.

Option+Shift+drag (Mac) or Alt+Shift+drag (Windows) a corner to resize diagonally, relative to the center point in a mirrored effect.

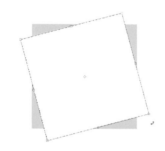

Option+drag (Mac) or Alt+drag (Windows) a center segment to resize both sides linearly in a mirrored effect.

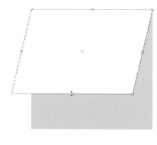

⌘+drag (Mac) or Ctrl+drag (Windows) a corner to distort freely in any direction.

⌘+drag (Mac) or Ctrl+drag (Windows) a center segment to skew the shape freely in any direction.

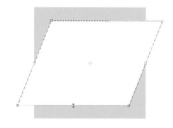

Option+⌘+drag (Mac) or Ctrl+Alt+drag (Windows) a corner point to distort both diagonal corners at once, with a mirrored effect.

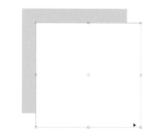

Option+⌘+drag (Mac) or Ctrl+Alt+drag (Windows) a center segment to skew freely, relative to a center point in a mirrored effect.

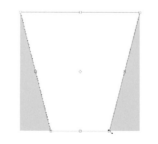

Option+⌘+Shift+drag (Mac) or Ctrl+Alt+Shift+drag (Windows) a corner point to create a perspective effect. Drag horizontally to pinch the opposite horizontal corner; drag vertically to pinch the opposite vertical corner.

Option+⌘+Shift+drag (Mac) or Ctrl+Alt+Shift+drag (Windows) a center segment to skew the shape around a center point.

Snow Hill

BUILDING THE IMAGE: *ABSENCE OF VOICE*

Figure 3.9

The raw image is opened and optimized

Figure 3.10

Duplicate the layer and flip it vertically.

Figure 3.11

Use the Multiply blending mode to combine the layers.

Copying and Flipping

Although *Absence of Voice* is not technically complex, it did rely heavily on the Transform commands to create the symmetrical pattern of the snow-covered tree branches.

I began with a raw image of a fresh snowfall on a hill of pine trees, which was optimized and sharpened (see Figure 3.9). I duplicated the initial Snow Hill image layer to a second layer and selected it in the Layers palette. The layer was then flipped vertically to create a mirror image. To do this, select

Edit, Transform, Flip Vertical (see Figure 3.10).

To complete the initial background pattern effect, the top layer was set to the Multiply blending mode by highlighting the layer and selecting Multiply from the Blending Mode pop-up menu in the Layers palette. The Multiply blending mode combined the image layers into a single, unified pattern (see Figure 3.11).

Applying the Distort Filter

Although the background pattern was interesting and compelling, it

was a little too perfect in its symmetry. It needed to loosen up a bit. I used the Wave filter in this instance because of its ability to create random, abstract distortions.

Launch the Wave filter (Filter, Distort, Wave) to see a dialog box with an array of control options. The most important thing to remember is that the general filter effect ranges from subtle modulations to staccato, kinetic waveforms. The Wavelength control slider primarily controls this range. Increase the Wavelength

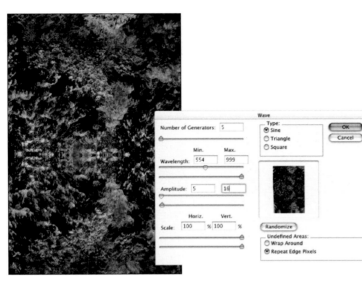

Figure 3.12

The Wave filter settings.

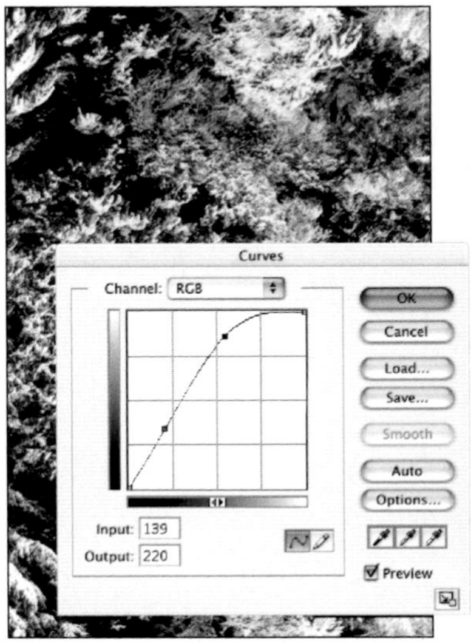

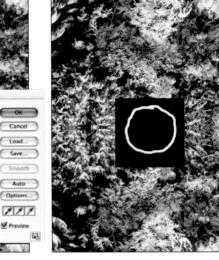

Figure 3.13

Apply Curves to the adjustment layer to lighten the image.

Figure 3.14

The final image.

Max value to create a subtle effect, or decrease it for an abstract, high-energy effect. Figure 3.12 shows the exact setting used in this instance to create a soft, subtle distortion to the background pattern. For details on the Distort filters, refer to Chapter 15, "Distort Filters."

Adding a Curves Adjustment Layer

Although the Multiply blending mode worked well to blend the two hill images, it darkened things quite a bit. To remedy this, I added a Curves Adjustment layer

to brighten things up.

To do this, click and hold the Adjustment Layer icon in the Layers palette and select Curves. Setting two curve points lightened the image: Input=52, Output=83, and Input=146, Output=225 (see Figure 3.13).

Drawing the Circle

To complete the image, I added the black square and white circle. I selected the Rectangular Marquee tool from the toolbox and drew a square by holding down the Shift key and dragging the shape. After the shape was drawn, I reposi-

tioned the selection by placing the cursor over the shape and dragging the shape into place. Then I filled the shape with black using the Paint Bucket tool.

I drew the circle by selecting the Paint Brush tool from the toolbox and setting a brush size of 35 pixels. I created a new layer and drew the circle freehand. I had to erase and redraw the circle several times to ensure that the end result held the space effectively (see Figure 3.14).

3

ABSENCE OF VOICE

1. Open the Snow Hill image.

2. Select Image, Adjustments, Curves; set a white point and a black point to optimize the tonal range.

3. Double-click the background image in the Layers palette and click OK to change it into a standard layer.

4. Select Layer, Duplicate Layer to duplicate the background layer. Rename the layer if desired and click OK in the dialog box to complete the command.

5. Flip the top layer by selecting Edit, Transform, Flip Vertical.

6. With the top layer active, select Multiply from the Blending Mode pop-up menu at the top of the Layers palette.

7. Select Filter, Distort, Wave to launch the Wave dialog box. Set the filter as follows: Wave Type: Triangle; Number of Generators: 5; Wavelength Min: 526; Wavelength Max: 999; Amplitude Min: 5; Amplitude Max: 16; Horizontal and Vertical Scale: 100%; Undefined Areas: Wrap Around.

8. Click and hold the Adjustment Layer icon in the Layers palette and select Curves. Set the input points on the curve to Input 50, Output 83 and Input 145, Output 225.

9. Create a new layer by selecting Layer, New, Layer.

10. Select the Rectangular Marquee tool from the toolbox. Shift+drag to draw a square selection; drag the selection to reposition it as necessary.

11. Select the Paint Bucket tool from the toolbox and set the foreground color to black. Click within the square selection to fill it with black.

12. Select the Brush tool from the toolbox, choose a 35-pixel round brush, and set the foreground color to white. Click and drag within the black square to paint the white circle.

CONTENTS

Chapter 4
Optimizing Images:
Impedance
84

Chapter 5
Enhancing Image Focus:
Requiem
96

Chapter 6
Mastering Curves:
Numerical Uncertainty
108

Chapter 7
Mastering Color Correction Techniques:
Oblique Ascension
122

Chapter 8
Making Hue and Saturation Adjustments:
Gesture
134

Chapter 9
Working with Adjustment Layers:
The Mystery of Folded Sleep
146

PART TWO

IMAGE EDITING

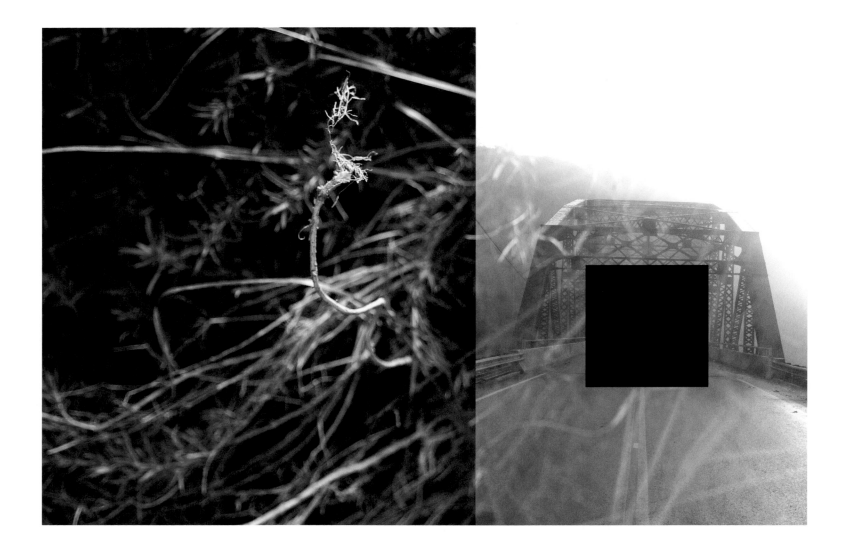

Image 4
Impedance | ©2002 Daniel Giordan

CHAPTER 4

OPTIMIZING IMAGES

It is immediately apparent that the image *Impedance* is a study in contrast and duality. The image is split in two sections that appear very different and distinct. On the left is a close-up of coarse grass presented in high-contrast black and white. On the other side is a trestle bridge with a large black square blocking the path.

The duality exists on a number of levels. The left side is organic and natural, with a single strand of grass that is dramatically illuminated. This provides a focal point that is compelling and reverential…almost transcendent.

In contrast, the right side is manmade and geometric. The bridge is composed of geometric shapes and angles that are echoed by the linear perspective of the road and guardrails. There's not a single straight edge in the image on the left, while the image on the right is composed almost exclusively of straight edges.

Beyond the aesthetic comparisons lie the emotional ones. The right side suggests a clear path that we are not allowed to follow. The black square punctuates this even further, as an absolute rejection of the obvious path. Conversely, the left side presents an infinite and accessible jumble of lines and areas that we can study and explore. The right side frustrates, while the left indulges and delights.

Finally, there is the issue of the transparency on the right side. The organic pattern is beginning to show through the bridge image, suggesting that the organic pattern is fundamental, even universal, and that the manmade world is temporal and finite. As a whole, the image is centered, complete, and cohesive—quite an accomplishment for a picture of a bridge and a clump of grass.

OPTIMIZING THE TONAL RANGE

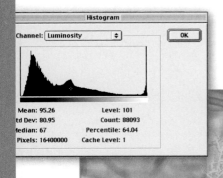

In case you haven't noticed, images usually don't come out of the camera, scanner, or stock photo agency all ready for National Geographic. Even high-end cameras and scanners can create images with flat highlights and muddy gray shadows, resulting in flat, lifeless images. That's where image optimization comes in.

You should attempt to optimize the tonal range of an image, regardless of its initial appearance. Contrast and color are subjective, and the monitor is deceptive. You will often find that an image that starts out looking good will look great with just a few minor tweaks.

Tonal Range and the Histogram

Digitally speaking, the tonal range of an image is expressed in numerical values from 0 to 255, with 0 being the darkest and 255 being the brightest. Optimizing the tonal range means that you are using all the available values in the RGB color space; your blacks are deep and rich with an RGB value near 0, your whites are maxed out at 255, and midtones are well distributed. An added dividend of tonal optimization is that it usually results in an even color balance and removes any unwanted color cast. Images with a poor tonal range usually appear flat and washed out, lacking depth and contrast.

The first step in image optimization is to evaluate the tonal range of the image and to identify how the various values are distributed.

How many pixels are in the highlights? What about the amount of information in the shadows? The histogram measures the relative number of pixels across the entire tonal spectrum; it is a quick and easy way to gauge the lightest and darkest values in an image.

Select Window, Histogram to launch the Histogram window. You'll be presented with a graph that measures pixel values from dark to light along a linear, left-to-right spectrum. By default, the Channel pop-up menu is set to Luminosity, which shows only the luminous grayscale values in the image.

Although this is a good place to start, you can also select and measure individual color channels from this pop-up menu.

In the histogram, the relative height of the black "mountain" along the spectrum represents the

TOOLS FOR OPTIMIZING TONAL RANGE

number of image pixels that correspond to that value. A higher peak on the graph means more pixels in the image with that corresponding value. On average, images have the highest peak in the mid and 3/4 tones and slope to the lowest points in the highlights and shadows.

By default, the histogram displays the mean pixel value for the image (average brightness) as well as the standard deviation (value range variation), median value (middle value), and total number of image pixels. More information is available by dragging the cursor within the black data portion of the histogram. The Level value represents the actual pixel value, the Count value shows the number of pixels with that value, and the Percentile value represents the percentage of pixels with a given value as compared to the total number of pixels. The Cache Level value corresponds to the Image Cache settings in the Photoshop Preferences dialog boxes.

As you examine the histogram, the first thing to check is the absolute darkest and lightest pixel values, referred to as the *black point* and the *white point*. Drag the cursor over the low and high pixel values and notice the count and percentage values that appear.

The Histogram Window

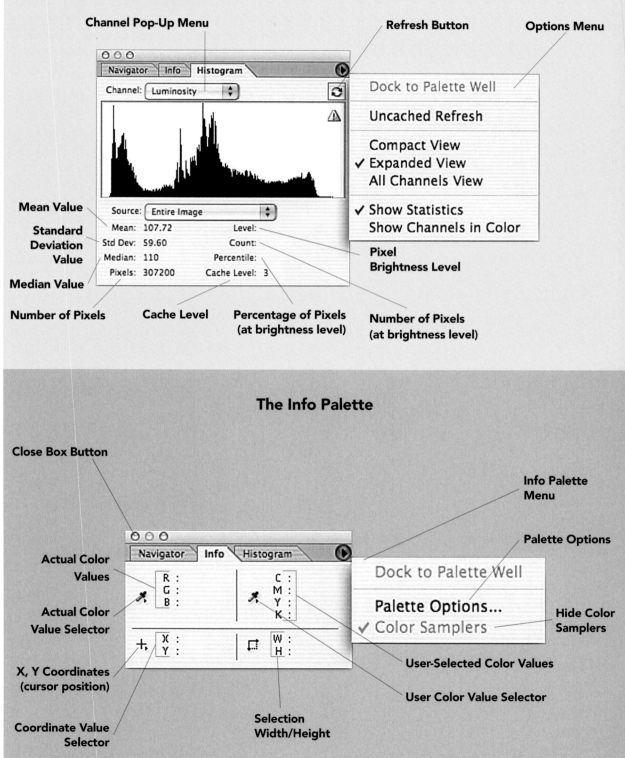

Channel Pop-Up Menu

Refresh Button

Options Menu

Dock to Palette Well

Uncached Refresh

Compact View
✓ Expanded View
All Channels View

✓ Show Statistics
Show Channels in Color

Mean Value

Standard Deviation Value

Median Value

Number of Pixels

Cache Level

Percentage of Pixels (at brightness level)

Pixel Brightness Level

Number of Pixels (at brightness level)

The Info Palette

Close Box Button

Info Palette Menu

Palette Options

Actual Color Values

Dock to Palette Well

Palette Options...
✓ Color Samplers

Hide Color Samplers

Actual Color Value Selector

X, Y Coordinates (cursor position)

Coordinate Value Selector

Selection Width/Height

User-Selected Color Values

User Color Value Selector

THE INFO PALETTE

Although the histogram charts the overall pixel brightness values in an image, it does not tell you where the pixel values are located. To check pixel values in specific areas of the image, use the Info palette. Open the Info palette by selecting Window, Info. The Info palette gives numeric readouts for pixel values based on cursor position. Select any Photoshop tool except the Type tool and move the cursor around the image. The numeric values change in the Info palette as you move the tool around in the image.

The numeric values displayed are based on the current color model in the image. Therefore, each pixel in an RGB image has a corresponding red, green, and blue value. The relative proportion of these values determines a pixel's color. For example, color values of 99R, 88G, 210B result in a blue color with hints of red. If the red value drops to 0, the color becomes blue with a greenish cast because the red is no longer there to cancel out the green. You can experiment further by adding color values in the Color Picker dialog box (double-click the foreground color swatch in the toolbox) to see how color variables affect overall color.

The first group of values in the Info palette represents the original saved color values in the image. The second group of values allows the user to select an alternative color space for comparison. Click and hold the eyedropper icon in either area to display a list of color-space options. Color model options for all color-based lists are Grayscale, RGB, Web Color, HSB, CMYK, Lab, Total Ink, and Opacity.

Setting the White Point and Black Point

The first step in tonal optimization is setting the black point and the white point. You can set these points from either the Curves or Levels dialog box (Image, Adjustments, Curves or Image, Adjustments, Levels). In this process, you set a selected brightness level to absolute black (0) or absolute white (255).

When setting white and black points, notice that some areas that look like flat black or pure white are actually dark grays and light tints based on their numeric readouts in the Info palette. Look for areas where the three color variables are close in value; never

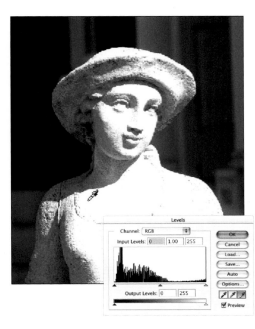

Figure 4.1

The sample image holds critical shadow detail between the RGB values of 10 and 50. The next image shows how setting the black point too low (in this case, RGB

values of 35/43/56) can flatten the shadow detail, even though it adds detail to the subject. The final image shows how setting white point too low (212/199/193

blows out highlight information in the subject even as it opens up the background shadows.

rely on your eyes when setting white and black points. If you accidentally specify a gray area as the absolute white or black point, you will clip the tonal range of the image.

Don't Trust the Monitor

Suppose that you have an area of pixels that show critical shadow details; these pixels have an RGB range of 10 to 50. Depending on the monitor used to view the image, this area could look flat black or light gray. If you click the black point eyedropper on a pixel with an RGB value of 50, all pixels in the image that have a value of 50 or less are instantly converted to absolute black. This means that all the shadow detail goes away, and the image becomes heavy and contrasty looking.

The inverse is also true: Highlight detail can be lost if you set the white point too low (see Figure 4.1). This is why you should never rely on what you see on your monitor to set the black point. To avoid degrading the tonal range, it's important to know the exact pixel values being selected.

Acceptable values vary from image to image, but if there are no values in the 0-to-10 and 245-to-255 ranges, consider resetting the white and black points. Be careful about resetting values that are too far into the grayscale range because they can adversely effect the image. If you make a mistake in setting the black or white point, remember that ⌘+Z (Mac users) or Ctrl+Z (Windows users) functions as the Undo command, even in the Curves or Levels dialog box. You can also click Cancel to exit the dialog box without making any changes.

TRACKING MULTIPLE PIXEL VALUES

When evaluating the tonal range of an image, you will usually want to monitor multiple areas, such as the highlights, shadows, and perhaps a skin tone area. Tracking multiple pixels can be a challenge in that it's hard to sample the exact pixel area repeatedly as you go back to evaluate the impact of various changes. The solution to this evaluation question is to use the Photoshop Color Sampler tool.

Figure 4.2

The Color Sampler tool lets you place sample points that you can reference from the Info palette.

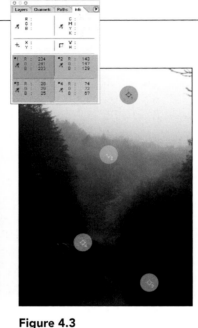

Figure 4.3

Four sample points are placed in the image, corresponding to the primary tonal areas of the image.

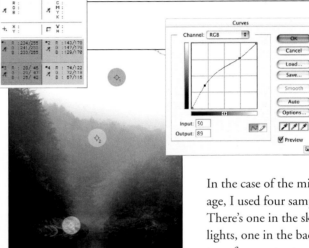

Figure 4.4

As the curve is modified, the before and after values for each point appear in the Info palette

In the case of the misty lake image, I used four sample points. There's one in the sky for highlights, one in the background trees for quarter-tones, one in the rocks for 3/4 tones, and one in the lake reflections for shadows (see Figure 4.3).

My goal was to monitor values in each of these areas, knowing that as I pushed the tonal range, some values would become clear at the expense of other values, which were in danger of disappearing altogether.

Going in, I had a game plan of lightening the image, forcing the sky to white to open the details in the foreground shadow areas. The curve shape shown in Figure 4.4 shows how point 1 is reduced to

The Color Sampler Tool

The Color Sampler tool allows you to place sample points throughout your image and monitor their associated values in the Info palette (see Figure 4.2). To do this, select the Color Sampler tool from the Eyedropper tool pop-out menu in the toolbox. Drag the cursor into the image and click to place sample points. After the points have been placed, you can drag them to other positions or drag them off the image window completely to delete them.

Each sample point you place has a number associated with it. In the Info palette, a new color set area is created with a corresponding number representing the values for that point. Use this approach to define and monitor critical areas within an image so that you can maintain consistent readings.

white, and that the lower shadow areas have been opened up and enhanced. It's a simple matter to reference the before and after numbers in each section to see how things have been affected. This is an especially valuable process when designing for print because you want to ensure that you hold detail in critical areas as you modify the overall image.

Color Models

Most images begin as RGB files; if you're working for the Web, the files may never change from that color model. Having said that, there are circumstances that dictate the use of other color models.

Remember that you can switch the color model by selecting Image, Adjustments and then selecting the desired model from the pop-out menu. These various models can then be selected from any of the pop-up lists in the Info palette (the lists are identified by small black triangles in each of the sections in the palette). By changing color models in the various Info palette sections, you can compare and measure the same pixel in multiple color models. The most common scenario for alternative color models is converting to CMYK for print purposes or to Grayscale for black and white work. But there are other color models listed in the Info palette that you should rely on when the time is right.

One of the most useful models is Lab color. Although Adobe bills Lab color as a great intermediate color space when moving between color gamuts, its most distinctive feature is how it isolates the black channel. The L channel controls the grayscale luminance, while the A channel controls the polar relationship between cyan and magenta. The B channel controls the polar relationship between blue and yellow. When you have the overall color balance right where you want it, switch to Lab color and tweak the Luminance channel to lighten and darken the image without changing the color.

HSB color is sort of the opposite of Lab color in that it gives you full control over color. The H variable controls the Hue, S controls Saturation, and B controls brightness. Switch to the HSB color model and modify the Hue variable to look at alternative colors without disturbing brightness or saturation. Alternatively, isolate the color intensity from the hue or brightness by changing the saturation variable.

One last color model that can help you as you build Web pages is the Web Color model. This color space converts color values to hexadecimal values that are used in prepping Web files.

OPTIMIZING THE TONAL RANGE

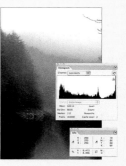

1. Select Window, Histogram to display the Histogram window. Note the black point, white point, and overall pixel distribution.

2. Choose Window, Info to open the Info palette.

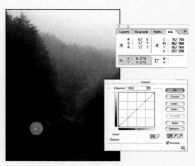

3. Close the Histogram window, then choose Image, Adjustments, Curves. Position the dialog boxes so that all are visible.

4. Click the black eyedropper icon. Use the Info palette readings to find the darkest point in the image and click to set the black point.

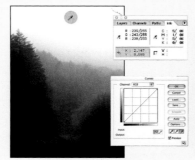
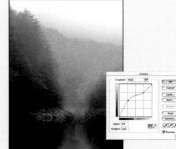

5. Click the white eyedropper icon. Use the Info palette to find the lightest point in the image and click to set the white point.

6. Adjust the curve shape to enhance shadows or highlights. Click OK to close the Curves dialog box and apply the effect.

Trestle Bridge

Coarse Grass

BUILDING THE IMAGE: *IMPEDANCE*

Figure 4.5
The original Coarse Grass image.

Figure 4.6
The Trestle Bridge matches the light direction and intensity of the grass.

Figure 4.7
The Screen blending mode integrates the two layers.

Finding the Right Images

The crucial skill used in creating this image was the image selection process itself. I have a vast library of images, many of which are seemingly obscure. Clumps of grass and a bridge on a foggy morning are two of thousands of images that I considered during the process.

Whenever multiple images are combined, tonal optimization becomes crucial. If the darks and lights don't match from image to image, things will feel forced and unnatural. This was certainly the case in *Impedance:* The white of the sky in the bridge image had to align itself with the highlights in the grass. In addition, the shadows in the grass had to be consistent with the heaviness of the black square.

Adding the Bridge

With the Coarse Grass image as the starting point (see Figure 4.5), I opened, cropped, resized, and rejected countless images before the bridge image asserted itself. The bridge image has a very strong directional light that matches the light on the strands of grass. In addition to the geometric and thematic contrasts mentioned at the beginning of this chapter, the bridge image fit well because the light intensity and direction were exactly right (see Figure 4.6).

Optimizing the Tonal Range

As I added and combined the two images, I optimized their tonal ranges as described earlier in this chapter. I left the Info palette constantly open, and I measured the values throughout the image. Special attention was paid to the shadows in the grass, making sure that they were as deep in value as the black square. This was a delicate task; making the grass shadows too dark would have sacrificed important shadow detail.

Figure 4.8

Attempts were made to integrate the two sides of the image.

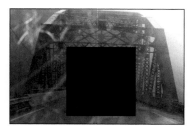

Figure 4.9

The black square is added.

Figure 4.10

A slight blur is brushed into the grass area to complete the effect.

Figure 4.11

The final image

To blend the two layers, the bridge layer was set to the Screen blending mode in the Layers palette. This mode preserved all the highlight intensity while creating a softer, transparent feeling in the shadows (see Figure 4.7).

Integrating the Halves

My next impulse was to try to integrate the two sides of the design with a number of transitional objects. Nothing seemed to connect with the directness of the two combined images. Any other object I tried to work in seemed to detract from the message rather than enhance it (see Figure 4.8).

In the end, adding a single black square to the bridge completed the image. This move enhanced the message because it blocked the secondary path that was distracting the viewer from the focal area of the grass. I added the black square by creating a new layer, dragging a square selection, and filling it with black (see Figure 4.9).

Completing the Images

The final nuance was to add a slight blur to the outer grass areas to make the strands of grass feel sharper (see Figure 4.10). To do this, I duplicated the Coarse Grass image and applied a 12-pixel mo-

tion blur at a 90-degree angle. Then I hid the entire layer with a layer mask and brushed back in specific blades of grass using a light transparency, creating a slight focus blur. The result added additional emphasis to the central strand (see Figure 4.11).

IMPEDANCE

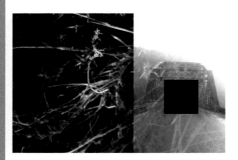

1. Open the Coarse Grass image.

2. Select Image, Adjustments, Curves; set the white point and the black point to optimize the tonal range.

3. Open the Trestle Bridge image.

4. Select Image, Adjustments, Curves; set the white point and the black point to optimize the tonal range.

5. Choose Select, All to select the entire bridge image.

6. Select Edit, Copy to copy the bridge image.

7. Activate the grass image and select Edit, Paste to paste the bridge image into the grass image as a separate layer.

8. Select Edit, Free Transform and drag a corner handle of the bridge layer to resize the bridge layer so that it's the same height as the grass layer.

9. Select the Move tool from the toolbox and drag the bridge layer into position on the right side of the grass image.

10. With the bridge layer active, choose the Screen blending mode from the pop-up menu at the top of the Layers palette, revealing the lower grass layer.

11. Create a new layer by selecting Layer, New Layer.

12. Select the Rectangular Marquee tool from the toolbox. Shift+drag to draw a square selection, and then drag it to reposition it over the bridge.

13. Select the Paint Bucket tool from the toolbox and set the foreground color to black. Click within the square selection to fill it with black.

Image 5
Requiem | ©2002 Daniel Giordan

CHAPTER 5

ENHANCING IMAGE FOCUS

The message in *Requiem* is an obvious one, expressing the temporal nature of beauty and the inevitable erosion of life. It's about getting old. It's about dying. The metaphor may be tired and a bit worn out, but its universal relevance makes it hard to ignore.

The composition features a kind of natural symmetry that feels solid and centered. The leaves form an impenetrable matrix that forces the gaze back to the immediate, "in your face" presence of the central flower image. The detail in the petals and the flower's center draws us in even further.

The flower itself is still quite beautiful, although the dark spots of decay around the edges might lead some to say that it is "aging gracefully." The petals are supple and sensuous, and there is a sense of natural beauty and vibrancy, despite some of the inevitable effects of time.

Although the symmetry of the image suggests one kind of mirroring, the overall metaphor suggests a different kind of reflection. The aging flower is presented in a stark frontal reality, resembling a head or a face. It feels almost like a portrait because it looks directly at the viewer—perhaps even staring him or her down. For some, the flower is a sentinel foretelling the inevitable. For me, it's as if I'm gazing into a mirror, taking inventory and wondering where I left my baseball cards.

●

ENHANCING IMAGE FOCUS

Chapter 5

THE ART OF PHOTOSHOP

ENHANCING IMAGE FOCUS

Image focus is the process of clearly communicating the important areas of an image so that the central message is delivered. Image focus can involve visual emphasis in one area of the image by making use of edge sharpening, color saturation, or other kinds of visual emphasis.

In some cases, image focus involves subtle area enhancement; in other cases, it requires the reduction of image clutter to give a clear view of the subject. After you understand what you want the image to say, all objects and areas should serve that central message. The hard part is maintaining visual clarity without sacrificing image complexity and detail. This involves making consistent creative decisions around a central theme and eliminating ambivalence and contradiction.

Controlling image focus begins when you compose an image in the viewfinder of your camera and extends through on-screen cropping, optimization, montage, and other digital effects. The end result is a cohesive, well crafted message that is both concise and meaningful.

Unsharp Mask Filter

Although the Unsharp Mask filter (Filter, Sharpen, Unsharp Mask) is not a solo act, it does play a critical role in *Requiem.* The Unsharp Mask filter enhances the contrast between adjoining pixels, making edges appear more distinct. It delivers full control of the sharpening process, dictating the amount of sharpening (contrast enhancement), the number of pixels affected (pixel radius), and the degree of contrast required between pixels for a pixel to be considered an edge pixel (called the *threshold*).

Gaussian Blur

There are many useful blur filters in Photoshop's arsenal, but the most useful for enhancing image focus is Gaussian Blur (Filter, Blur, Gaussian Blur). Although specialty filters such as Motion Blur, Radial, and Smart Blur have their place, they don't offer Gaussian Blur's degree of control. The filter offers a single slider that controls the pixel radius of the filter application. The higher the radius value, the more extreme the effect.

Add Noise

The Add Noise filter (Filter, Noise, Add Noise) is useful in creating a soft effect that can act as a counterpoint to sharp focus. It offers a single slider that controls the amount of effect, along with radio buttons that offer Uniform or Gaussian distribution.

By default, the Add Noise filter creates pixilated noise made up of red, green, and blue pixels. This colored "noise" can create an unwanted color cast in some images. Understanding this, the filter also includes a Monochromatic check box that lets you apply a tonal effect with no colorization.

Sharpen, Blur, Dodge, Burn, and Sponge Tools

In addition to filters, Photoshop also features the Sharpen, Blur, and Sponge tools. As you know, filters are applied globally to an entire image; in contrast, these tools can be discreetly applied to specific areas of the image.

The Blur and Sharpen tools are located in a single pop-out menu in the toolbox; you can also select and toggle through them by pressing Shift+R. The tools work as you would expect—sharpening and blurring areas as you brush over them. You control the pressure, blend mode, and brush size of these tools from the Options bar.

The Dodge and Burn tools lighten or darken an image, respectively, while the Sponge tool brushes in saturation or desaturation effects. These tools are located in the toolbox and can be selected and toggled by pressing Shift+O. You control the pressure and brush size of these tools from the Options bar. The Dodge and Burn tools also allow you to select which areas of the image should be modified. Select Highlights, Midtones, or Shadows from the Range menu in the Options bar to modify only those areas in the image. The Sponge tool controls saturation; select Saturate or Desaturate from the Mode menu in the Options bar to increase or decrease color intensity.

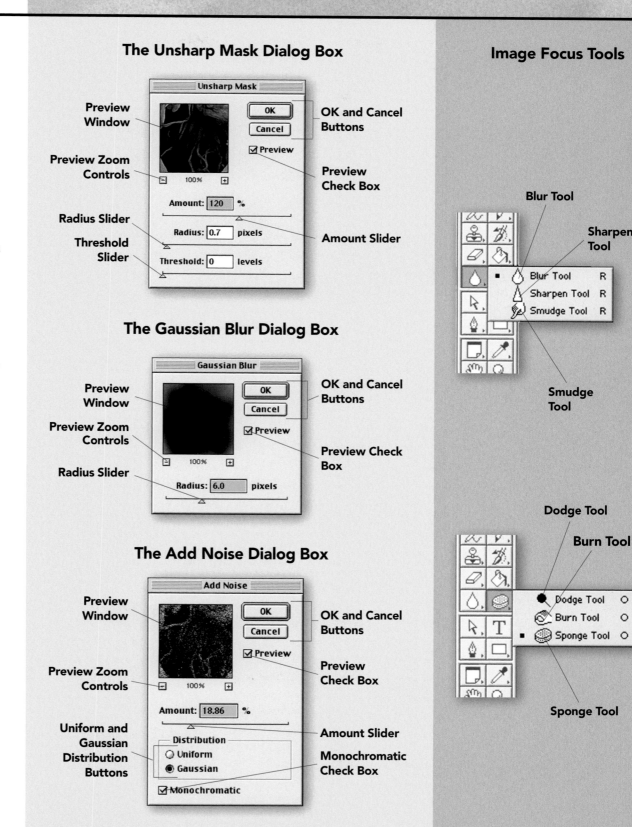

The Unsharp Mask Dialog Box

Preview Window
Preview Zoom Controls
Radius Slider
Threshold Slider
OK and Cancel Buttons
Preview Check Box
Amount Slider

The Gaussian Blur Dialog Box

Preview Window
Preview Zoom Controls
Radius Slider
OK and Cancel Buttons
Preview Check Box

The Add Noise Dialog Box

Preview Window
Preview Zoom Controls
Uniform and Gaussian Distribution Buttons
OK and Cancel Buttons
Preview Check Box
Amount Slider
Monochromatic Check Box

Image Focus Tools

Blur Tool
Sharpen Tool
Smudge Tool

Blur Tool   R
Sharpen Tool R
Smudge Tool R

Dodge Tool
Burn Tool
Sponge Tool

Dodge Tool   O
Burn Tool   O
Sponge Tool O

ENHANCING IMAGE FOCUS

Chapter 5

THE ART OF PHOTOSHOP

IMAGE FOCUS STRATEGIES

When working with photographs, the most basic form of image focus is to move from a soft blur to a sharp-edged focus. This strategy is intrinsic to the

Sharpen Selective Areas

Unfortunately, many designers apply a single sharpening treatment across an entire image and assume that their job is done. Yes, the subject's face is sharp, but so are its shoes, the mountains behind it, and even the birds flying a mile away. Are the birds as important as the subject supporting the central message? Probably not. And if something is not supporting the subject, it's probably distracting.

The first strategy in lending focus to the image is to sharpen selective areas of the image as a way of emphasizing important areas. The "Controlling Image Focus with Multiple Layers" steps that follow present a good way to do this; the Sharpen and Blur tools, which can be brushed directly into the image, are another way to focus the viewer's attention on a particular area of the image.

The Blur tool can create some subtle effects, but beware the Sharpen tool. It can easily get out of hand and create an unwanted pixilated noise effect. To avoid this, lower the Pressure setting in the Options bar. It is often necessary to set the Pressure value in the single digits to gain the necessary

Figure 5.1

Blurring the background can make a soft image appear sharper, as shown in these before and after images.

CONTROLLING IMAGE FOCUS WITH MULTIPLE LAYERS

photographic process and is the most familiar way to control the composition of an image. Large-format view cameras illustrate this approach because their rear film plates tilt and swivel to control the focal plane.

degree of control. With a low Pressure setting, repeatedly brush over the desired area, building the effect slowly. Undo the effect as necessary to gain perspective on the overall progress of the effect.

Another way to sharpen a selected area is by using the Threshold slider in the Unsharp Mask dialog box. The Threshold setting applies the sharpening effect based on the contrast between edge pixels. You can set it to ignore low-contrast edges and apply it only to high-contrast edges. If the objective is to sharpen only the outer edges that define objects and areas, raise the Threshold setting so that more subtle areas are left untouched.

Don't Over Sharpen

Another common mistake when setting image focus is to create too much sharpness. Sharpness is not always desirable. Extreme over-sharpening creates an unnatural halo effect around shapes and objects that looks even worse in print than it does onscreen.

But even when a sharpened image looks technically acceptable, it can still be the wrong thing to do. If sharpness accentuates unwanted facial flaws or creates an unnatural level of detail, for example, avoid it. Many subjects, such as some wedding portraits or landscapes, are more effective if they are rendered in a style that is soft and elusive. There are no firm guidelines here, but you should allow the subject to blur if it helps in communicating the message.

Blur to Sharpen

Occasionally, we are forced to use a poor-quality image that is hopelessly out of focus. For images such as these, all the sharpening in the world won't achieve the desired results—at least not by itself. In addition to sharpening the area of focus as much as possible, it can be helpful to blur unwanted areas such as the background or foreground. In many cases, this blurring makes the subject areas seem sharper and more distinct (see Figure 5.1).

1. Open the desired image and duplicate it by selecting Layer, Duplicate Layer. In the dialog box that opens, click OK.

2. Select the upper duplicate layer (the top one) in the Layers palette. Apply the desired filter such as Blur or Add Noise.

3. Click the Add A Mask icon in the Layers palette to create a blank layer mask on the upper duplicate layer.

4. Select the Brush tool, set black as the foreground color and paint the layer mask to reveal the lower layer.

5. Decrease brush opacity to incrementally apply the filter effect. In this instance, the blur shows through a transparent mask, making it slightly sharper.

6. Repeat steps 1 through 4 to create additional effects. In this example, the saturation was reduced on a separate layer and integrated with the mask.

IT'S ABOUT FOCUS, NOT SHARPNESS

It's important to remember that focus is not necessarily the same thing as sharpness. There are ways to deliver the optimum level of information into the central subject areas other than sharpening the central subject area. Consider the following options as alternatives to the standard image-focus techniques of blurring and sharpening.

Original image

Figure 5.2
Adding shadows or highlights is an effective way to control image focus.

Light to Dark

Information can be veiled or revealed using shadows and light. By combining multiple layers (as explained in the "Controlling Image Focus with Multiple Layers" steps on the preceding page), it's possible to drop unwanted image areas into shadows or stark highlights. In addition, you can use the Dodge and Burn tools to selectively brush shadows and highlights into specific areas. Lower the Pressure setting in the Options bar and use a large brush to ensure a smooth and gradual build-up of the effect (see Figure 5.2).

Figure 5.3

Use the Sponge tool to control color saturation.

Figure 5.4

Consider using a texture or filtered pattern in place of a soft blur to help focus the image.

Monochrome to Color

Color is a powerful and compelling tool for creating image focus. Consider using the multiple layers technique described in the "Controlling Image Focus with Multiple Layers" steps on the preceding page to transition from grayscale to color. In addition, you can use the Sponge tool to brush saturation or desaturation effects into selected areas (see Figure 5.3).

Texture to Sharp

Instead of simply blurring the details, consider obscuring them by using a textured filter effect. This approach works if you use any filter that produces a textured result (try the Add Noise, Brush Strokes, Artistic, and Sketch filter sets). In fact, almost any filter can be applied to specific areas of the image with interesting and sometimes beautiful results (see Figure 5.4). Again, use the multiple layers technique described in the "Controlling Image Focus with Multiple Layers" steps on the preceding page, substituting the filtered areas for those that should be soft and out of focus.

BUILDING THE IMAGE: *REQUIEM*

Figure 5.5

The Rose image is cropped and colorized.

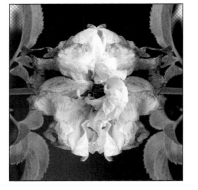

Figure 5.6

The Rose layer is rotated, duplicated, and flipped to create a mirror image.

Figure 5.7

The image is rotated, and a layer mask is used to create a cross-pattern.

Building the Rose

The interesting thing about *Requiem* is that it started with a fairly ugly picture. When I shot the image of the rose, I was drawn to the detail in the wilting petals, but I was uninspired with the overall composition and design.

I began by cropping the image to a square by selecting the Crop tool from the toolbox, dragging a marquee to define the selection, and double-clicking inside the image to apply the crop. To create the soft, monochrome effect, I selected Image, Adjustments, Hue/Saturation, and enabled the Colorize check box. I set the Hue slider to

64 and the Saturation slider to 27 to fine-tune the hue and saturation (see Figure 5.5).

Building the Symmetry

Then I rotated the entire image by selecting Image, Rotate Canvas, 90° CW. With the image on its side, I double-clicked the layer and then clicked OK in the dialog box that opened to change the layer from a background to a standard layer. Then I selected Layer, Duplicate Layer to create a copy of the layer, and Edit, Transform, Flip Horizontal to flip the copied layer.

I reduced the Opacity in the Layers palette to 45 percent, selected the Move tool, and moved the upper layer to align the flowers in the center. With the layers aligned, I reset the transparency to 100 percent, added a layer mask to the top layer, and masked out the right side of the layer to reveal the lower flower image and to integrate the two sides into one (see Figure 5.6).

At this point, the central flower itself was shaping up, but the edges of the image were lacking, and there were a few holes that needed to be patched. To address this, I selected the entire image, chose

Figure 5.8

The Liquify filter is used to create movement and break up the symmetry.

Figure 5.9

A Curves adjustment layer increases the contrast.

Figure 5.10

The Noise filter is applied to the background.

Figure 5.11

A second Curves adjustment layer lowers the background contrast.

Edit, Copy Merged to copy the full composite, and then pasted the image as a third layer. I rotated the new layer 90° clockwise, added another layer mask, and concealed the top and bottom edges to create the cross effect with the stems (see Figure 5.7). Although the image was getting more interesting, at this point it was too symmetrical. To counteract this, I selected the Liquify filter (Filter, Liquify), and lightly brushed it into the leaves to create a soft, swirling effect (see Figure 5.8).

Adding Tones and Texture

With the background coming together, I began to consider the overall feel and tonality of the image. I clicked the Adjustment Layer icon in the Layers palette and created a Curves layer in an effort to increase the contrast and darken the background. I added two curve points, moving them from Input=39 to Output=11 and from Input=175 to Output=155. I then clicked the Add a Mask icon and brushed in the mask to lighten the petals and selected areas of the background (see Figure 5.9).

To add the noise texture to the background, I started by selecting the full image, chose Edit, Copy Merged, and pasted the entire image as a single layer. I then selected Filter, Noise, Add Noise so that I could apply the filter to the entire image. I set the Amount slider to 18.86 and enabled the Gaussian and Monochromatic options. Then I clicked the Add a Mask icon and created a mask to hide the noise area in the flower image, allowing the underlying flower layer to show through (see Figure 5.10).

The final step was to lower the contrast in the noise background to allow the flower to come forward. I clicked the Adjustment Layer icon again and created another Curves layer. I added two curve points, moving them from Input=0 to Output=26 and from Input=255 to Output=182. The final step was to restrict the Curves effect to the background only, leaving the flower untouched. To do this, I created a clipping mask, using the noise layer as the base of the group. I positioned the cursor between the adjustment layer and the noise layer, held down the Option key (the Alt key for Windows users) and clicked, creating the clipping mask. Because of the mask in the noise layer, the curve reduced the contrast in the background only (see Figure 5.11).

5

REQUIEM

1. Open the Rose image.

2. Crop the image to show just the flower and a few adjoining leaves.

3. Select Image, Adjustments, Hue/Saturation. In the dialog box, enable the Colorize check box, set the Hue slider to 64 and Saturation to 27, and click OK.

4. Select Image, Rotate Canvas, 90° CW.

5. Double-click the layer and click OK to change it from a background layer to a standard layer.

6. Duplicate the layer by selecting Layer, Duplicate Layer. Click OK in the dialog box that appears.

7. Flip the new layer horizontally by selecting Edit, Transform, Flip Horizontal.

8. Lower opacity to 45 percent, select the Move tool, and align the two layers.

9. Reset the transparency to 100 percent. Click the Add a Mask icon to add a layer mask to the top layer.

10. Select a large, feathered brush with black as the background, and paint out the top layer, merging the two halves of the image.

11. Choose Select, All, and then Edit, Copy Merged, and paste the entire image to a new layer.

12. Select Edit, Transform, Rotate 90° CW.

13. Click the Add a Mask icon in the Layers palette to add a layer mask to the top layer.

14. Select a 65-pixel feathered brush with black as the background, and mask the top and bottom edges of the image.

15. Choose Select, All, and then Edit, Copy Merged, and paste the entire image to a new layer.

16. Select Filter, Liquify. In the dialog box that appears, distort the leaves in the background.

17. Add a Curves adjustment layer to darken the image. Create two curve points. Move the first from Input=39 to Output=11, and the second from Input=175 to Output=155.

18. Select the Add a Mask icon and airbrush over some of the petals with the foreground color set to black so that some of the lighter petals from the lower layers show through.

19. Select the image and copy all the layers by choosing Edit, Copy Merged.

20. Paste the image into a new layer and select Filter, Noise, Add Noise. In the Add Noise dialog box,, set the Amount slider to 18.86, select the Gaussian Distribution radio button, and enable the Monochromatic check box. Click OK.

21. Mask the Add Noise layer to restore the flower: Select the Add a Mask icon and airbrush over the flower area with the foreground color set to black.

22. Add a Curves adjustment layer to lighten the background and lower the contrast. Create two curve points. Move the first from Input=255 to Output=182, and the second from Input=0 to Output=26.

23. Place the cursor between the Noise and Adjustment layers and Option+click (Alt+click for Windows users) to create a clipping mask.

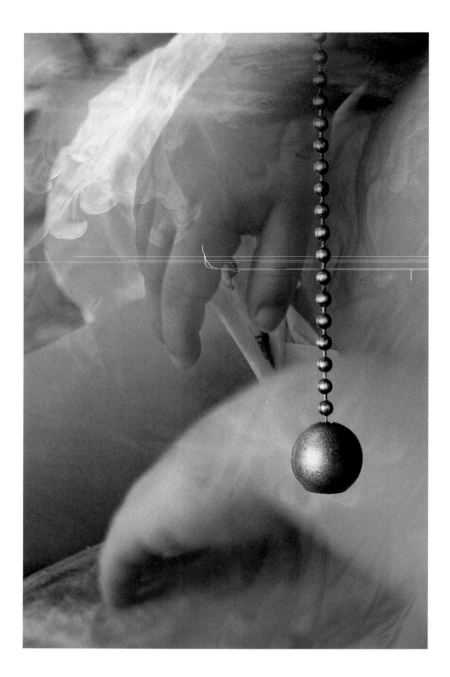

Image 6
Numerical Uncertainty | ©2002 Daniel Giordan

CHAPTER 6

MASTERING CURVES

Rudolph Arnheim expounded on the relationship between Entropy and Art in a 1983 essay of the same title. The premise contrasted man's compulsion for order against the entropic second law of thermodynamics. *Webster's Collegiate Dictionary* defines *entropy* as the degradation of the matter and energy in the universe to an ultimate state of inert uniformity. Simply put, Arnheim's essay addresses the cliché scenario of order versus disorder.

Numerical Uncertainty explores some of Arnheim's ideas. A pair of child's hands lies limp and motionless, pulled down by the effects of gravity and unconsciousness. This irresistible pull is reinforced by the taut vertical tension of the chain, drawing the eye down to the lower-right corner of the image. This sense of gravity dissipates the energy from the objects, rendering them lifeless and inert.

Four thin white lines run horizontally across the upper third of the image, as a buoyant counter to the vertical pull. The lines are broken in places, and occasionally they jump the track, moving from their linear course into random scribbles. The horizontal lines are a slower read compared to the fast linear pull of the verticals, resulting in a suspended, directional tension between horizontal and vertical.

The feeling of suspension is repeated in the slow, billowing clouds of liquid that swirl through the image. These clouds infuse the image with a sense of timelessness that is compelling and energizing. The suspended liquid and lines contrast with the strong vertical pull of the composition, creating a dynamic tension that resists Arnheim's inert uniformity.

●

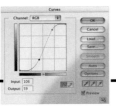

ANATOMY OF A CURVE

Although the Photoshop Curves feature promises complete flexibility over the tonal range, color balance, and overall image appearance, casual Photoshop users still tend toward the use of the Levels feature (or worse) as their color-corrective tool of choice.

The Curves command allows you to make subtle color variations; you can also use it to completely abstract the color relationships within the piece. Curves allow for global corrections, local corrections to single channels, and everything in between. Curves are flexible, powerful, and indispen-

sable. In fact, if I were stranded on a deserted island with just one Photoshop color control, my hands-down choice would be Curves.

Curves are often ignored because they do take a certain amount of study before you understand how all the components interact with each other—while still representing the image's tonal structure. If you take the time to understand how the tonal range of your image maps to the controls in the Curves dialog box, there's a good chance you'll be as convinced as I am of the power of Curves.

The Grid

The Curves dialog box is dominated by a grid of five intersecting lines, arranged horizontally and vertically. These lines correspond to tonal areas in the image: highlights, 1/4 tones, midtones, 3/4 tones, and blacks. Hold the Option key and click the grid (Mac users) or Alt+click (Windows users) to change to an 11-section grid, which further subdivides the tonal range.

The Gamma Line

The image's tonal range is represented by the diagonal gamma line running from the lower-left to the upper-right corner of the grid. Curves allow you to modify pixels within a given tonal

range by clicking and dragging the gamma line up or down. Drag the midpoint of the gamma line up or down to modify the midtones in the image itself. Because the horizontal grid lines represent the tonal scale (divided into quarters), dragging the vertical midtone point (represented by the middle gray areas in the image) up to the 1/4 tones lightens all the midtones in the image to the 1/4 tone values. Think of the horizontal tonal divisions as the starting point for the tonal range; the vertical tonal divisions can be thought of as a reference for image modifications: They help you measure how much you're changing the pixel values.

Notice that when you move a point on the gamma line, the curve bows in a gradual fashion,

changing similar pixels around the actual point value. This is an algorithmic feature of the Curves control that ensures that the changes themselves are gradual, and that they integrate with other unaffected areas in the image. For example, if you changed only those pixels with a 50% value and did nothing to those pixels with a 55% value, the image would break apart and become very abstract. The first basic rule for using the Curves control is that you should keep the gamma line as smooth as possible if you want to create a natural, photographic effect. Too many points or abrupt peaks and valleys in the gamma line seldom creates acceptable results.

110

Other Controls

The Channel pop-up menu on the Curves dialog box allows you to modify the curve of your entire image or of each individual channel. Whether you're working with RGB, CMYK, or Lab color, you can modify each color channel separately. At the bottom of the Curves dialog box is a gradient bar going from black to white (or from white to black), with a set of double arrows in the middle. This gradient tells you the tonal direction of your curve. The tone in the lower-left corner of your curve tells you what value is represented there. Click the double arrows in the middle of the gradient bar to reverse the tonal direction of the curve. The Input field reflects the original curve point position; the Output field reflects the curve's modified position. The Standard Curve and Arbitrary Map icons reside at the bottom of the dialog box; click the Standard Curve icon to return to the default curve state or click the Arbitrary Map icon to draw the curve shape manually.

The right side of the Curves dialog box contains the remaining controls and the various buttons. Under the buttons are the Black Point, Midpoint, and Highlight eyedropper controls, the Preview check box, and the Scale dialog box icon (which enlarges or reduces the size of the Curves dialog box).

Curves Dialog Box

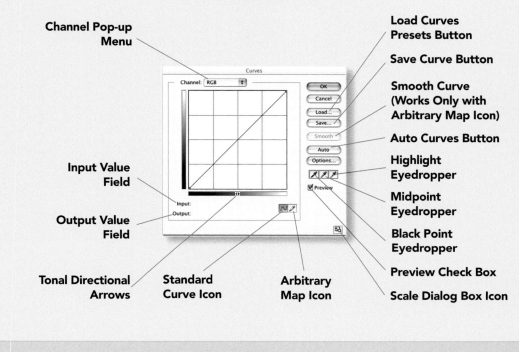

- Channel Pop-up Menu
- Input Value Field
- Output Value Field
- Tonal Directional Arrows
- Standard Curve Icon
- Arbitrary Map Icon
- Load Curves Presets Button
- Save Curve Button
- Smooth Curve (Works Only with Arbitrary Map Icon)
- Auto Curves Button
- Highlight Eyedropper
- Midpoint Eyedropper
- Black Point Eyedropper
- Preview Check Box
- Scale Dialog Box Icon

Curves Tonal Grid

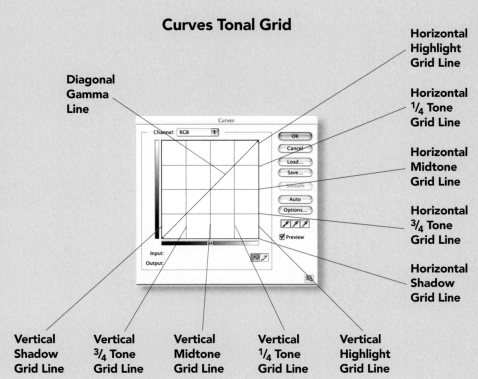

- Diagonal Gamma Line
- Vertical Shadow Grid Line
- Vertical 3/4 Tone Grid Line
- Vertical Midtone Grid Line
- Vertical 1/4 Tone Grid Line
- Vertical Highlight Grid Line
- Horizontal Highlight Grid Line
- Horizontal 1/4 Tone Grid Line
- Horizontal Midtone Grid Line
- Horizontal 3/4 Tone Grid Line
- Horizontal Shadow Grid Line

BASIC CURVE TECHNIQUES

Curves can be confusing at first because it's hard to translate the dynamic tonal range of an image into the sterile, diagonal black line of the Curves dialog box. A good way to understand this relationship is to open the Curves dialog box and then click and drag the mouse pointer over an RGB image. The pointer changes to an eyedropper when you do this, and a dot appears on

the diagonal line, corresponding to the pixel values you are currently "sampling."

You can also access individual color channels using the Channels pop-up menu in the Curves dialog box, Notice how the sampled point in the image

Original Image

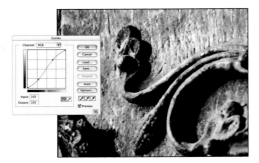

Standard "S" Curve

Extreme "S" Curve

Adding Points to the Curve

Although you could just start dragging the line in the Curves dialog box around, it's a much better idea to add points to the line and modify them. These points give you more control—and a better understanding of the adjustments you're making. To add a point, place the mouse pointer on the diagonal gamma line and click to create a fixed point. You can drag this point to modify that tonal area, or you can use it as an anchor. If you want to leave a portion of the tonal range unchanged by the surrounding

curve modifications, click an anchor point without moving the curve.

When you create a point, a value appears in the Input field at the bottom of the Curves dialog box. When you move the point, the Output value changes to represent what the original Input value will change to. For example, click a point on the curve at the 128 mark and drag it down until the Output field reads 66; this action changes the midtone values (from the original value 128) to 3/4 tones (down to the value 66), reducing the brightness by half. Be

aware that the curve is dynamic; if you slide horizontally, you will move the Input point as well as the Output point.

Arbitrary Mapping

In addition to setting points on a curve, you can also draw a curve with a pencil tool. To do this, click the Arbitrary Map icon in the Curves dialog box and begin to draw in the grid. This approach creates an erratic result that is often abstract and colorful.

After you have drawn the curve, you can temper the result using the Smooth button. Click the

Smooth button to see the curve shape smooth out, as the image reverts to a more normal appearance. Click the Standard Curve icon and points appear on the curve you drew, ready for further modifications.

Curve Shapes

Anyone who has played with curves can tell you that too many points and an erratic curve shape will distort and abstract the color in the image. Although you can occasionally use these distortions to your advantage, they have served to scare more people away

relates to that single channel (the location of flesh tone information along just the red curve, for example). Although you cannot apply this technique to the composite channel of a CMYK image, you can apply it to the individual CMYK channels. Experimenting like this is a great way to understand how the tonal range of an image is dispersed along the diagonal gamma line.

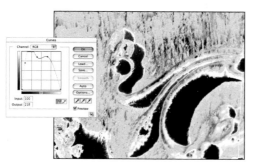

Erratic Curve Setting

from Curves than to endear them to the feature. For a naturalistic image, minimize the number of points in the curve and keep the slope smooth and gradual.

Let me underscore the fact that the basic shape of the curve affects the overall image. Specifically, steeper areas of the curve reflect greater contrast, and the flatter curve areas reflect reduced contrast. Therefore, if you want to see more detail in the midtones of your image, raise the highlights and lower the shadow areas, creating a steep curve slope in the midtone area of the graph. As you

raise and lower these areas, notice that the curve shape of the highlight and shadow areas gets flatter. The midtone area gets steeper, however, which creates more contrast and detail in this area.

Raising the highlights and lowering the shadows creates a classic "S" curve, which works well for flat or normal-balanced images that need an overall contrast boost. Overdoing it can cause a loss of detail in the shadows, blown-out highlights, and an artificial, high-contrast look.

CREATING AN "S" CURVE

The "S" curve increases the contrast in flat or normal contrast images. The same basic approach can be used to create any of the other curve shapes.

1. Open an image file and select Image, Adjustments, Curves to launch the Curves dialog box.

2. Move mouse pointer over the curve until the Input value is 191. Click to place the first point on the gamma line.

3. Move mouse pointer over the curve until the Input value is 64. Click to place the second point.

4. Drag the first point up until the highlights open up, but still look natural. (A typical Output value range can be 210–230.)

5. Drag the second point down until the midtone contrast increases without completely closing up the shadows. (A typical Output value range can be 45–30.)

6. Click OK to close the dialog box and apply the effect.

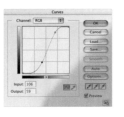

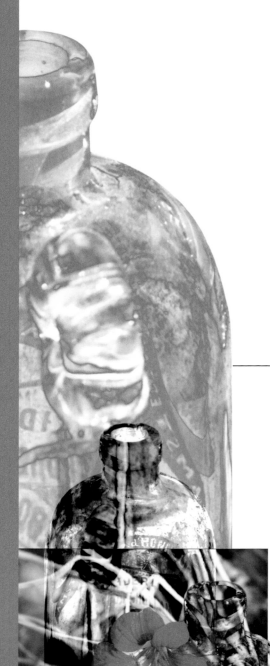

OTHER CURVE SHAPES

Understanding how tones are dispersed on the curve, along with the power of a basic "S" curve, will take you far in your work with the Curves command. You should be aware of other curve shapes, however, that will allow you to invert an image or cause interesting and sometimes useful abstractions.

Figure 6.1

The original Image.

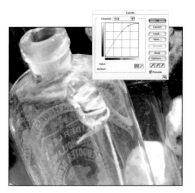

Figure 6.2

Notice how the sharp-rise curve brings out the text in the bottles

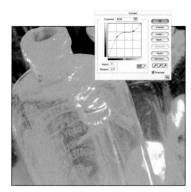

Figure 6.3

The mid-plateau curve flattens the midtones

Sharp Rise

Raising the highlights to an upper plateau results in a steeper curve in the 1/4 tones to midtones. This curve shape can open up an image that's too dark, although it can also flatten out fine detail in the lightest highlights (compare the original image in Figure 6.1 with Figure 6.2).

Mid-Plateau Curve

Raising the shadows and lowering the highlights results in a chair-like shape, with a flat plateau in the midtones. Although a balanced image might suffer from this treatment, images that are primarily light or dark will benefit from the extra range this gives the lights and shadows (see Figure 6.3).

With a solid understanding of which areas of the curve impact the final image, you will discover numerous other shapes for this curve as well. Think about applying these curves to single channels (which you can select from the Channels pop-up menu in the Curves dialog box) or to specific selections. The curve shapes are listed here, accompanied by the resulting changes in a reference image.

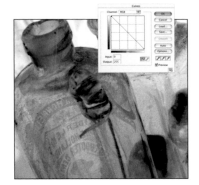

Figure 6.4
An inverted curve creates a negative image

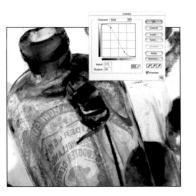

Figure 6.5
An inverted "S" curve creates more detail in the (inverted) midtones

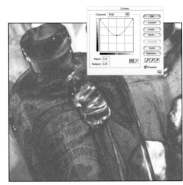

Figure 6.6
The "U" curve inverts only the shadows.

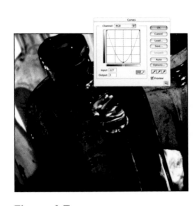

Figure 6.7
The deep "U" curve inverts the shadows while changing the midtones to shadows

Inverted Straight Curve

Making a curve move from the upper-left to the lower-right corners of the grid results in the inversion of the original image to a negative image. This does the same as the Invert command, although using the Curves dialog box allows you additional fine-tuning of the curve (see Figure 6.4).

Inverted "S" Curve

Modifying an inverted curve to show a backwards S results in a negative image with the heightened contrast characteristics of the aforementioned "S" curve (see Figure 6.5).

The "U" Curve

Raising the highlights up to the top-left shadow area while anchoring the midpoint results in an image in which the midtones and highlights remain the same while the shadows invert to highlight values (see Figure 6.6).

The Deep "U" Curve

In addition to raising the shadow point, the deep "U" curve also lowers the midpoints to the shadows. At this point, the only tonal values that remain constant are the highlights, while the midtones go dark, and the shadows go light (see Figure 6.7).

COLOR CORRECTING WITH CURVES

Up to this point, we've looked at how the Curve controls map to the tonal range of the image. We've also learned to use the curve shapes to make global corrections and abstractions. This brings us to specific strategies for color corrections that respond directly to the unique requirements of an image.

Using the Curves dialog box to color-correct an image requires even more study because we must stop and understand a bit about color spaces, numeric representation of color, and color channels. This page should set the stage for getting you started on the path of numeric color correction.

Original image

Figure 6.8

This chart shows the polar relationships between red/cyan, green/magenta, and blue/yellow.

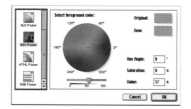

Red curve up

Red curve down, add cyan

Green curve up

Green curve down, add magenta

Blue curve up

Blue curve down, add yellow

Understanding Additive and Subtractive Color

RGB (which stands for red, green, and blue) is the native color space for the digital medium. The monitor you look at uses red, green, and blue pixels to describe every color on your screen. In addition, most scanners capture their images using red, green, and blue filters, capturing raw data in the RGB format.

RGB is a *luminous* color space in that the light is passed through an object from behind, registering on receptors in front of the device. Other examples of luminous devices are your television, stained glass windows, and one of my favorite toys of all time, the Lite Brite. (Although the windows and Lite Brite don't qualify as RGB color spaces, they are examples of luminous color.) RGB color is an *additive* color space in that the maximum combination of all three color variables equals white; the minimum combina-

  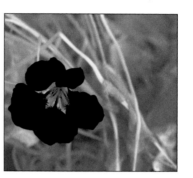

tion of all three color variables equals black.

By contrast, CMYK space is a *subtractive* color space in that the maximum combination of all four variables equals black, and the minimum combo is white (no ink on white paper). The CMYK color space is *reflective* rather than luminous: light bounces off the paper or substrate into our eyes. CMYK stands for Cyan, Magenta, Yellow, and blacK.

The main point to remember for color correction is that RGB and CMYK are not just contrasting color spaces, they are exact polar opposites. If you take away the black plate for each color space (which is a printer's addition, not a theoretical requirement), the colors align at opposite ends of the same poles. The polar relationships are Red/Cyan, Green/Magenta, and Blue/Yellow. This means that when you increase the Red variable (in an RGB image), the image not only

looks more red, it looks less cyan. More green means less magenta, and so on. Figure 6.8 shows examples of these color polarities.

Understanding Tonal Values in Channels

Your education in additive and subtractive color spaces comes into play when you look at individual channels in an attempt to correct color. Open the Channels palette and choose an individual color channel to view it. In RGB, dark tones signal the absence of color and white signals the presence of color. For example, in the RGB color space, looking at the Red channel for a picture of a red flower would show a white flower shape. For an image in the CMYK color space, the opposite is true: dark areas signal a color's presence, which would create a dark flower shape in the Magenta channel (the channel closest to red). Figure 6.9 shows the original image and how it looks in the RGB and CMYK color spaces. If

the flower image were yellow, the Yellow channel in the CMYK color space would be black. For a yellow flower in the RGB color space, the Blue channel would be black (blue is the inverse of yellow).

When correcting color with Curves, you should start with an audit of the color distribution across the channels. You can do this by using the Info palette or by checking the individual color channels in the Channels palette. Make adjustments by selecting a color from the Channels pop-up menu at the top of the Curves dialog box and adjusting the curve to be lighter or darker. You can also select multiple channels and adjust each one individually to create a cumulative result.

Using the Info Palette to Set a Strategy

The Info palette is crucial when you're doing curve-based color corrections. We covered the

Info palette in some detail in Chapter 4, "Optimizing Images," so flip back a few chapters if you need a refresher on the details. The main application here is that the Info palette shows interactive readouts of color values as you roll over different areas of the image. Open the Info palette before you launch the Curves dialog box so that you can measure specific areas as you're correcting colors in the image.

IMAGES USED

Hands

Green Liquid

Chain

BUILDING THE IMAGE: *NUMERICAL UNCERTAINTY*

Figure 6.10
Curves are applied to the hand image

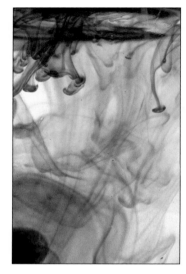

Figure 6.11
Curves are used to change the image of the liquid from green to blue

Figure 6.12
The liquid image is added to the hands with the Difference blending mode.

Starting with the Hands

Any time you're compositing a design from multiple sources, Curves should play a vital role. This is because it's important to optimize each image being added. Curves also help set a consistent color balance and nudge tonal areas to make sure that everything fits together as it should.

I started with the Hands image, which was taken of my four-year-old son as he slept. It was captured in black and white in a dark room, so the exposure was a bit on the

dark side. I used Curves to set the black and white points in the image, opening up the image and adding more detail to the hands. The best white point I could find in the original image was at 160 (out of a possible 255), which signifies how overexposed the image was. The black point was a more reasonable value, however, and a basic curve adjustment was made, with a point at Input=148, Output=176 (see Figure 6.10).

Adding the Water

Then I opened and optimized the Green Liquid image. After applying the Unsharp Mask, I used Curves to change the image from green to blue. Specifically, I shifted the Blue channel from Input=64 to Output=194. I moved the Green channel from Input=146 to Output=88 (see Figure 6.11).

I placed the water image on top of the hands layer and applied the Difference blending mode to the water layer (see Figure 6.12). To temper the strong saturation ef-

Figure 6.13

The Hands layer is duplicated, placed over the water layer, and blended with a mask.

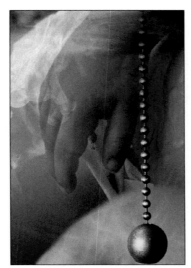

Figure 6.14

The chain is added and silhouetted against the background.

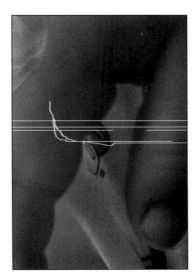

Figure 6.15

Lines are drawn on a separate layer.

Figure 6.16

The final image.

fect, I duplicated the hands layer and moved it over the water layer. A layer mask was applied; a light gray was applied to the entire mask using the Paint Bucket tool to achieve a transparency of 33%. Then I used the Brush tool, with the color set to white, to darken some of the shadows in the hands (see Figure 6.13).

Pulling the Chain

The image really started coming together with the addition of the Chain image. After dragging the chain into its own layer, I used a layer mask to silhouette it against the rest of the design. Once the mask was set, I needed to find a way to fade the chain into the cloud pattern in the top. After experimenting with the burn and brush tools, the lighting effects filter was applied to it in order to fade the chain as it moved towards the top (Figure 6.14). With the mask thumbnail selected, a single spotlight with a white light was used pointing down from the top.

Finishing with Lines

The final step was to select the pencil tool with a one-pixel brush, and add the lines. These lines were added to a separate layer so that the cycle of drawing, erasing, and redrawing could be repeated until things felt right (Figure 6.15). Once the lines were drawn, the layer was repositioned to ensure that the placement was optimum (Figure 6.16).

6

NUMERICAL UNCERTAINTY

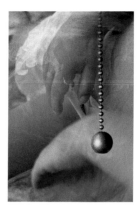

1. Open the Hands image.

2. Open the Curves dialog (Image, Adjustments, Curves). Set the black point and white point to optimize the image, and raise the midpoint of the curve (from Input=148 to Output=176).

3. Open the Green Liquid image and Copy/Paste it into the composite image.

4. Open the Curves dialog box (Image, Adjust, Curves). Select the Blue channel from the channel pop-up menu and raise the midpoint of the curve (from Input=64 to Output= 194).

5. Select the Green Channel from the Channel pop-up menu and lower the midpoint (from In-put=146 to Output=88). Click OK to apply the curve.

6. Highlight the Green Liquid layer in the Layers palette and select Difference from the Blending Mode pop-up menu in the Layers palette.

7. Highlight the Hands layer and select Duplicate from the Lay-ers palette menu.

8. Drag the new Hands layer above the modified Green Liquid layer.

9. Click the Layer Mask icon to add a layer mask to the dupli-cated Hands layer. Click the mask thumbnail in the Layers palette to highlight it.

10. Select the Paint Bucket tool and make black the fore-ground color. Set the opacity to 33% in the Options bar and click in the image to fill the mask with light gray.

11. Select the Brush tool with a 45-pixel brush and set the foreground color to white. Paint the mask in the areas of the hand shadows to darken them.

12. Paste the Chain image as a separate layer.

13. Click the Layer Mask icon in the Layers palette to add a lay-er mask to the Chain layer. Highlight the mask thumbnail in the Layers palette.

14. Select Filter, Render, Lighting Effects. Create a thin spotlight shining down over the chain mask. Set the light source to white and click OK to apply it.

15. Select New Layer from the Layers palette menu to create a new layer.

16. Select the Pencil tool from the toolbox with a one-pixel brush and the foreground color set to white. Draw horizontal lines, holding down the Shift key as necessary to constrain the di-rection.

17. Reposition the lines layer to complete the effect.

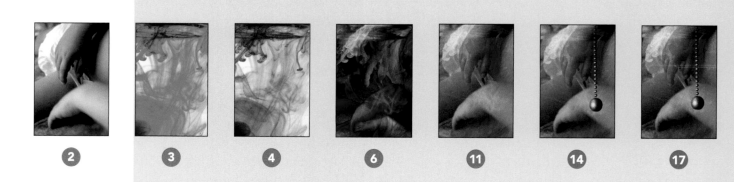

2   3   4   6   11   14   17

Image 7
Oblique Ascension | ©2002 Daniel Giordan

CHAPTER 7

MASTERING COLOR CORRECTION TECHNIQUES

After being featured in *Requiem*, the White Rose image makes another appearance in *Oblique Ascension*, although it delivers a very different message in the process. In *Requiem*, the rose reflected on aging, death, and the inevitable passage of time; in *Ascension*, it rises…floats in a way that is almost transcendent.

Oblique Ascension is imbued with a pervasive sense of mystery and ambiguity that keeps us from feeling any resolution or security in the moment. The fog and the water create an infinite periphery that extends so far that our only real point of focus is what's right in front of us. The rose is shrouded and veiled, hiding within itself as it elevates above the water. Even the trees make us feel off-balance, as their symmetry and mirrored arrangement imply that something is not quite right. Thus we have a mysterious, transcendent moment; stepping outside of our normative experience into something we still cannot quite grasp.

The title comes from the astronomical reference to a rising star. In an elusive yet hopeful gesture, the rose rises over the implied horizon of the water's edge. In fact, *oblique ascension* is a little-used astronomy term that refers to the alignment of the equator with Aries, creating the shape of an oblique sphere.

The title also borrows from the bodily ascent of Jesus into heaven after his resurrection. He told his disciples that he was going to prepare a better place for them; a place that was beautiful, mysterious, and transcendent. They placed their hope in this improbable mystery, and in a benefactor whose promise was punctuated by an unnatural movement upward.

●

CORRECTING IMAGE COLOR

Adobe created Photoshop with the basic idea that choice and variation in software design is a good thing. They don't provide just one way to correct color; they deliver 12 different correction options. Why have 12 options when you need only one? The idea is twofold (if not twelvefold). First, there are many different kinds of Photoshop users. Some are very technical and understand complex color theory; others are casual users who own Photoshop only because it was bundled with their $200 scanner. Twelve color options allow Photoshop to

deliver as much or as little control as necessary to meet the needs of the user and the image.

The second reason for so many controls is that the science of color involves a number of variables that can be manipulated globally or in smaller subsets. Sometimes you want to change just one of these components using a more specialized tool rather than using a general-purpose tool for global corrections. For example, changing a slight color cast involves a different approach than making radical changes to the hue or saturation of an image. Conversely, making a global change in overall contrast would be very difficult if you had to change hue, saturation, and brightness independently. In short, each tool has its place, depending on the task at hand..

The Basic Categories

The 12 color options can be grouped into four basic categories: global controls, component controls, isolation controls, and specialty controls. These categories contain options for both beginners and advanced users, from the basic slider metaphor of Brightness/

Contrast to the complexities of Curves and the Channel Mixer. The color controls and their respective categories are outlined in the sections that follow.

Global Controls

Global controls tend to have fewer control variables. The most basic control is Brightness/Contrast, followed in complexity by Levels and Curves. Although Curves is perhaps the single most powerful color tool (it's detailed in Chapter 6, "Mastering Curves"), the Levels and Brightness/Contrast controls tend to be more simplified. They

offer two or three basic variables that modify the entire image.

You wouldn't use Brightness/Contrast to modify only the red ribbon in a girl's hair for example. This approach would be cumbersome at best…not unlike doing surgery wearing boxing gloves. Global controls modify an image in broad strokes, as evidenced by single command variations such as Auto Levels, Auto Contrast, Auto Color, and Desaturate.

As is the Curves control, Selective Color is another powerful global control. Selective Color allows you

to select a specific color range—such as all the reds, greens, or blacks—and add or subtract cyan, magenta, yellow, or black to just that range.

Component Controls

Component controls allow pinpoint control over specific color building blocks, such as color or spectral variables. The Variations, Color Balance, and Hue/Saturation controls fall into this category.

Variations is a beginner's tool that can help you visualize color relationships and how they impact your image. It uses thumbnails of the image arranged in a color wheel, showing the impact of incremental color adjustments.

The strength of the Color Balance control is in the way it isolates polar color variables on a sliding scale, which can be modified specifically in highlights, midtones, or shadows. Although these variables exist in the Levels palette, for example, the controls are reversed there and are harder to control than in the Color Balance dialog box.

The Hue/Saturation control isolates specific attributes of a given color. Hue, Saturation, and Brightness can be modified independently, allowing you to maintain one variable (such as a specific shade of blue) while changing the others (its saturation or brightness).

Isolation Controls

The isolation color controls perform as promised: They isolate specific colors or color variables, allowing you to get at that red ribbon or make subtle changes to the color range. This category includes the Replace Color and Color Range commands.

The Replace Color control works in a direct way, allowing you to specify an exact color within an image and replace it with another

color. The sole purpose of the Color Range command is to allow you to make a selection based on the colors in an image.

Specialty Controls

Frankly, this category is for the stuff that's left over and doesn't fit in any other category. You'll find the Channel Mixer and Gradient Map in this category.

The Channel Mixer control is hard for many people to grasp in that it blends multiple grayscale channel values into a single grayscale channel that affects how a single color variable displays its color. Even now it sounds kind of mystical, although I do go into it in some detail in the following pages.

The Gradient Map also uses grayscale data, although it's a bit more straightforward than the Channel Mixer. Gradient Map applies the values of a predefined gradient to the grayscale channel data of an image. The result is a graphic, duotone effect that can be very powerful. The Gradient Map control is detailed in Chapter 17, "Using Gradients and Gradient Maps."

The Adjustments Submenu

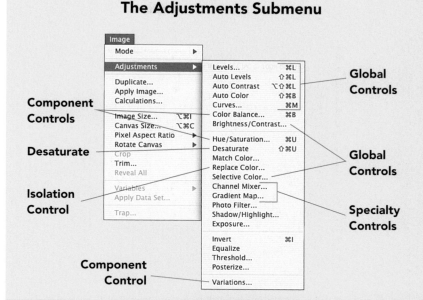

The Color Balance Dialog Box

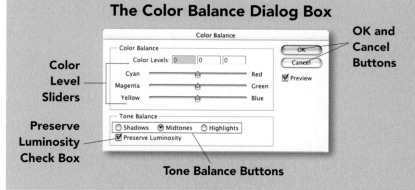

USING COLOR BALANCE

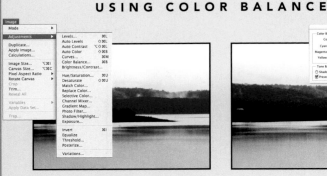

1. Choose Image, Adjustments, Color Balance to launch the Color Balance dialog box. If desired, choose Window, Info to open the Info palette and track the color values.

2. To adjust the color cast in the highlights, click the Highlights option in the Tone Balance section and drag the color balance sliders. In this example, the green slider was raised 5 points.

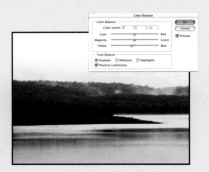

3. To adjust the color cast in the midtones, click the Midtones button in the Tone Balance section and drag the color balance sliders. In this example, yellow was increased by 47 points and green by 12 points.

4. To adjust the color cast of any shadows, click the Shadows button in the Tone Balance section and adjust the color balance sliders. In this example, yellow was increased by 12 points.

5. Click OK to close the Color Balance dialog box and apply the effect.

CORRECTING COLOR CASTS

Color correction involves correcting the flaws in an image to bring it back in line with its natural appearance. Photographs and scans can take on unnatural color casts that must be corrected to make things look normal. In addition, artificial light sources such as fluorescent or incandescent lights can add a green or yellow cast to an image.

Color Balance or Selective Color

Photoshop offers two color correction controls that are very similar in approach and operation. Color Balance and Selective Color both feature a slider approach that modifies specific areas of the color range. It's important to understand the similarities and differences to ensure that you use the proper tool at the right time.

As you learned in the Step-by-Step sidebar on this page, the Color Balance dialog box lets you isolate a specific tonal range (such as highlights or shadows) and make slider-based color changes within that range. This approach works well for images that have a predominant color cast in specific tonal areas. In many cases, poor exposure, sun damage, or poor scanning can create this cast. To check for color casts, use the Info palette to measure similar hues across the three tonal areas.

Rather than isolating tonal areas, the Selective Color dialog box (Image, Adjustments, Selective Color) allows you to isolate specific color areas. You can select all the reds, yellows, greens, cyans, blues, or magentas in an image and add or subtract cyan, magenta, yellow, or black from each color area. You can even isolate the whites, neutrals, and blacks in an image.

Key to using these tools is getting a feel for where these variables start and stop. Most areas are not solid green or red—they tend to be a combination of multiple colors. When you use Color Balance, you will find that color casts tend to exist in more than one tonal area. In fact, if you've been paying attention, you may be asking why you need Color Balance at all if Selective Color lets you isolate the whites, neutrals, and blacks. The answer is in how well each tool isolates the tonal range. Figure 7.1 shows an image that I modified by adding 50% magenta with both Color Balance and Selective Color. You can see that Selective Color darkened the shadows significantly, indicating that Selective Color does not isolate color changes in tonal areas as effectively as does Color Balance; Selective Color tends to be more of a global adjustment tool.

Fluorescent Lighting

Fluorescent lighting is a common correction scenario. In the example in Figure 7.2, the original image of a fish tank shows the effect of the cold green fluorescent light attached to the top of the tank. The Info palette shows high readings in the green channel; the image is also washed out, which is typical of fluorescent lighting. The green cast was most prominent in the white area just below the fish's eye. I used the Curves control to set the white point in this area, which corrected most of the green cast. Chapter 4, "Optimizing Images," has more on setting the white and black points. I also used the Color Balance tool to make additional tweaks.

After the fish image was balanced, creative changes dictated an increase in saturation, so I added a slight reddish cast using the Hue/Saturation control. Although the actual scene was not so vibrant as what appears in the figure, the correction enhances the subject and the overall feel of the image.

Color Cast in Scans

Scans with a color cast are another reason to unpack Photoshop's color controls. Bad scans can result from sloppy scan prep, a cheap scanner, or even a faded original. In many cases, clients may send you poor digital files, and you will have no idea why they look as bad as they do.

The example in Figure 7.3 shows a color cast and a poor exposure. The image is flat with little contrast. In addition, it's green in the midtones and shadows, and blue/magenta in the highlights. The corrective changes involved opening up the exposure by raising the composite RGB curve from Input=32 to Output=56. Then I used Color Balance to modify the highlight, midtone, and shadow areas to balance the color and make things look natural. Then I got creative by applying a curve with an adjustment layer by changing the settings from Input=183 to Output=230. Doing so dramatically increased the contrast in the face, creating a stark, washed out effect. I added a mask to the adjustment layer to maintain more of a normal exposure in the toy figure.

Original Image   *Modified with Color Balance*   *Modified with Selective Color*

Figure 7.1
Color Balance did a better job of restricting the magenta color change to the midtones. Selective Color modified the magenta throughout the image, sacrificing detail in the shadows.

Original Image   *Black and White Points Added*   *Color Adjusted with Hue/Saturation Controls*

Figure 7.2
Adjusting the white and black points corrects the washed out, green cast from the fluorescent lights; creative color adjustments increase the color intensity.

Original Image   *Color Balanced Image*   *Adjustment Layer Skews Contrast*

Figure 7.3
Creative color adjustments increase the color intensity and saturation, enhancing the subject matter.

USING REPLACE COLOR

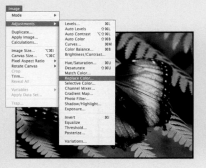

1. Choose Image, Adjustments, Replace Color to launch the Replace Color dialog box.

2. Choose the Color Sample eye-dropper tool and click in the main image window to sample the target color. Adjust the Fuzziness slider to expand or contract the sample range.

3. Choose the Add to Sample eye-dropper and click any other colors in the main image to define the full color range to be modified. Use the Subtract from Sample eyedropper if necessary.

4. Adjust the Hue slider in the Transform section of the Replace Color dialog box to change the sampled colors.

5. Click OK to close the Replace Color dialog box and apply the effect.

USING COLOR CONTROLS TO OPTIMIZE GRAYSCALE

It may sound like a contradiction in terms, but color controls can be very effective in creating and optimizing grayscale images. When color is out of the picture, the tonal values in a grayscale image must be clean and distinct. They must describe the details in the image, define texture and light quality, and communicate spatial relationships.

In addition, the graphic nature of black-and-white images creates a certain emotional impact that is unique to the medium. Therefore, it's important to control how color maps to grayscale if you want to maintain image detail and deliver an emotional impact.

Grayscale Conversion Options

As with most Photoshop tasks, there are many ways to convert color images to grayscale. Some of these options should never be attempted; others can be used to suit your preference or the requirements of the image.

Options to Avoid

If you're guilty of using any of these methods to convert a color image to grayscale, you should resolve to mend your ways and adopt some of the painless alternatives that follow. The list of things not to do includes:

- **Grayscale:** It sounds like a good idea on the surface: Selecting the Grayscale command

(Image, Mode, Grayscale) *does* turn the image to black and white, but the sacrifices are significant. All color channels are replaced with one grayscale channel, making it very hard to isolate tonal areas. I know that there are times when an image must be converted to grayscale—for the Web, for duotones, and the like—but for the most part, avoid this command until the grayscale image has been optimized.

- **Desaturate:** Using the Desaturate command (Image, Adjustments, Desaturate) sucks the color out of an image with no regard for tonal relationships or optimum contrast. This command offers no preview or control.

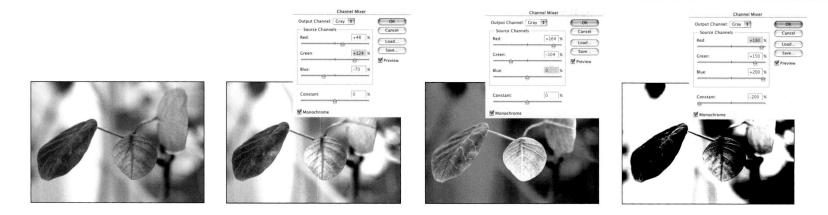

Figure 7.4

All these grayscale variations were created from a single RGB image using Channel Mixer. The Channel Mixer settings are displayed next to each result.

- **Hue/Saturation:** Reducing the Saturation slider in the Hue/Saturation dialog box (Image, Adjustments, Hue/Saturate) eliminates the color in an image or layer, but again, there is no control over how the gray values are mapped.

- **Variations:** Yes, it is possible to select the Saturation radio button in the Variations dialog box and click your way to a black-and-white image. Not only is this approach difficult to control, it's way too much work.

Acceptable Grayscale Conversion Options

By now, it should be clear that you're looking for a grayscale conversion option that will allow you to preview the results and modify the color relationships as needed. The following options offer acceptable levels of preview and color control:

- **Color Channels:** Open the Channels palette and click each channel color to view its grayscale information. The grayscale info will be different in each case because tonal arrangement is dictated by the colors in the image. For example, high concentrations of a channel's color will appear lighter or even white in the preview. In the green channel, for example, grass or trees would be the lightest areas.

  Remember that you can modify this grayscale channel image using Curves, Levels, or any other color controls. If you get a result you like, highlight it, select Duplicate Channel from the Channel palette menu, and select New as the destination in the dialog box that appears. A new file is created with the grayscale info you just previewed.

- **Lab Color:** Because Lab color isolates a file's tonal information in the L channel (*L* stands for Luminance), this can be a good area to check. Convert the image to Lab color by selecting Image, Mode, Lab Color. Then proceed with the Channels palette as just described.

- **Gradient Map:** You can apply a Gradient Map using a black-to-white gradient. With this method, you can modify the break in the gradient transition to control how the grayscale data maps to the color image. Chapter 17 provides complete details on using the Gradient Map tool.

- **Channel Mixer:** One of the easiest and most powerful color controls in your repertoire is the Channel Mixer. This control allows you to combine data from all channels into a single grayscale result. It also includes a master slider to control the overall contrast.

  Choose Image, Adjustments, Channel Mixer to launch the Channel Mixer dialog box. Select the Monochrome check box and modify the Source Channels sliders to combine the channel data. Modify the Constant slider for global control over lightness and contrast. This approach allows you to achieve multiple results from a single color image (see Figure 7.4).

White Rose

Lake Trees 1

BUILDING THE IMAGE: *OBLIQUE ASCENSION*

Figure 7.5

The Lake Trees 1 image is optimized using the Curves dialog box..

Figure 7.6

Free Transform is used to compress the Lake Trees 1 image from a rectangle into a square

Figure 7.7

After doubling the canvas width, the image is duplicated and flipped

Setting the Table

Oblique Ascension got off to a very inauspicious start with the overexposed image of a misty lake. The image was brought back into service by setting the black and white points and making a simple curve adjustment (see Figure 7.5). Even at this point, the image had such a strong left-to-right narrative that it was hard to use. I considered flipping it so that the trees were on the left, but this, too, was less than satisfactory.

The final solution was twofold: First I compressed the image horizontally using Free Transform (see Figure 7.6). After selecting the Free Transform command (Edit, Free Transform), I moved the left middle handle of the bounding box toward the center, compressing the image into a square aspect ratio that compressed things horizontally, without modifying the vertical proportions. With the image feeling like more of a square, I doubled the width of the canvas, duplicated the background layer, and flipped and aligned the two layers (see Figure 7.7). This created an interesting backdrop for the central figure of the rose, setting the table for the steps that followed.

Adding the Rose

The White Rose image was added and dragged into position in the lower center of the canvas (see Figure 7.8). I added a layer mask and carefully painted out the background to create the silhouette of the flower. In creating the mask, it was important to zoom in very closely to make sure that the edges were properly defined. It was also necessary to turn off lower layers and to use a combination of soft-edged and hard-edged brushes to create an acceptable result (see Figure 7.9).

The placement of the flower was another point of experimentation. Initially, I placed it in the center, in agreement with the mirrored nature of the overall composition. I also tried placing multiple flowers off-center, to the right, and to the lower left of the image.

Figure 7.8

The White Rose image is added to the composition.

Figure 7.9

A layer mask is used to silhouette the rose.

Figure 7.10

A Color Balance adjustment layer is added to complete the effect.

Figure 7.11

The final image

Ultimately, placing the flower in the lower center of the image accentuated the feeling of elevation, which played well against the tree limbs springing from the center of the image.

Completing the Image

Completing the image involved adding the last touches of detail and nuance to the White Rose. First I used the Replace Color controls to isolate the center shadow areas of the rose and to push in a soft blue with a slight increase in saturation and lightness. The blue created some interesting color variations, while remaining in the cool color range suggested by the trees and water. One of the most

difficult imaging challenges is to create nuance in the shadows. This shade of blue held the overall shadow effect while delivering expressive, saturated color.

Then I tweaked the overall color of the flower to align it with the blue I had added in the Replace Color step. Changes centered around the shadows and midtones; I added a slight blue cast to the overall flower and pushed magenta into the shadows (see Figure 7.10). Zooming back out, Figure 7.11 shows the final result.

7

**OBLIQUE
ASSENSION**

1. Open the Lake Trees 1 image.

2. Select Image, Adjustments, Curves and set white point and black point to optimize tonal range. Modify the composite in the Curves dialog box from Input=193 to Output=214.

3. Choose Edit, Free Transform and drag the left handle to the right to form a square image.

4. Choose Image, Canvas Size. In the dialog box that appears, double the width dimension and set the Anchor placement to the left middle square. Click OK to double the canvas width.

5. Highlight the background layer in the Layers palette and select Duplicate Layer from the Layers palette menu.

6. With the new layer active, choose Edit, Transform, Flip Horizontal.

7. Drag the new layer to the right and align the edges of the two layers to create a single, mirrored image.

8. Open the White Rose image and drag it into the composition.

9. Lower the opacity in the White Rose layer to aid in aligning it with the background. Drag the rose into position and reset the opacity to 100%.

10. Click the Add Layer Mask icon in the Layers palette to add a layer mask to the White Rose image.

11. Set the foreground color to black and set the brush size parameters; then paint the mask to erase the background and silhouette the rose.

12. Choose Image, Adjustments, Replace Color. In the dialog box that appears, click the Color Sample eyedropper tool and click the light pink tones in the center of the rose. Adjust the Fuzziness slider to select the desired color area.

13. In the Transform area of the Replace Color dialog box, adjust the hue slider to +180 to specify a warm blue color. Increase the Saturation slider to +12 and click OK.

14. Click the Adjustment Layer icon in the Layers palette and select Color Balance from the pop-up menu.

15. In the Color Balance dialog box, enable the Shadows radio button and move the Magenta slider to −32. Enable the Mid-tones radio button and adjust the Cyan slider to −54, the Magenta slider to −11, and the Yellow slider to +27. Click OK to create the adjustment layer.

16. If necessary, drag the adjustment layer to the top position in the Layers palette, just above the White Rose layer.

17. Position the cursor on the line between the adjustment layer and the White Rose layer. Hold down the Option key (Mac users) or the Alt key (Windows users) and click to create a clipping mask that restricts the adjustment layer to the rose only.

1 3 7 9 13 17

Image 8
Gesture | ©2002 Daniel Giordan

CHAPTER 8

MAKING HUE AND SATURATION ADJUSTMENTS

Gesture is silent and peaceful, its drama unfolding in static slow motion like time-lapse photography. A single hand lies draped across the lower-right corner of the image—motionless, vulnerable, perhaps even sleeping. Above it is a landscape dominated by a tree shrouded in a morning mist. The atmosphere is high chroma, saturated and intense, blending with its surroundings to create a sense of color that is almost palpable.

At the top of the image, the tree fades into a brilliant light that is cleansing, pure…perhaps even epiphanous. Our eyes are led down the right side of the image by the billowing organic branches that gain in contrast, picking up speed as they tumble towards the earth. The tree shape ends with the abrupt flip of one of its limbs, stopping in deference to the resting hand.

The hand is the destination of our eyes and the recipient of the light. The light and the hand come together in a way that is almost tactile; skin and finger details are revealed, while the form of the hand slips into the shadows of the foreground. As the branch and hand create a visual tension, the composition moves across the bottom of the image, moving downward, until the alignment of the trunk and the fingertips pulls our gaze straight up to the top of the image and into the blinding light.

●

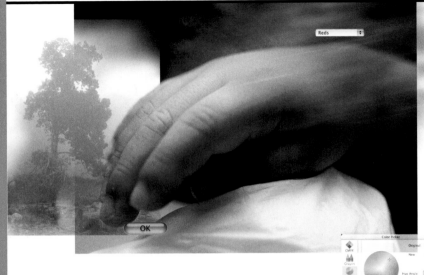

HUE/SATURATION AND HSB COLOR

The Hue/Saturation tools are a great way to control color shade and intensity for a single color or a range of colors within an image. Although other color controls allow you to control the color within specific areas of the tonal range, Hue/Saturation controls the colors across the actual color spectrum. It's a great choice for changing a ball from red to blue, or perhaps for punching up the color intensity in a sunset.

Introduction to Hue/Saturation

The Hue/Saturation controls are located in the Hue/Saturation dialog box and comprise three primary slider variables: Hue, Saturation, and Lightness. These controls allow you to change the actual hue of a selection, the intensity (saturation) of the color, and the lightness of the color.

You can also select specific color areas for editing from the dialog box's Edit menu. Edit menu options include the RGB and CMY variables of red, yellow, green, cyan, blue, and magenta. Using this menu, it's a relatively easy task to select a color area such as red and then modify the slider values for all the reds in the image.

The HSB Color Model

The Hue/Saturation controls are related to the HSB color model, which stands for Hue/Saturation/ Brightness. The HSB color model allows you to view your image or selection using the same variables shown in the Hue/Saturation controls.

The HSB color model allows you to measure the current hue or saturation before you make any changes. The easiest way to do this is to open the Info palette (choose Window, Info) and set the User Value Color Selector to HSB. (For full details on the Info palette, see Chapter 4, "Optimizing Images.") Although this does not actually change the color model being used in the image, it does allow you to

measure pixel values with HSB variables. With the HSB color model active, you can drag the cursor through the image and measure the hue position on the color wheel (hue is measured in degrees) or the percentage of saturation or brightness of the color.

The Apple and Adobe Color Pickers are two Photoshop controls that can help you understand HSB color—and consequently the Hue/Saturation controls. The Adobe Color Picker is the default picker and the one most people use, but for an introduction to HSB, you should start with the Apple Color Picker. To activate it, you must choose it in the Preferences dialog box (choose Photoshop, Preferences, General) and

then click OK. Click the foreground color swatch in the toolbox to launch the Apple Color Picker.

The buttons across the top of the Apple Color Picker allow you to choose the color mode you want to work in. Click the Color Sliders Mode button and then choose HSB from the Color Options pull-down menu. Yes, although Photoshop uses different terms for the lightening variable (Brightness, Lightness, Value), all the terms have the same impact: each lightens the color. The Hue angle is measured in degrees and starts at zero, which is the equivalent of 3 o'clock; zero degrees is red. Experiment by entering a numerical value in the Hue Angle entry field.

The Hue/Saturation Dialog Box

Edit Menu

Hue Slider

Saturation Slider

Lightness Slider

Colorize Check Box

Preview Check Box

Pre-Adjustment Color Bar

Eyedropper Tool

Add To Sample Tool

Subtract From Sample Tool

When you move the Hue slider in the Hue/Saturation dialog box, you're moving around this color wheel for your selection. Moving towards the center of the wheel decreases color saturation, tinting the color towards the absence of saturation, expressed as pure white. Moving the Brightness slider darkens the color.

With this basic visualization of the Apple Color Picker, take another look at the Adobe Color Picker. Select the Adobe Color Picker in the Preferences dialog box (choose Photoshop, Preferences, General) and click the Foreground color swatch to launch the Adobe Color Picker. The H, S, and B radio buttons display the Hue, Saturation, and Brightness relationship in a slightly different way. The radio button variable is displayed in the vertical slider bar, and the other two variables are mapped to the X/Y axis in the color display window. Thus, if you select the S radio button, saturation is displayed in the vertical bar, moving from pure color down to pure white. Hue is displayed in the window along the horizontal axis, and Brightness runs vertically.

The Apple Color Picker

Color Wheel

The Adobe Color Picker

Hue Radio Button

Saturation Radio Button

Brightness Radio Button

Color Display Window

Vertical Slider Bar

ADJUSTING HUE AND SATURATION

1. Choose Image, Adjustments, Hue/Saturation to launch the Hue/Saturation dialog box.

2. If desired, use the Edit drop-down menu to select a range of colors to modify; alternatively, leave the Edit menu set to Master.

3. With the Preview check box selected, enter a value or drag the Hue slider to change the color relationships.

4. Move the Saturation slider to the left or right to decrease or increase color intensity.

5. Move the Lightness slider to the left or right to darken or lighten the image.

6. Click OK to accept the results.

LOCALIZED HUE/SATURATION TECHNIQUES

Most people never go past using Hue/Saturation as a global tool to modify an entire image or selection. One of the real strengths of the tool is its capability to isolate and modify specific colors. Mastering these techniques will allow you to exercise full control over color changes that embrace the entire spectrum or that fall within a very narrow range.

Understanding the Color Bars

Although the three sliders in the Hue/Saturation dialog box are pretty easy to understand, the re-mainder of the controls in the dialog box are less intuitive. The two color bars at the bottom of the dialog box with the triangles and slider bars do not explain them-selves visually. What makes it even more difficult to figure out is that, most of the time, these controls are grayed out and inaccessible.

The top color bar represents the starting color values; the bottom bar represents the changes to the color spectrum. As you move the Hue slider, notice that the color in the bottom bar shifts. Thus, by comparing the top bar with the bottom bar, you can predict how the color changes will map to the entire spectrum (see Figure 8.1). For example, if you want to change a red flower to yellow, move the Hue slider until the yellow area of the bottom bar is under the red area in the top bar, showing that the reds have shifted to yellow. For global changes, you will probably just look at the im-age until you like the color that results, but you'll see that an un-derstanding of the relationship

Figure 8.1

The top color bar reflects original color relationships; the bottom bar reflects the changes.

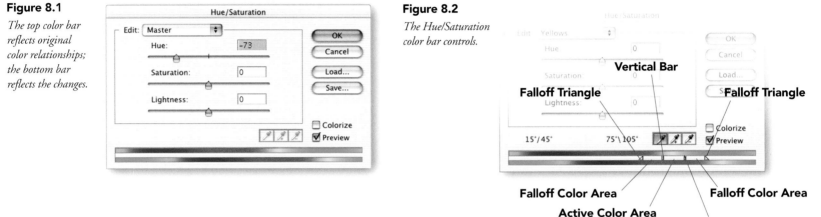

Figure 8.2

The Hue/Saturation color bar controls.

between the two color bars in the Hue/Saturation dialog box is crucial when using localized techniques.

Isolating the Color Range

You can isolate a portion of the total color range in an image for modification. It is impossible to do this when the Edit pop-up menu is set to Master, so click and hold the menu and select one of the preset range values. The range controls (a series of triangles and vertical bars) appear between the two color bars (see Figure 8.2). The bars and triangles work to define an active color area and a

falloff color area. The space between the two vertical bars is the active color area, and the two spaces between the bars and the triangles represent the two falloff areas.

If you select Yellows from the Edit pop-up menu, the active color area centers on the yellow area of the color bars; when the effect is applied, it will fade out across the color spectrum up to the points marked by the triangles. You can modify the controls to adjust both the position and the range of the effect. Drag one of the triangles to increase the falloff range. To modi-

fy the active color area, click and drag one of the spaces between the triangles and bars. As you drag, the active color area expands or contracts, while repositioning the falloff area across the color spectrum. To increase the active color area without changing the position of the falloff area, click and drag one of the bars. The triangle remains stationary, and the size of the falloff area is altered. To shift the active color area and the falloff areas without changing any of their proportions, click and drag the active color area.

Above the color bars in the dialog box are two sets of numbers. The

first represents the hue angle position of the left falloff triangle and the first active color bar. The second represents the second active color bar and the right falloff triangle. If you know that the target color in your image is at 297° on the hue circle, you can drag the controls to the exact position based on these readouts. If you're not one for referring to the Info palette, you can instead use the eyedropper tools to select the colors in the image that you want to modify.

HUE/SATURATION STRATEGIES

Now that we've discussed the details of how the Hue/Saturation dialog box works, it's time to cover selective strategies and techniques. The ideas presented *here should serve as a starting point for further exploration, while providing additional examples of how the Hue/Saturation dialog box is used*

Using the Colorize Check Box

The Colorize check box can be thought of as the lazy man's duotone. It converts the entire image to a tint of a single color, which can be modified by the control sliders. Select the Colorize check box to get started; the image is automatically reduced to one color and the Saturation slider is lowered to 25, simulating the aforementioned duotone effect. The bottom color bar changes to a flat color, which changes as you move the sliders (see Figure 8.3).

Figure 8.3

The original image, the Colorize effect, and the Hue/Saturation dialog box settings.

Isolating a Single Object

With careful manipulation of the active color area and falloff ranges, it is possible to isolate an object of a dominant color, while de-emphasizing the background. Possible effects could include desaturating the background to black and white, lightening the background to a tint, or any other combination of variables that creates a strong contrast (see Figure 8.4).

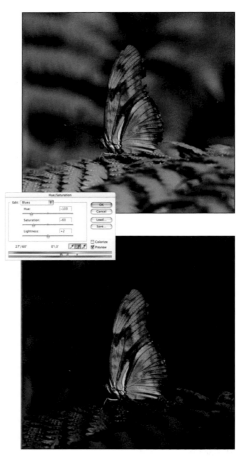

Figure 8.4

The original image, the isolation effect, and the Hue/Saturation dialog box settings.

EDITING A COLOR RANGE WITH HUE/SATURATION

1. Choose Image, Adjustments, Hue/Saturation to launch the Hue/Saturation dialog box.

2. From the Edit pop-up menu, select the range of colors you want to modify. In this example, the Reds option is selected.

3. Drag the Saturation slider to –100, turning the preset red range in the image to gray.

4. Click the Subtract From Sample Eyedropper tool and click any colors in the image you want to subtract from the effect.

5. Click the Add To Sample Eyedropper tool and click in the image to add back any desired colors.

6. Modify the sliders as desired to achieve the final effect within the defined color range.

Excluding a Single Color

To activate the color range controls, you must select a color variable such as Reds from the Edit pop-up menu. The best way to include all colors except for one is to position the falloff triangles on opposite sides of the isolated color. When you drag the controls off one side of the color bar, they appear on the opposite side (see Figure 8.5). If you drag the falloff triangle off the left side, it reappears on the right side. You can then position the falloff triangle in the green, excluding the yellow. You can drag the bar as well, further defining the active area and falloff characteristics.

Figure 8.5

The original image, the Single Color effect, and the dialog box settings.

Fog Tree

Hand

BUILDING THE IMAGE: *GESTURE*

Figure 8.6
The optimized image, Motion Blur, and darkened image layers are combined.

Figure 8.7
A pair of Curves adjustment layers heighten contrast and stretch the tonal range.

Figure 8.8
Adding the first hand layer sets the shadows and foreground detail.

A Gesture of Color

Gesture is a careful combination of two images, fused together with color and light effects. A total of six separate adjustment layers were used to modify the layer stack, with a host of layer masks thrown in to isolate the effects to specific areas.

After optimizing the Fog Tree image, I knew I had to minimize the foreground to serve as a backdrop for the Hand image that was to follow. The solution was to apply a motion blur set to a distance of 182 pixels at a 0° angle. Then I applied a layer mask using a black-to-white vertical gradient, hiding the motion effect in the tree area (Chapter 17, "Using Gradients and Gradient Maps," details the use of gradients). I painted in more of the mask to remove the remaining motion effects from the leaves.

At this point, the blur was integrated into the foggy landscape, but the details in the tree were still pretty sketchy. To remedy this, I duplicated the original tree image and dragged it to the top of the layer stack. I applied a curve to heighten the contrast and used a mask to brush the details into only the leaves and roots of the tree. The final result was a tree image with solid detail, a blurred foreground, and a misty ambience (see Figure 8.6).

Curves Adjustment Layers

To push the tonal range further, I added a Curves adjustment layer to brighten the image and fade the tree out at the top. With the top of the tree fading out, a second Curves layer darkened down the remainder of the image while increasing the contrast (see Figure 8.7).

Adding the Hand

I created the hand area of the image in two stages. The first application set up an interesting foreground base for the hand to rest on, while defining interesting shadow areas and darker details. To do this, I added the Hand image to the layer stack and used

Figure 8.9

The second hand layer adds back the details.

Figure 8.10

Red color accents are added with a Hue/Saturation adjustment layer.

Figure 8.11

Another Hue/Saturation adjustment layer adds a violet color cast and transforms the red accents.

Figure 8.12

A Curves and Hue/Saturation Adjustment layer creates the final image.

a layer mask to silhouette the hand from its background. After I had the proper extraction, I used the Hard Light blending mode to create the stark contrast effect (see Figure 8.8).

Then I duplicated the Hand layer and set the layer blending mode to Normal. I painted in the layer mask to isolate the effect of the Normal Hand layer to just the hand, ignoring the white foreground area (see Figure 8.9).

Adding Hue/Saturation Effects

The filter effects and the images were working well together at this point, but the overall color in the image was a flat and monochrome green. In an effort to modify the overall color cast in the image, I added a Hue/Saturation adjustment layer. I shifted the Hue slider to −66 and increased the Saturation slider to +28 to create an ambient red glow. Then I added a layer mask to the adjustment layer to push the red coloration into the edges of the tree and the roots (see Figure 8.10). By this time, I knew that I was going to add a second adjustment layer, and I wanted to use the red to create color contrast and differentiation.

I added the second Hue/Saturation adjustment layer to create a global color cast. I lowered the Hue slider to −125 and the Saturation slider to −40 (see Figure 8.11). Notice

that the hand is untouched by the color effect because the hand is a black-and-white image that contains neither hue nor saturation.

Finishing the Image

Although the color was better at this point, things still felt a little flat and tepid. To create more drama, I created a Curves adjustment layer and positioned it in the layers stack below the Hue/Saturation adjustment layers created in the previous section. I darkened the shadows by changing the black and white point values from Input=138 to Output=67 and Input=188 to Output=162. I masked out this effect from parts of the tree and the thumb area of the hand.

I created a final Hue/Saturation adjustment layer to desaturate part of the hand. To do this, I set the Saturation slider to −100 and used a mask to push the effect into the fingers. Although I could have achieved this effect by adding to the layer mask of the previous layer, I decided to create a separate layer so that I would have the flexibility to revert without upsetting the current effect of the mask (see Figure 8.12).

8

GESTURE

1. Open the Fog Tree image.

2. Open the Curves dialog box (choose Image, Adjustments, Curves). Set the black point and the white point.

3. Select Duplicate Layer from the Layers palette menu.

4. Choose Filter, Blur, Motion Blur. Set the distance slider to 182 pixels and the Angle position to 0°.

5. Click the Add Layer Mask icon to apply a layer mask to the filtered layer.

6. Click the Gradient tool in the toolbox and click the gradient icon in the Options bar. Set the gradient colors to black and white.

7. Hold down the Shift key and draw a vertical gradient from the top to the bottom of the image, with black at the bottom.

8. Select the Brush tool and touch up the mask so that the leaves and roots of the tree are sharp.

9. Duplicate the original Fog Tree layer and drag the duplicate to the top of the stack.

10. Choose Image, Adjustments, Curves to launch the Curves dialog box. Move the points from Input=64 to Output=52, and from Input=178 to Output=210.

11. Click the Add Layer Mask icon to apply a layer mask. Choose a paintbrush with black as the foreground color and paint in the mask to show the contrast details in the leaves and roots of the image.

12. Click and hold the Adjustment Layer icon in the Layers palette and select Curves from the pop-up menu. Move the points from Input=176 to Output=231, and from Input=56 to Output=50.

13. Click and hold the Adjustment Layer icon in the Layers palette and select Curves from the pop-up menu. Move the points from Input=53 to Output=20, and from Input=211 to Output=175.

14. Add the Hand image to the composite and set the blending mode in the Layers palette to Hard Light.

15. Click the Add Layer Mask icon to apply a layer mask. Choose a paintbrush with black as the foreground color and paint in the mask to silhouette the hand and foreground.

16. Select Duplicate Layer from the Layers palette menu.

17. Choose a paintbrush with black as the foreground color and paint in the mask to silhouette the hand.

18. Click and hold the Adjustment Layer icon in the Layers palette and select Hue/Saturation from the pop-up menu. Specify these settings: Hue: −66, Saturation: +28, Lightness: 0.

11   13   15   17   19   20   24

19. Choose a paintbrush with black as the foreground color and paint in the mask to apply the Hue/Saturation effect to the edges of the objects.

20. Click and hold the Adjustment Layer icon in the Layers palette and select Hue/Saturation from the pop-up menu. Specify these settings: Hue: −125, Saturation: −40, Lightness: +1.

21. Click and hold the Adjustment Layer icon in the Layers palette and select Curves from the pop-up menu. Move the points from Input=126 to Output=68, and from Input=184 to Output=156.

22. In the Layers palette, drag the Curves adjustment layer under the previous two Hue/Saturation adjustment layers.

23. Click and hold the Adjustment Layer icon in the Layers palette and select Hue/Saturation from the pop-up menu. Specify these settings: Hue: 0, Saturation: −100, Lightness: 0.

24. Choose a paintbrush with black as the foreground color and paint in the mask to apply the Hue/Saturation effect to the fingers in the hand.

Image 9
The Mystery of Folded Sleep | ©2002 Daniel Giordan

CHAPTER 9

WORKING WITH ADJUSTMENT LAYERS

To Say Before Going to Sleep *by Ranier Maria Rilke*

Translation by Albert Ernest Flemming

I would like to sing someone to sleep,
have someone to sit by and be with.
I would like to cradle you and softly sing,
be your companion while you sleep or wake.
I would like to be the only person
in the house who knew: the night outside was cold.
And would like to listen to you
and outside to the world and to the woods.

The clocks are striking, calling to each other,
and one can see right to the edge of time.
Outside the house a strange man is afoot
and a strange dog barks, wakened from his sleep.
Beyond that there is silence.

My eyes rest upon your face wide-open;
and they hold you gently, letting you go
when something in the dark begins to move.

Rilke's poem and *The Mystery of Folded Sleep* both speak of the unique and primitive vulnerability that comes with sleep and dreams. We have all known the protective care we take before going to sleep: locking the door, looking outside, and perhaps lying in bed wondering whether we've left a window unlocked. Have we left an opening? Is the danger real or imagined? Does our safety depend on our actions or, for most of us, is it a byproduct of random chance?

There's no denying that the sleeping boy is dreaming. His dreams are veiled, mysterious, and yet compelling. We get a glimpse of something just behind the trees—just around the corner so to speak. And the desire to look and to push forward is almost irresistible. Looking for that strange man, listening to the barking dog, and hoping that a pair of eyes rest on us…wide open…gently holding.

●

USING ADJUSTMENT LAYERS

Adjustment layers are for those who can't make up their mind, or at least for those who like to leave their options open. With all the progress we've made with the undo commands and the History palette, there's still a degree of finality about image editing. At some point, we pass the point of no return; the point where we can't revert to a previous state. And it's usually at this point that the composition changes and you wish you could trace your steps back and go in another direction.

This is where adjustment layers come in. They allow you to make edits within a separate layer that can be applied to the entire image or to just a single layer. Turn the layer on or off, and keep the process fluid forever. Make as many changes as you want to the adjustment layer without ever compromising the original image

Using Adjustment Layers

Adjustment layers are special layers that allow you to modify all or part of an image without altering the actual source material in any individual layer. To be specific, an adjustment layer contains image editing settings that are applied to the layers beneath it in the layer stack.

Photoshop offers 15 different commands you can associate with an adjustment layer: Solid Color, Gradient, Pattern, Levels, Curves, Color Balance, Brightness/Contrast, Hue/Saturation, Selective Color, Channel Mixer, Gradient Map, Photo Filter, Invert, Threshold, and Posterize. When you create an adjustment layer, an icon representing the specific adjustment appears in the Layers palette. In addition, a layer mask is automatically created and linked to the layer.

To apply the layer mask, highlight a target layer, click the Adjustment Layer icon in the Layers palette, and select an editing option from the pop-up menu that appears. This action launches the corresponding control for the selected option, allowing you to apply the desired settings. Clicking OK creates the adjustment layer, which will appear in the stack of layers in the Layers palette just above the target layer.

If you have just one layer, the process is simple and straightforward; the process can get a bit more complicated when you're working with a multi-layered image. The reason is that an adjustment layer affects all the layers beneath it in the stack, and there will be times when you want to change just a portion of the lower layers. There are two approaches to take in these instances: clipping groups and layer sets.

Clipping Masks

Clipping masks create subgroups of layers that are controlled by the transparency of the lowest layer in the group. In other words, the transparency in the lowest layer acts like a mask that restricts the visibility of the higher layers. If the lower layer is a circle on a transparent background, the upper layers will only appear within that circle.

Clipping masks work well to restrict an adjustment layer to the layer just beneath it (or to other layers in the group that may be visible with transparency). The next pages feature step-by-step instructions with details on setting up clipping masks with adjustment layers.

Group Layers

An alternative to a clipping mask is a group layer. Group layers are subfolders in the Layers palette that isolate a group of layers so that you can apply the adjustment layer to them.

To create a layer group, select New Group from the Layers palette menu, assign a name as desired to the new layer in the dialog box that appears, and click OK. When the layer group folder appears in the Layers palette, drag any layer to the layer group folder to add to that group. You can also rearrange the layers within that group. The key thing to remember with adjustment layers and layer groups is that you must change the blending mode from Pass Through to Normal. By default, layer groups are set to the Pass Through blending mode, which makes the set behave as though it were part of a normal layer group as far as blending modes, adjustment layers, and other forms of layer interaction are concerned. Changing this setting to Normal restricts the effect of the adjustment layer to only the layer group.

If these approaches don't work for your image, remember that you can always duplicate an adjustment layer and drag it to any other layer in the group, combining the layers with a clipping mask, as just described. This works well when the order of the layer stack does not allow placing all the layers to be adjusted in the same group or set.

The Layers Palette

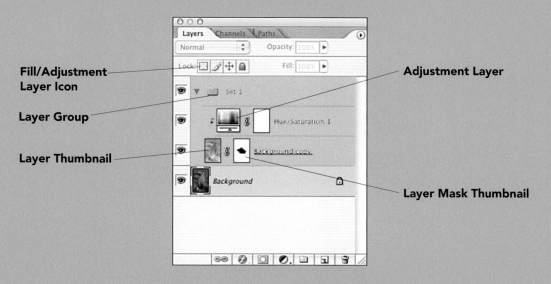

Fill/Adjustment Layer Icon

Layer Group

Layer Thumbnail

Adjustment Layer

Layer Mask Thumbnail

The Adjustment Layer Options

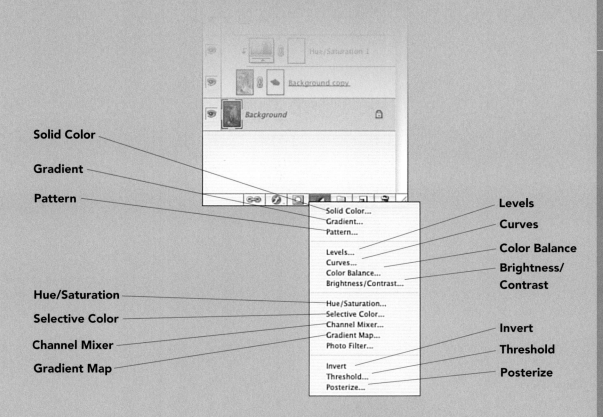

Solid Color

Gradient

Pattern

Hue/Saturation

Selective Color

Channel Mixer

Gradient Map

Levels

Curves

Color Balance

Brightness/Contrast

Invert

Threshold

Posterize

ADJUSTMENT LAYER STRATEGIES

It's one thing to understand the mechanics for creating adjustment layers, and another thing to develop a feel for how and when to use them. The following sections show how a multilayered file can change dramatically based on the adjustment layer choices that are made. The following text also gives additional tips and insights on how to push things further, exploring more advanced techniques.

Figure 9.1
The original image and its associated Layers palette.

The Original Image

The original image for this exploration is the sleeping child superimposed over a water droplet (see Figure 9.1). This image starts with four separate layers for the droplet and two layers for the child. Adjustment layers will be applied to different layers within the stack and controlled with clipping groups.

Figure 9.2

A clipping mask isolates the Hue/Saturation effects on just one layer, harmonizing the color set. The bottom image shows the result without the clipping mask.

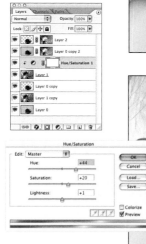

Figure 9.3

A Gradient Map and a clipping mask isolate this dramatic effect to just the droplet area. The bottom image shows the result without the clipping mask.

Hue/Saturation

Hue/Saturation is a valuable adjustment layer option because it allows you to intuitively cycle through an entire gamut of color changes. The biggest challenge is to understand how and where to apply this command—to one layer or to the entire stack? Figure 9.2 shows two different results created by a single adjustment layer in the same place in the layer stack. The top image isolates the adjustment layer to the next layer in the stack, using a clipping mask.

Gradient Map

The Gradient Map option plots the colors of a gradient to the tonal range of an image and is thus a great way to add a graphic, duotone effect to an image or layer. In the top image in Figure 9.3, a Gradient Map adjustment layer is applied to only the top droplet layer.

Figure 9.4

A Solid Color fill creates a strong color mood.

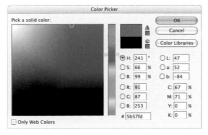

Figure 9.5

The layer mask for the Hue/Saturation layer was filtered with the Noise and Halftone Pattern filters. The alternative image shows the result before filtering the mask.

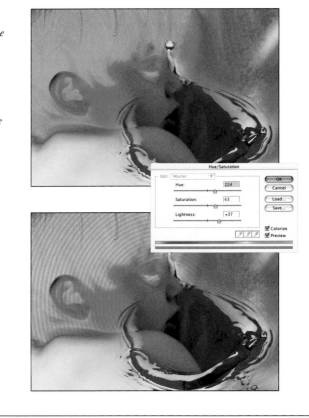

Fills

It is also possible to create layers that are filled with a color or pattern. Although such layers are not technically "adjustment layers," they are created in the same way and are associated with the adjustment layer tool set (see Figure 9.4). Specific fill layer options are Solid Color, Gradient, and Pattern.

Using Filters on the Mask

You can push adjustment layers further by modifying their layer masks. A good way to do this is with filters. In Figure 9.5, a Hue/Saturation layer was created, and the Noise and Halftone Pattern filters were applied to the mask. Slight adjustments to the Curves dialog box were also applied to tweak the final effect.

CREATING ADJUSTMENT LAYER
CLIPPING MASKS

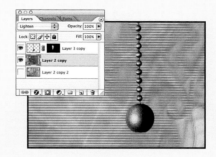

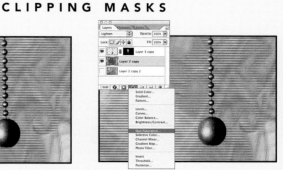

1. In the Layers palette, select the target layer, which will serve as the base for the clipping mask.

2. Click and hold the Fill/Adjustment Layer icon at the bottom of the Layers palette. Select the desired effect from the list.

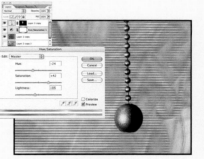

3. In the dialog box that appears, set the adjustment controls and click OK. The new adjustment layer will appear in the Layers palette.

4. Place the cursor between the target and adjustment layers. Hold the Option key or the Alt key; the cursor changes to the clipping mask icon. Click to create the clipping mask.

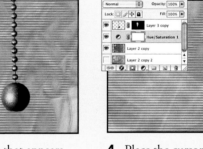

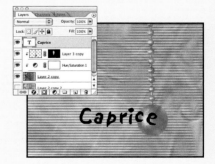

5. To edit the adjustment settings, double-click the layer mask thumbnail. The adjustment dialog box reappears. Change options and click OK.

6. To add more layers, drag them to the top of the group and Option/Alt+click.Option/Alt+click between clipping mask layers to return to normal.

Figure 9.6

The layer mask for the Hue/Saturation layer was modified with the Color Dodge blending mode.

Blending Modes

One last option in the adjustment layer arsenal is to use blending modes. Blending modes control how an adjustment layer is applied to the lower layers. In Figure 9.6, the filtered adjustment layer from the example in Figure 9.5 is applied using the Color Dodge blending mode, and the layer mask is altered slightly to show more of the face.

Dry Lily

Fog Trees

Face

BUILDING THE IMAGE: *THE MYSTERY OF FOLDED SLEEP*

Figure 9.7
The Dry Lily is added to the Fog Trees image.

Figure 9.8
Multiple flower layers are blended to complete the top of the image

Figure 9.9
The first Face layer is added.

Flowers in the Trees

The *Mystery of Folded Sleep* was an interesting image to create in that the initial design came together quite quickly. In contrast, the final steps of finessing the balance between figure, ground, and color took quite a long time.

The initial step involved combining the Dry Lily image with the Fog Trees background image. The Dry Lily image was an actual flower that was dried, pressed, and scanned on a flatbed scanner. After dragging the Dry Lily image onto the Fog Trees image, the Lily

was silhouetted with the Extract tool and moved into position, using just a portion of the overall image. (See Chapter 10 "Silhouetting with the Extract Filter," for details on this technique.) The flower scan was at a very high resolution, which brought out a fair amount of texture and detail. This detail was used to its full advantage, given that the Fog Trees image was a bit flat and blurry (see Figure 9.7).

The lily layer was duplicated, flipped horizontally, and scaled to create a second flower area in the upper-right corner. Because the

orange area was a bit light, the flipped layer was duplicated again, darkened with the Curves dialog box, and lightly painted into selected highlight areas with a layer mask (see Figure 9.8).

Adding Faces

The Face image was rotated 90° CCW and cropped just to the face and shoulder area. The Hue/Saturation option was applied to the image with the Colorize check box enabled, adding a soft sepia tone feeling.

The modified face layer was added to the image and dragged to the bottom of the layer stack. The

Figure 9.10
A Curves adjustment layer color-corrects the face.

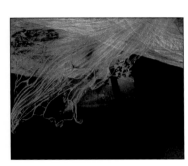

Figure 9.11
The results of the Hue/Saturation adjustment layer.

Figure 9.12
The Layers palette shows the layer structure for the file.

Figure 9.13
The final image.

Face layer was duplicated and de-saturated by reducing the Saturation slider to −100 in the Hue/Saturation dialog box.

This black-and-white face image was hidden by an opaque mask (Layer, Layer Mask, Hide All) and lightly brushed into the lower layer using a paintbrush with the fore-ground color set to white (see Figure 9.9).

Nuance and Finesse

After placing the Face layers, the main components were in place. All that remained was tweaking the layer relationships to solidify the design. The first step in this process was adding a Curves adjustment layer in an attempt to warm up the color in the trees and face (see Figure 9.10). In working with the Curves dialog box. I low-ered the Green channel from 137 to 118, I lowered the Red channel from 135 to 117, and I applied an "S" curve to the RGB composite channel (from 184 to 208 and from 36 to 27).

Next I added a Hue/Saturation adjustment layer (Hue +23, Satu-ration +41, Brightness −27). This layer toned things down slightly and shifted the color tint towards yellow (see Figure 9.11).

The final adjustment layer was an-other Curves layer that added an extra measure of brightness in the face and trees. The settings for that Curves dialog box modified just the RGB composite from 129 to 190 and from 53 to 70.

At this point, I should mention that the process for creating this image was not a linear process. Because there was so much explo-ration, I created extra layers and adjustment layers, which might not be necessary if I were to re-build this image from scratch (see Figure 9.12). Multiple adjustment layers and image layers are a good way to try various approaches while still leaving your options open.

The end result is a strong yet subtle image that remains open and flexi-ble at all times (see Figure 9.13).

9

THE MYSTERY OF FOLDED SLEEP

1. Open the Fog Trees image.

2. Open the Dry Lily image and copy and paste it into the composite image.

3. Choose Filter, Extract. In the dialog box that appears, trace the inside and outside of the lily shape and silhouette the image (refer to Chapter 10, "Silhouetting with the Extract Filter," for details).

4. Set the layer blending mode to Screen and drag the lily layer into position in the upper-left edge of the image.

5. Duplicate the lily layer, rotate it, and drag it into position in the upper-right corner of the image.

6. Duplicate the lily layer a third time, setting the blending mode to Multiply.

7. Click the Layer Mask icon at the bottom of the Layers palette to add a mask to the third lily layer. Lightly brush transparency into the mask, slightly darkening the flower shapes.

8. Open the Face image and rotate it 90° CCW.

9. Choose Image, Adjustments, Hue/Saturation. Enable the Colorize check box and adjust the Hue slider to reflect a warm yellow-ochre color.

10. Select the Crop tool and crop the Face image tightly to the face and shoulder.

11. Drag the face into the composite image; align the face with the bottom of the image.

12. Duplicate the face layer and choose Image, Adjustments, Hue/Saturation. Move the Saturation slider to −100 and click OK to desaturate the layer.

13. Click the Layer Mask icon at the bottom of the Layers palette to add a mask to the desaturated face layer. Lightly brush transparency into the mask, slightly graying out the face.

14. Click and hold the Fill/Adjustment Layer icon at the bottom of the Layers palette and select Curves from the pop-up menu that appears.

15. Create an "S" curve (from Input=184 to Output=208 and from Input=36 to

Output=27), and modify the Green and Blue channels slightly (move the Green channel from Input=137 to Output=118 and move the Blue channel from Input=135 to Output=117).

16. Click and hold the Fill/Adjustment Layer icon at the bottom of the Layers palette and select Hue/Saturation from the pop-up menu that appears.

17. Set the sliders as follows: Hue +23, Saturation +41, and Lightness −27.

18. Click and hold the Fill/Adjustment Layer icon at the bottom of the Layers palette and select Curves from the pop-up menu that appears.

19. Create a curve that rises sharply (from Input=129 to Output=190 and from Input=53 to Output=70) to complete the effect.

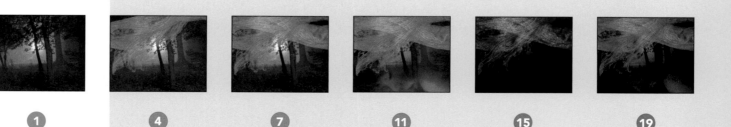

1   4   7   11   15   19

CONTENTS

Chapter 10
Silhouetting with the Extract Filter:
Occupation
160

Chapter 11
Working with Layer Masks:
Dark with Excessive Bright
170

Chapter 12
Using the Clone Stamp Tool:
The Space Between
182

Chapter 13
Understanding the Blending Modes:
Ominous Botanicus
192

PART THREE

MONTAGE

Image 10
Occupation ©2002 Daniel Giordan

CHAPTER 10

SILHOUETTING WITH THE EXTRACT FILTER

Occupation considers how we relate to the places we live in. In this case, that space is a living room, presented in high-contrast black and white, with gloomy shadows and a patina of age. A bright, almost blinding light breaks into the room from a central window, although it is thwarted and pushed back by the darkness and shadows. The couch is ominous and uninviting, threatening to swallow you up should you make the mistake of sitting down.

Holding court in the middle of the room is a large, dry lily—floating above the scene, separate yet central. It seems to be watching over the space, or perhaps reliving it as a memory. It reaches out with a petal that is rendered in ultra-sharp clarity, drawing the viewer into the turbid atmosphere of the scene.

And yet when you look closely, the scene is not ghostly or foreboding. It's more reminiscent and nostalgic. The unsettling part is that the room has a feeling of approximation rather than specificity, as though it is being recalled in the generalized mist of a dream.

All this begs the question: When you live in a place for a long time, or when you experience traumatic events in a specific location, how much of you remains in that place? Does your presence haunt a location (as the occultists would have us believe) as a ghost or spiritual presence?

In the example of *Occupation*, perhaps the opposite is true. When a place is marked with significance, it gains a foothold in our consciousness; it leaves a unique mark. Ultimately, because the flower in the image is real and the place is spectral, it may be fair to say that it's the *place* that haunt *us*.

●

The act of silhouetting an object is central to the process of image montage and composition. Separating an object from its background and integrating it convincingly into another scene is a basic test of true Photoshop skills.

To that end, Adobe has created a host of new tools in recent releases of the software that offer help with the silhouetting task. The Magic Eraser, Background Eraser, Magnetic Lasso, and Paths tools all offer their assistance. In fact, any tool that allows an organic selection is a possible option for creating image silhouettes.

Of all the available tools, the most powerful is the Extract filter. Extract allows you to define the edge position and opacity in minute detail, separating objects from backgrounds with relative ease.

Introduction to Extract

The Extract filter provides a clean and professional way to isolate an object, erasing its background layer. It is especially useful with objects that have soft, elusive edges, such as smoke, mist, or hair. The filter takes some skill and patience, but with a bit of both, Extract can deliver results that no other Photoshop tool can match.

The Extract command is driven by the Extract dialog box, which can be launched by selecting Filter, Extract. The basic approach for extraction is to define the edge that separates the object from the background. After this is done, you fill the interior of the object and preview or finish the extraction process.

The key to success in extraction is in accurately defining the background and interior. When Extract deletes the background, it also examines any pixels in the edge area, eliminating any color components that are derived from the background.

The Painting Tools

In the Extract dialog box, Adobe offers a wide range of tools for edge definition, filling, and viewing the results. Although the painting tools control basic functions, the Tool Options area of the dialog box provides the finesse needed to achieve professional results.

On the left side of the dialog box are the painting tools, which are arranged in logical groups. The first group contains the three creation tools: Edge Highlighter, Fill, and Eraser. Use these tools to define the edge, erase the edge, or fill the area to be preserved. The next tool is the Eyedropper, which is used to sample a foreground color, and to force a foreground for a hard-to-define subject. The third group is the editing tools: Cleanup and Edge Touchup. The last group of two tools allows you to navigate the preview window and examine the image: the Zoom and Hand tools.

The Tool Controls

On the right side of the dialog box are the Tool Options, Extraction, and Preview areas. The Tool Options area allows you to select all painting parameters, including brush size, highlight and fill colors, and smart highlighting. Default fill colors are green and blue; to select another fill color with the Color Picker, choose Other from the Fill menu.

The Extraction controls provide some interesting options:

• The Channel drop-down menu allows you to start an extraction based on the contents of a current channel. This is effective if you have already created a channel for the object you want to silhouette. This menu also provides a good way to use the channel data as a starting point for further changes. Saving a selection (Select, Save Selection) is the easiest way to create a separate channel, which you can name and customize in the Save dialog box that appears. After you have named and saved a channel, its name appears in the Channel drop-down menu.

• The Force Foreground check box allows you to select a foreground color with the Eyedropper tool for images that have soft edges. This approach involves selecting the entire object with the highlight tool and then selecting a solid color to key on as the foreground color. Although this approach does not always work, it is very effective for images with a predominant color.

The Preview area offers the Show menu, from which you can toggle between the original image and the mask layer. The Display menu controls the preview effect, and the two check boxes control the visibility of the highlight and fill.

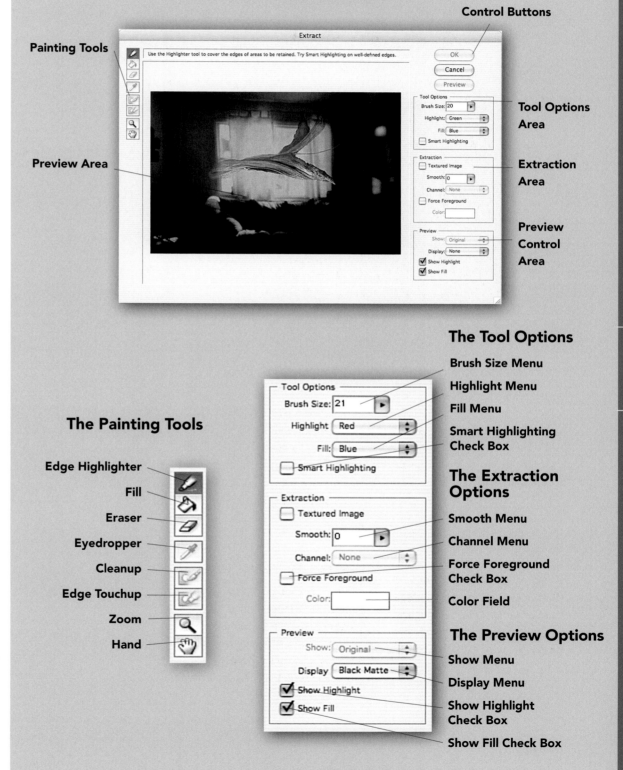

The Extract Dialog Box

Control Buttons

Painting Tools

Preview Area

Tool Options Area

Extraction Area

Preview Control Area

The Painting Tools

Edge Highlighter

Fill

Eraser

Eyedropper

Cleanup

Edge Touchup

Zoom

Hand

The Tool Options

Brush Size Menu

Highlight Menu

Fill Menu

Smart Highlighting Check Box

The Extraction Options

Smooth Menu

Channel Menu

Force Foreground Check Box

Color Field

The Preview Options

Show Menu

Display Menu

Show Highlight Check Box

Show Fill Check Box

USING EXTRACT TO DELETE A BACKGROUND

1. Select Filter, Extract to open the Extract dialog box.

2. Select the Edge Highlighter tool and use the Tool Options area to set brush size and color.

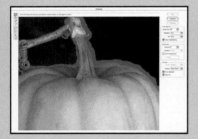

3. Paint the outside edge of the object, making sure that you cover the full edge of the object along with any anti-aliased edges.

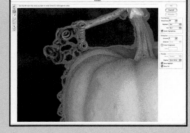

4. If necessary, select the Eraser tool and clean up the edges. Use the Zoom tool to set the proper magnification as you work.

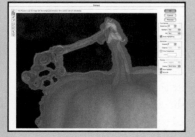

5. Select the Fill tool and click anywhere inside the outlined object; all the areas to be preserved are covered with the fill color.

6. Click the Preview button to view the results. If they're acceptable, click OK. If necessary use the Cleanup or Edge Touchup tools.

ADVANCED EXTRACTION TECHNIQUES

The basic extraction techniques discussed so far will deliver solid results for most images. For images that are more challenging, however, you'll have to push your skills further to the get the best results. In many cases, it's just a matter of redrawing the edge, zooming in closer, or taking your time with things. If the results are still falling short of expectations, try employing some of the techniques described on these pages.

Smart Highlighting

Smart Highlighting is similar to the Magic Lasso tool in that it snaps a thin, sharp edge line around the object. This approach works best with objects that have clear, distinct edges and good contrast. To use this feature, enable the Smart Highlighting check box in the Tool Options area of the Extract dialog box before you paint the edge line (see Figure 10.1).

Editing an Edge

When previewing an extraction, it is sometimes necessary to tweak an edge to get the silhouette to read properly. The easiest way to do this is with the Cleanup and Edge Touchup tools, found in the Extract dialog box. The Cleanup tool eliminates background residue and holes in the main image; the Edge Touchup tool sharpens edges. Both tools have a cumulative effect (see Figure 10.2).

Force Foreground

The Force Foreground option is an effective way to extract complicated images such as smoke or clouds, especially when the object is all the same color. The process is slightly different from the standard process of outlining the edge and filling the object in that you cover the entire shape with the outline color. For best results, use a very large brush and click to cover the shape rather than outlining and filling. After the object is filled in, enable the Force Foreground check box in the Extraction area of the Extract dialog box,

Figure 10.1

The original image, the extract mask, and the final result of Smart Highlighting.

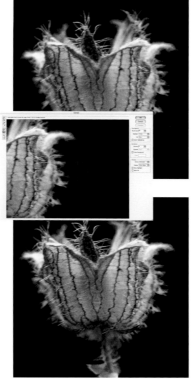

Figure 10.2

The original preview, the modified extract mask, and the final result of edge editing.

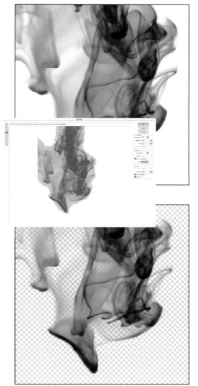

Figure 10.3

The original image, the modified extract mask, and the final result of forcing the image foreground.

Figure 10.4

The original preview, the channel-based extract mask, and the final result over a texture layer.

select the Eyedropper tool from the dialog box, and click the image to select a foreground color. Click the Preview button to check the image. Reselect the color and click Preview again as necessary to achieve the desired results (see Figure 10.3).

Using Channels

You can also use channel information as a starting point for an extract mask. Open the Channels palette to see whether any channels outline the shape of the object. Black in the channel will come into the Extract dialog box as an outline, leaving the remain-

der as fill area. Alternatively, you can use the Force Foreground feature, using the highlight color to define the entire object. The example shown in Figure 10.4 started as the cyan channel. It was duplicated and inverted to change the clouds to black. In the Extract dialog box, the cyan copy was selected

from the Channel menu in the Extraction area, and the Force Foreground check box was enabled, with white as the color. The final result is shown in a separate layer, positioned over a texture layer.

●

Dried Lily 2

Red Room

BUILDING THE IMAGE: *OCCUPATION*

Figure 10.5
Curves are applied to the Red Room image.

Figure 10.6
Application of the Hue/Saturation command changes the image from red to blue.

Figure 10.7
The Extract Highlight mask is applied using the Smart Highlighting feature.

The Red Room

The picture of the red room is unique; it's a perfect example of how the immediacy of digital cameras can influence art and design. With my digital camera, I impulsively took a picture of my living room through a drinking glass made of red blown glass. The result was so effective that I went through the house for the next hour taking pictures through the glass. The Red Room image was the first to make it into a composition.

Although the image was very strong to start with, the glass effect did leave the shadows a bit gray, and the entire image was somewhat flat. To compensate, I used the Curves command to add a single anchor point at an input value of 147 and dragged it up to an output value of 172 (see Figure 10.5).

From Red to Blue

As I began thinking about he Dried Lily image as a compliment to the Red Room image, I realized that the red was too strong. My first response was to use the Hue/Saturation command to shift the color towards the blue/violet color set of the flower. The settings I used were Hue +111, Saturation +73, and Lightness −18 (see Figure 10.6). With the correct color and contrast changes, the Red Room image was now ready to function as the backdrop for the final composite.

Adding the Lily

The first step in adding the Dried Lily image was to drag it into the Red Room image as a separate layer. After dragging it to the center of the image, I selected Filter, Extract to open the Extract dialog box.

Because it had relatively hard edges with good contrast, the Smart Highlighting check box was a very effective option. After selecting the Edge Highlighter tool, I enabled the Smart Highlighting check box and zoomed in closely to make sure that I was painting the highlight right on the edge

Figure 10.8
The extraction results.

Figure 10.9
The lily is flipped, and a layer mask is added to create transparency.

Figure 10.10
A Hue/Saturation adjustment layer changes the background to black and white.

Figure 10.11
A strong Curves adjustment layer creates the final image.

(see Figure 10.7). Even though I strayed off the edge a few times, I completed the outline of the lily shape and then erased and redrew the edge highlights. With a good edge highlight in place, I filled the image and completed the extraction (see Figure 10.8).

The bulb end of the flower needed further tweaks and I also wanted to modify the edges to soften them in places. To do this, I added a layer mask and used transparent fills and brush strokes to get the proper effect. I also flipped the image horizontally, reduced it slightly, and repositioned it over the window area in the Red Room image (see Figure 10.9).

Finishing with Adjustment Layers

I added a Hue/Saturation adjustment layer above the room layer and lowered the Saturation slider to −100 to remove all the color in the background (see Figure 10.10). Although the black-and-white color palette worked better, the process lowered the contrast in the image again. To compensate and complete the image, I added a Curves adjustment layer above the previous adjustment layer. I adjusted the curve settings from Input=56 to Output=3, from Input=123 to Output=128, and from Unput=191 to Output=208 (see Figure 10.11).

1. Open the Red Room image.

2. Open the Curves dialog box (Image, Adjustments, Curves). Set the black point and the white point and raise the midpoint of the curve from Input=147 to Output=172.

3. Select Image, Adjustments, Hue/Saturation. Adjust the sliders to Hue +111, Saturation +73, and Lightness -18.

4. Open the Dried Lily image.

5. Select Filter, Extract to launch the Extract dialog box.

6. Select the Edge Highlighter tool, enable the Smart Highlighting check box in the Extract dialog box, and zoom to 100%.

7. Place the mouse pointer on the object edge and paint the highlight all around the object.

8. Select the Eraser tool and touch up any mistakes. Redraw the outline again using the Edge Highlighter.

9. Fill the image and click OK to extract the image.

10. Select Edit, Transform, Flip Horizontal to flip the image.

11. Select Edit, Free Transform and Shift+drag a corner to scale the image in proportion to make it smaller. Click and drag the center and reposition the lily in front of the window.

12. With the lily image still selected, click the Add Layer Mask icon in the Layers palette to add a layer mask.

13. Select the Brush tool and specify a soft edge, a 110-pixel brush size, and 40% opacity. With black as the foreground color, paint the left end of the flower to soften and blend it into the background.

14. Increase the brush size and lower its opacity. Paint this transparent mask into the flower to blend it into background.

15. With the background layer selected, click and hold the Fill/Adjustment Layer icon in the Layers palette. Select the Hue/Saturation option from the pop-up menu that appears to add a Hue/Saturation adjustment layer. Lower the Saturation slider to -100 to remove all the color from the image.

16. Click and hold the Fill/Adjustment Layer icon in the Layers palette. Select Curves from the pop-up menu that appears to add a Curves adjustment layer.

17. Adjust the curve points from Input=56 to Output=3, from Input=123 to Output=128, and from Input=191 to Output=208.

2   3   14   15   16

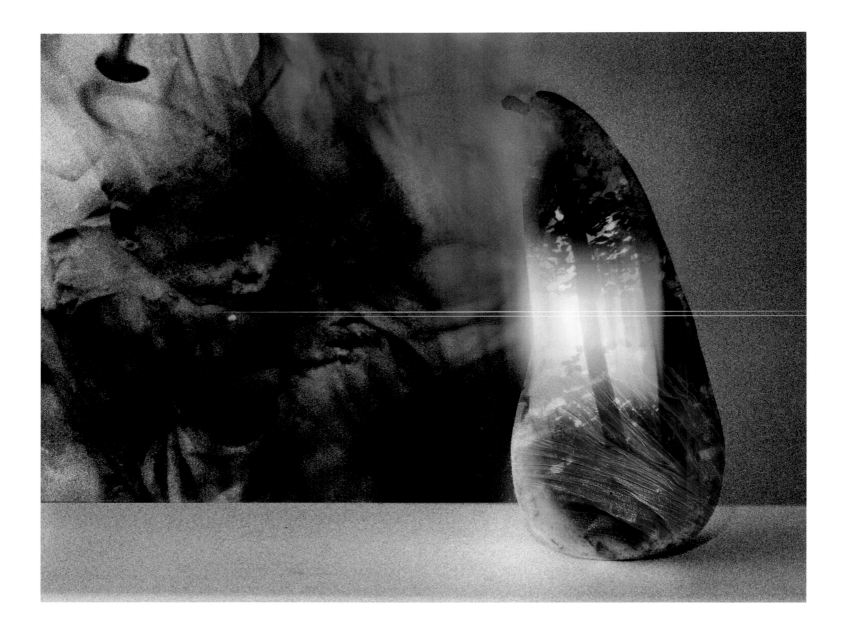

Image 11
Dark with Excessive Bright | ©2002 Daniel Giordan

CHAPTER 11

WORKING WITH LAYER MASKS

…Fountain of Light, thyself invisible
Amidst the glorious brightness where thou sit'st
Thron'd inaccessible, but when thou shad'st
The full blaze of thy beams, and through a cloud
Drawn round about thee like a radiant Shrine,
Dark with excessive bright thy skirts appear,
Yet dazzle Heav'n, that brightest Seraphim
Approach not, but with both wings veil their eyes.
—excerpt from Paradise Lost, Book III, *by John Milton*

Milton allegorically presents the divine nature of truth as an ambiguous contradiction, turning to an oxymoron to express the inexpressible. The phrase "dark with excessive bright" presents a surprising juxtaposition of opposites that uniquely expresses these elusive truths.

Dark with Excessive Bright is one of the most dramatic images in this series; it presents a series of visual and aesthetic opposites that fit well within Milton's context. An excessively bright light emanates from inside a pear, allowing a glimpse into another world, like Alice through the looking glass. This is not a parallel world, however. This world is markedly different.

The world of the still life is dark and pixilated, providing the perfect counterpoint to the illuminated warmth and brightness. The brightness is rendered in a smooth, well-defined texture that stands in further contrast to the dark pixelation. In the shadows, you can discern the outline of a seraphim that seems drawn to the light, yet hesitates to embrace it. Perhaps the most interesting contrast is between the miraculous and the commonplace: That God's skirts might appear through the most common of everyday objects, a piece of fruit.

●

MASTERING LAYER MASKS

It's hard to believe there was ever a time when we had no layer masks in Photoshop. It's kind of like remembering a world without remote controls or garage door openers. Layer masks are indispensable to using Photoshop effectively because they allow you to hide or reveal areas within the layer, creating smooth, seamless transitions to the other layers in the stack.

There are numerous ways to create a layer mask, and even more ways to manipulate one. Because each layer mask exists in a separate channel, it is similar to a Quick Mask selection in the way you can view and edit the mask (see Chapter 2, "Using Quick Mask to Make Selections"). This chapter looks at the basics of using layer masks and also explores more advanced options for creating masks that are unique and powerful.

Add layer mask

Creating a Layer Mask

To create a layer mask, you can either use the Add Layer Mask icon in the Layers menu, or click the Add Layer Mask icon at the bottom of the Layers palette. The Add Layer Mask command in the Layers menu offers a submenu from which you can choose to hide or reveal the full layer, or hide or reveal a current selection. Clicking the Add Layer Mask icon automatically creates a mask that reveals the entire layer, with nothing hidden. Option+click (Mac users) or Alt+click (Windows users) the Add Layer Mask icon to create a mask that conceals the entire layer. If a selection is active, Option+clicking or Alt+clicking the Add Layer Mask icon creates a mask that hides the selection.

When working with layer masks, it is important to remember that black conceals the layer, while white reveals it. Keep this in mind as you notice the mask thumbnail that appears next to the layer's image thumbnail in the Layers palette. The black and white areas of the mask thumbnail correspond to the visible areas in the layer. The active mask and image thumbnails are highlighted with a black frame to help you keep track of what mode you're in.

Painting into a Layer Mask

With the mask thumbnail selected in the Layers palette, you can manipulate the mask using any of Photoshop's paint tools. In addition to the Paintbrush and Airbrush tools, which are obvious

choices, the Smudge, Sharpen, and Toning tools can also be effective.

To use Photoshop's paint tools with a layer mask, select the mask thumbnail, make sure that white or black is active in the color swatches in the toolbox, and paint into the image. When you create a layer mask, Photoshop automatically changes the color options to grayscale, reflecting the channel mask that is active at the time. As you paint with black selected, the image disappears under your brush. Painting with white selected makes the image appear.

As you work, you can temporarily turn a layer mask on or off by Shift+clicking the mask thumbnail or by selecting Mask Enabled from the Layers menu. If you would

Layer Mask Controls in the Layers Menu

rather edit the mask without looking at the image in the layer, you can Option+click (Mac users) or Alt+click (Windows users) the layer mask thumbnail to view just the grayscale mask. As you can with the Quick Mask feature, you can see the entire layer with a colored "film" representing the mask by Option+Shift+clicking (Mac users) or Alt+Shift+clicking (Windows users) the mask thumbnail. The default film color is red, but you can change this by double-clicking the mask thumbnail, clicking the color swatch, and choosing another color.

To keep the file size small and nimble, Photoshop will allow you to apply or discard the mask at any time. To remove the mask, highlight the mask thumbnail and either click the trash icon at the bottom of the Layers palette or choose Remove Layer Mask from the Layers menu. The ensuing dialog box prompts you to apply the mask to the layer or to discard the mask, leaving the layer untouched.

Reveal All
Creates a Layer Mask, Leaving Layer Contents Visible

Hide All
Creates a Layer Mask, Hiding the Layer Contents)

Reveal Selection
Creates a Layer Mask, Leaving Selection Contents Visible While Masking the Rest of the Layer

Hide Selection
Creates a Layer Mask, Hiding the Selection Contents While Making the Rest of the Layer Visible

Layer Mask Controls in the Layers Palette

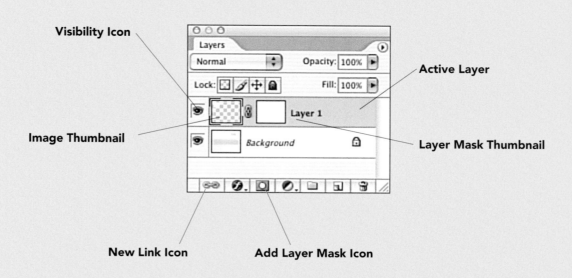

Visibility Icon

Active Layer

Image Thumbnail

Layer Mask Thumbnail

New Link Icon

Add Layer Mask Icon

WORKING WITH LAYER MASKS

Chapter 11

THE ART OF PHOTOSHOP

CREATING A TYPE-BASED LAYER MASK

This approach creates a layer mask in the shape of user-formatted text.

1. Click and hold the Type tool in the toolbox and select the Horizontal Type Mask tool (or the Vertical Type Mask tool).

2. Set the desired text parameters in the Options bar, including type font and size.

3. Click to place the cursor in the image; a colored mask fills the screen when you click.

4. Type the text as desired.

5. When finished typing, click the Add Layer Mask icon in the Layers palette.

6. If desired, click the Mask Link icon between the image and mask thumbnails in the Layers palette and reposition the mask with the Move tool.

ADVANCED LAYER MASKING AND RELATED TECHNIQUES

The basic layer mask is a simple approach to hiding, revealing, and combining layer components. There are variations and strategies that can be employed to take things even further. Consider these techniques when you want to modify masks, create text effects, and manage the various components that go into making a mask work.

Repositioning the Mask

When you create a layer mask, Photoshop automatically creates a link between the layer and the mask. The assumption is that if you reposition the layer in the image, you would want the mask to move along with it. Although this is normally true, there are times when you may want to move the mask shape around the image to look for just the right crop.

The link between the layer and layer mask is represented by the chain icon that appears between the image and the mask thumbnails. To break the link, click the chain icon so that it disappears (see Figure 11.1). You can now select the Move tool and drag the mask around the image without bringing the image with it.

Masks with Adjustment Layers

Masks are very effective when combined with adjustment layers. Adjustment layers allow you to modify the layer stack with a number of editing tools without modifying the layers themselves (see Chapter 9, "Working with Adjustment Layers"). The challenge is that you usually want to modify certain areas but leave others unaffected. This is where layer masks come in.

After creating the adjustment layer, click the Add Layer Mask icon in the Layers palette and paint the mask as desired; in the example shown in Figure 11.2, the mask isolates the pepper shape from the background. Using the mask, you can apply the adjustment to specific areas and leave other areas untouched.

Chain Icon

Figure 11.1

Click the chain icon to link or unlink a mask and its layer.

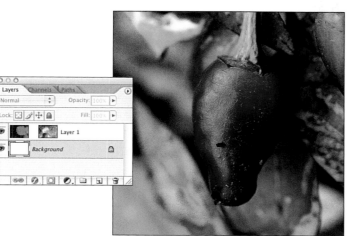

Figure 11.2

A layer mask is applied to an adjustment layer, controlling the visibility of the adjustment effect.

Figure 11.3

The original image, the grayscale mask image, and the final result.

Using an Image as a Layer Mask

Because a layer mask is actually a grayscale image, it is possible to paste a copied grayscale image that will function as the mask. This approach allows you to reveal the masked layer through the white areas of the pasted image, the masked layer is concealed by the dark areas in the pasted image. Follow these steps to create an image-based layer mask:

1. Open the image you want to use as mask and convert it to grayscale if necessary (Image, Mode, Grayscale). In the example in Figure 11.3, an image of a sleeping child is used.
2. Select the image (Select, All) and copy the image to the Clipboard (Edit, Copy).
3. Open the full-color image and highlight the target layer for the mask in the Layers palette. In the example in Figure 11.3,

highlight the layer with a flower petal.
4. Click the Add Layer Mask icon in the Layers palette.
5. Open the Channels palette and highlight the mask name that corresponds to the active layer from step 3.
6. Paste the copied image (Edit, Paste), which will appear as a mask when the mask channel is selected and visible.

After the mask is created, you may have to make further edits to achieve the right balance between mask and image. Also, because the original image will be most visible in the black areas of the mask, you may have to invert the mask (select the mask icon and choose Image, Adjustments, Invert) to make things read properly.

EXPLORING THE APPLY IMAGE AND CALCULATIONS COMMANDS

Although the techniques discussed on these pages are not technically considered layer masks, the Apply Image and Calculations commands do involve manipulating channel data to combine images and layers. Because of this manipulation, the end results of these two effects are very similar to a layer mask, while allowing an exponential degree of control over a host of variables.

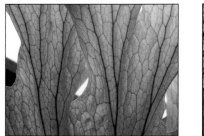   

Figure 11.4

The source image, the target image, and the final result of the Apply Image command. The settings used the Green channel of the source image, with the Linear Light blending mode.

Apply Image Command

The approach to pasting an image as a mask, described on the preceding page, is a very good technique for learning how layer and channel components work together to create a mask. The Apply Image command takes things a step further, however, because it allows you to combine a separate source image, layer, or channel with a target image. This capability allows for any combination of blending modes, opacity, image inversion, and even masks in the target image.

Access the Apply Image command by choosing Image, Apply Image. The settings are self-explanatory, and the preview results give instant feedback on your progress (just make sure that the Preview check box is selected). In addition, the source and target images must be in the same color mode if you want to combine their composite channels, although individual channels can be combined regardless of mode (see Figure 11.4).

Calculations Command

The Calculations command functions in a way similar to the Apply Image command except that it creates a channel or selection rather than an actual image. Because of this, the Calculations command does not allow you to work with composite channels. You should use Calculations to create a complex grayscale channel that can be used for further editing (see Figure 11.5).

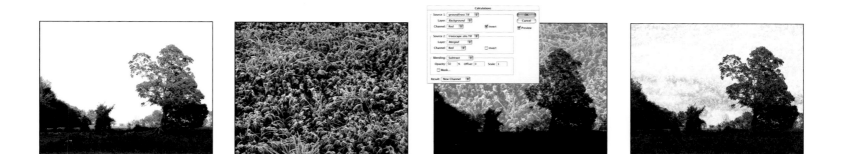

Figure 11.5

The source image, the second source, the Calculations settings, and the final editing result.

Notes on the Add and Subtract Blending Modes

Although the blending modes are discussed in detail in Chapter 13, "Understanding the Blending Modes," there are two special blending modes we should discus within the context of layer masks. Because the Add and Subtract blending modes appear only in the Apply Image dialog box, we will discuss these specific options here.

The Add mode combines the two sets of pixel data, lightening any overlapping pixels without touching the black values. The Subtract mode subtracts the pixel values as it darkens the image.

For either the Add or Subtract mode, you can throw in extra calculations to make further changes. The Scale field lets you enter a value between 1.0 and 2.0 to lighten or darken the entire image. The Offset field allows a value from −255 to +255 to be added or subtracted from each pixel value in the image. With this modification, you can lighten or darken the image while maintaining the tonal relationships.

Fog Trees

Pear

Dried Lily

Abstract Trees

Statue

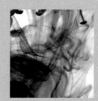

Liquid

BUILDING THE IMAGE: *DARK WITH EXCESSIVE BRIGHT*

Figure 11.6
A layer mask is applied to the Pear image, allowing the lower layer to show.

Figure 11.7
The Dried Lilly and Abstract Trees images are added and positioned behind the mask.

Figure 11.8
Two curves layers add color to the image.

Building the Pear

After trying to integrate the pear into the Fog Trees landscape, I began exploring the idea of putting the landscape into the pear. In *Dark with Excessive Bright,* the pear was shifted to the top of the layer stack and aligned over the highlights in the lower images. I explored the use of blending modes and decided that the best way to combine the layers was with a layer mask. The challenge was in creating a mask that would reveal the lower layer while still retaining the volumetric shape of the pear itself. I used a large feathered brush to build up the effect, alternating between black and white to achieve the proper edge and transparency (see Figure 11.6).

Because the Dried Lily image worked so well with the earlier Fog Trees composition, it was only natural to add it here. After trying a number of positions, I was delighted to see how well it anchored the bottom of the pear, setting up the highlight and helping to describe the volume. The Screen blending mode created the proper balance for the composite.

To finish off the details, I opened the Abstract Trees image and added it as a separate layer, above the lily and under the pear. This order forced the Abstract Trees image to comply with the mask; a Soft Light blending mode created a soft mottled effect (see Figure 11.7)

Developing the Background

The pear image I started with was not of great quality. Because I knew that I couldn't smooth out the noise without a ton of work, I decided to go in the other direction and emphasize the noise even further. I applied the Add Noise filter set to Monochrome, Gaussian, and 7.16%. Next I added a Curves adjustment layer with the intention of pushing an accent color into the background. The curve modified each of the color channels separately, as well as the composite RGB channel. The overall effect added a green tint to the highlights and a dark blue to the shadows (see Figure 11.8).

A second Curves adjustment layer was added with the intent of creating more contrast and darker values in the shadows. The

Figure 11.9

A Hue/Saturation layer reduces the image back to monochrome, but with an improved tonal range.

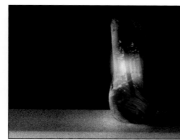

Figure 11.10

A motion blur is used to create the diffuse highlight.

Figure 11.11

The Statue/Liquid composite is added, and the shadows are darkened.

Figure 11.12

The flare lines are added to complete the image..

extreme darkness caused by this layer was controlled by choosing Layer, Layer Mask, Hide All and painting the dark areas into the shadows, creating contrast between the background and the ledge (see Figure 11.9).

At this point, I saw that although the colors in the adjustment layers were not working, they had done a good job of defining the tonal relationships and adding contrast. To eliminate the color while keeping the tonal changes, I desaturated with a Hue/Saturation adjustment layer.

Building the Pear Flare

Next I drew a rectangular selection over the highlight area within the pear. I then chose Image, Copy Merged to copy everything within the selection. The Edit, Paste command pasted the composite rectangle in its own layer. I used the Lens Flare filter to create the motion flare, and placed the flare center in the highlight area of the image. (To place the flare center, drag the plus sign in the dialog box's Preview window.) I applied a vertical motion blur to complete the effect.

Adding the Figure

I brought the Statue image into the composite and flipped it horizontally (Edit, Transform, Flip Horizontal). I also added the Liquid image below the Statue figure. I set the Statue layer's blending mode to Multiply and added a layer mask to hide the unwanted background behind the figure. Then I merged the Statue and Liquid layers by linking them in the Layers palette and selecting

Merge Layers from the palette menu. I added another layer mask and softened and blended the merged layer into the dark background. I inverted the final result by selecting Difference as the merged layer's blending mode.

At this point, the figure of the statue was not as visible as I would have liked, so I duplicated the Statue layer and lightened it with the Curves command. Then I selected Layer, Layer Mask, Hide All to conceal the entire layer. After selecting a paintbrush with black as my foreground color, I painted back the highlights in the face of the figure to complete the area (see Figure 11.11).

Finishing the Flare

I created a new layer for the first horizontal flare line by selecting

New Layer from the Layers palette menu. I selected the pencil tool with a 3-pixel hard brush and a white foreground color and drew a horizontal line through the highlight area, holding down the Shift key to keep things straight. To taper the ends and create the flare effect, I selected Filter, Blur, Motion Blur, set the distance to 713 pixels, and used a 0° angle.

Because the flare line was on its own layer, I selected the Move tool and tweaked the positioning. I then copied the layer by selecting Duplicate Layer from the Layers palette menu and moved the copy of the line down and to the right to complete the image (see Figure 11.12).

11

DARK WITH EXCESSIVE BRIGHT

1. Open the Fog Trees image.

2. Open the Dried Lily image and drag it into the Fog Trees image to begin the composite.

3. Select Filter, Extract and define the outer edge and inner shape of the lily using the Extract tools. Click OK to silhouette the image (see Chapter 10, "Silhouetting with the Extract Filter," for details on this tool).

4. Open the Abstract Trees image and drag it into the composite.

5. Open the Pear image and drag it into the composite, positioning it at the top of the layer stack.

6. With the Pear layer selected, click the Add Layer Mask icon in the Layers palette.

7. Select the Brush tool with black as the foreground color. In the Options bar, select 18% opacity and a 220-pixel feathered brush.

8. Paint lightly into the pear area of the image to build up a mask that shows the background, while still retaining the volume of the pear.

9. In the Layers palette, select the Dried Lily layer and set the blending mode to Screen.

10. In the Layers palette, select the Abstract Trees layer and set the blending mode to Soft Light.

11. Highlight the Pear layer and select Filter, Noise, Add Noise.

12. In the Add Noise dialog box, specify a 7.16% noise addition and enable the Gaussian and Monochromatic options.

13. Click and hold the Adjustment Layer icon in the Layers palette and choose Curves from the pop-up menu that appears.

14. Modify the Curves for the individual RGB channels as well as for the composite. Move the Composite channel from Input=82 to Output=71 and Input=190 to Output=214; move the Red channel from Input=115 to Output=82; move the Green channel from Input=35 to Output=26 and from Input=184 to Output=193; move the Blue channel from Input=83 to Output=77, from Input=126 to Output=91, and from Input=205 to Output=182.

15. Click and hold the Adjustment Layer icon in the Layers palette and choose Curves from the pop-up menu that appears.

16. Move the curve's points from Input=74 to Output=44 and from Input=161 to Output=232.

17. With the second Curves adjustment layer still selected, select the layer mask and fill it with black.

18. Select the Marquee tool and draw a rectangle that encompasses the wall behind the pear, aligning the bottom of the rectangle with the back edge of the shelf.

19. Select the Brush tool with black as the foreground. In the Options bar, specify a 22% opacity and a 300-pixel feathered brush.

20. Paint lightly into the image to build up a mask that darkens the background and creates contrast against the shelf.

21. Click and hold the Adjustment Layer icon in the Layers palette and choose Hue/Saturation from the pop-up menu that appears.

22. Lower the Saturation slider to −100 and click OK.

23. Select the Marquee tool and draw a rectangular selection around the highlight area at the top of the pear.

24. Select Edit, Copy Merged.

25. Select Edit, Paste to paste a flat version of the layers within the selection as a separate layer.

26. Select Filter, Render, Lens Flare. Set the controls in the dialog box to 50–300mm and 154%; drag the flare center in the thumbnail to align it with the image highlight.

27. Select Filter, Blur, Motion Blur. Set the controls in the dialog box to Angle: 90°and Distance: 182.

28. Open the Liquid image and drag it into the composite.

29. Open the Statue image and drag it into the composite.

30. With the Statue layer still selected, choose Edit, Transform, Flip Horizontal.

31. Choose Multiply from the blending mode menu in the Layers palette.

32. Click the Add Layer Mask icon in the Layers palette.

33. Select the Brush tool with black as the foreground color. In the Options bar, specify a 12% opacity and a 300-pixel feathered brush.

34. Paint lightly into the image to build up a mask that blends the Statue with the Liquid and the background.

35. In the Layers palette, ⌘+click (Mac users) or Ctrl+click (Windows users) to select the Statue and the Liquid layers. Then click the link icon at the bottom of the Layers palette.

36. Select Merged Layers from the Layers palette menu to combine the linked layers.

37. Choose Difference from the Blending Mode menu in the Layers palette.

38. Click the Add Layer Mask icon in the Layers palette.

39. Select the Brush tool with black as the foreground color. In the Options bar, specify a 09% opacity and a 300-pixel feathered brush.

40. Paint lightly into the image to build up a mask that blends the Statue/Liquid layer with the background.

41. Select Duplicate Layer from the Layers palette menu.

42. Select Layer, Add a Mask, Hide All from the menu bar.

43. Select the Brush tool with white as the foreground color. In the Options bar, specify a 09% opacity and a 45-pixel feathered brush.

44. Paint lightly into the image to build up a mask that brings out the details in the statue's face.

45. Select New Layer from the Layers palette menu.

46. Select the Pencil tool with white as the foreground color and a 3-pixel hard brush.

47. Hold down the Shift key and draw a horizontal line through the highlight area of the image.

48. Select Filter, Blur, Motion Blur. Set the controls in the dialog box to Angle: 0° and Distance: 721.

49. Select Duplicate Layer from the Layers palette menu to make a copy of the flare line layer.

50. Drag the new layer below and to the right of the first flare line to complete the image.

Image 12
The Space Between ©2002 Daniel Giordan

U S I N G   T H E   C L O N E   S T A M P   T O O L

The Space Between is a study in contrast and comparison. It's hot and cold, light and dark, calm and chaotic. And yet the piece still resonates because it resists the categorization and cliché interpretations usually elicited by these polarities.

A strong contrasting line cuts across the upper third of the image, delineating the boundaries of two different worlds. The top is a landscape dusted in snow, with a clean and direct presentation that pulls forward to dominate the viewer's attention.

But even as you look at the top, you can feel the cavernous space in the lower area. The space is dark and mysterious; it recedes into space in the same way that the top pulls forward. The light in this space is veiled and indirect, like a flickering fire on the walls of a cave, illuminating the strange textures and strata.

And then there's the tricycle.

The tricycle is as young as the tree is old. And yet, while the tree is presented with stark clarity, the tricycle is veiled; poignant and nostalgic. It speaks of time past…it's as intangible as a memory, threatening to dissolve in an instant. The tricycle is felt before it is seen. It lurks beneath the surface.

In the end, we're left to orient ourselves between the polarities. Where do we live? Where do we fit? How do we relate to these parameters? Mortality, security, and a sense of the past are parameters that define human existence. And yet, perhaps it's not the parameters that define us, perhaps we're defined by how we operate in the space between.

●

THE CLONE STAMP TOOL

Given the structure of this book, it may seem like overkill to devote a single chapter to just one tool. Other chapters deal with broader issues and commands, seldom drilling down to the specificity of a single tool. We don't give a chapter to the Brush or Eraser, so why single out the Clone Stamp tool?

First of all, the Clone Stamp tool is unique in what it does. Other tools usually belong to larger groups of tools that can be addressed as a group. In addition, the act of pixel cloning is central to image montage. The Clone Stamp tool's capability of integrating disparate image sources, blending two areas, or replicating a texture make it an irreplaceable image-editing tool, earning it the right to its own chapter.

Introduction to the Clone Stamp Tool

The Clone Stamp tool samples pixel values from one area and replicates them in another. It's kind of like the transporter device in *Star Trek* in that it duplicates the pixel values in one set of coordinates and paints them in another. Don't let the notion of X and Y coordinates scare you though; the Clone Stamp tool lets you click to select the reference point where you want to start. As you paint, the tool brushes in the pixels values from the reference point. With the Clone Stamp tool selected, press the Option key (Mac users) or Alt key (Windows users) to specify the input point. Any painting done after that uses the input point as the source for pixel data.

As you paint, you can specify whether the reference point moves with the cursor or remains stationary. If the reference point remains stationary, it paints from the same point every time you start a new brush stroke. For example, if you set your reference point to the petal of a flower, each brush stroke you make anywhere else in the image begins in the same spot: the petal of the flower. The stationary reference point is the default state of the Clone Stamp tool.

To make the reference point move with the cursor, enable the Align option. When you select an input point and begin painting, Photoshop looks at the relationship between the reference point and where you started to paint. Let's

say that the initial paint stroke began 100 pixels up and 300 pixels across from the input point. That X/Y relationship is maintained between the input point and the paint stroke. Move the cursor to the left, and the input point also moves to the left, continuously reflecting the spatial relationship between the input source point and the paint stroke. Enable the Align check box in the Options bar for the Clone Stamp tool to select this option.

The Options Bar Settings

The Clone Stamp tool offers most of the standard brush settings. You can set the brush size, blending mode, opacity, flow, and airbrush options, just as you can with any other brush.

An interesting option offered by the Clone Stamp tool is the Use All Layers option. When this check box is enabled, the option samples the reference point data in all the layers of the layer stack. If this check box is disabled, the reference point samples only the information in the currently selected layer.

The Pattern Stamp Tool

The Pattern Stamp tool is similar to the Clone Stamp tool and is located in the same fly-out menu in the toolbox. Instead of selecting a reference point as you do with Clone Stamp, with Pattern Stamp, you select a predefined pattern from the Options bar and paint with that. The Pattern Stamp tool offers the other standard brush options, and also features an Impressionist check box that blurs the pattern, creating a painterly effect.

The Stamp Tools

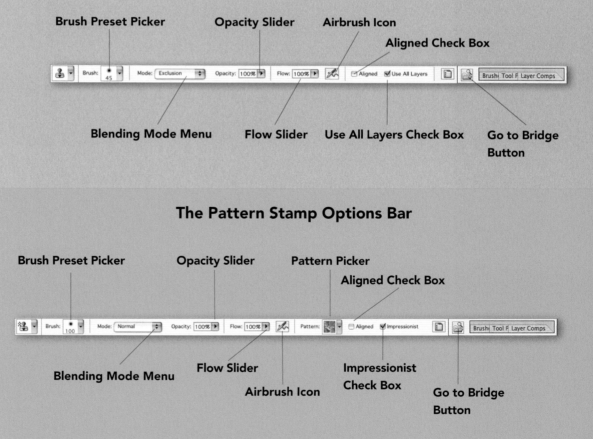

Clone Stamp Tool

Pattern Stamp Tool

The Clone Stamp Options Bar

Brush Preset Picker · Opacity Slider · Airbrush Icon · Aligned Check Box

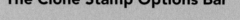

Blending Mode Menu · Flow Slider · Use All Layers Check Box · Go to Bridge Button

The Pattern Stamp Options Bar

Brush Preset Picker · Opacity Slider · Pattern Picker · Aligned Check Box

Blending Mode Menu · Flow Slider · Airbrush Icon · Impressionist Check Box · Go to Bridge Button

USING THE CLONE STAMP TOOL

1. Select the Clone Stamp tool from the toolbox.

2. Specify the brush size, opacity, and other brush settings in the Options bar.

3. Enable the Align check box if desired.

4. Move the cursor into the image and Option/Alt+click to set the reference point defining the center of the clone brush stroke.

5. Move the cursor elsewhere in the image to the starting point and paint as desired.

CLONE STAMP TECHNIQUES

The Clone Stamp's capability of duplicating an image area in a single brush stroke can create a wide range of special effects. This section looks at a few techniques and options that can extend the possibilities of this useful tool. In addition, remember that you can combine these effects; for example you can add opacity variation to custom brushes or blending modes to create even more variations.

Repairing Scratches and Dust

The Clone Stamp tool is indispensable as a resource for cleaning up spots and blemishes in scans and digital images. The best approach to fixing such blotches is to enable the Align check box and set the reference point as close to the blemish as possible, taking care to select a value that matches the area being corrected (see Figure 12.1). This approach is also effective for painting out scratches and telephone wires because the reference point follows the brush to pick up any variation in the background.

Lowering Opacity to Blend

Lowering the Opacity setting is an effective technique when you're trying to cover a large area, or when replicating the pattern would be noticeable. As you clone an area, lower the Opacity slider in the Options bar and reset the reference point as you paint. This approach will create a build-up of multiple texture areas in one spot, creating a unique area rather than a carbon copy of a single reference point.

Using Blending Modes

As you paint with the Clone Stamp tool, experiment with different blending modes to modify how the reference area is applied to the image. With the Clone Stamp tool selected, click and hold the Blending Mode pop-up menu in the Options bar to select the desired mode option.

Cloning a Channel

Cloning a layer is a special effect that allows you to duplicate an image or object in a single color channel. When you clone a single layer, you create a double image graphic effect that can be used to create a double image, 3D effect, or overall pattern based on the cloned object.

To clone a channel, open the Channels palette and highlight the target channel to select it. This

Figure 12.1

The first image shows the reference point placement, and the second shows the corrected image.

Figure 12.2

The original image, the Channels palette settings, and the final result.

Figure 12.3

Using Lab color to clone in grayscale. The Channels palette shows that the Lightness channel is selected.

Figure 12.4

The original image and the textured clone result.

action changes the image to grayscale, reflecting the contents of the selected channel. Click the Channel Visibility icon in the composite channel (the icon is titled after the file's color model—RGB, CMYK, and so on). This action shows the image in full color, even though only one channel is selected. The target channel should still be highlighted, which ensures that your edits will be applied to the only the selected

channel as you view the composite results. Select the Clone Stamp tool and set the reference point on the desired area; paint with the Clone Stamp tool to create the effect. You should see a ghosted image in the color of the selected channel (see Figure 12.2).

As a variation, if you switch to Lab color (Image, Mode, Lab Color) and target the Lightness channel, you can clone the reference area in grayscale without disturbing the

underlying color relationships. This effect is similar to the Luminosity blending mode (see Figure 12.3).

Using a Custom Brush

Photoshop CS's custom brushes provide a wide range of painting and digital effects. In the context of the Clone Stamp tool, the custom brushes allow you to clone an object or area with a texture brush, creating an abstraction that is still

based on the reference area (see Figure 12.4). Make modifications in the Scattering, Texture, and Dual Brush sections of the Brush Presets area of the Brushes palette for the most effective textures. See Chapter 14, "Painting and Custom Brushes," for details.

Red Deck

Corn

Winterscape

Tricycle

BUILDING THE IMAGE: *THE SPACE BETWEEN*

Figure 12.5
The Corn image is added to the Red Deck image.

Figure 12.6
The Corn image is silhouetted and scaled down..

Figure 12.7
The kernel texture is cloned.

Cloning a Textured Background

The design began with the Red Deck image, a digital photograph of the deck of a house, shot through a tumbler made of red blown glass. Thus, the red coloration and edge distortion were created by the glass itself, rather than with any Photoshop effects. My intent was to find another image that would work with the color and structure of the Red Deck image to create a textured background. After some experimentation, I decided that the kernels in the Corn image would work nicely.

After copying the Corn image into the Red Deck image to begin the composite (see Figure 12.5), I had to silhouette the Corn image to isolate the corn kernels. I selected Filter, Extract to open the Extract filter, defined the edges of the corn, and created the silhouette (see Figure 12.6). The result required a small amount of touch-up using the History brush, but I wasn't being too careful because I knew that I was going to abstract the kernels and that the original object would be obscured.

With the silhouette completed, I created a new layer and then selected the Clone Stamp tool. I specified a small brush and 100% opacity. I Option+clicked (Alt+click for Windows users) to set the reference point in the center of the corn shape. Then I moved the mouse and began to paint, extending the kernel pattern. I changed the reference point several times to create the texture overlap, and I followed the shapes of the trees to define the pattern placement (see Figure 12.7). To create the areas of semi-transparent texture, I lowered the Opacity slider in the Options bar to 45%. When I was done cloning the texture into the image, I set the blending mode in the Layers palette to Hard Light and added a Curves adjustment layer to integrate the texture with the background (see Figure 12.8).

At this point, the foreground was still not working with the overall

Figure 12.8
The texture is completed using transparency and a Curves adjustment layer.

Figure 12.9
A mirror image is created with the Copy, Paste, and Flip Vertical commands..

Figure 12.10
The image is rotated, and a gradient mask is used to blend the colors.

Figure 12.11
The landscape and tricycle are added to create the final image.

background, so I decided to cover it completely. I selected the Marquee tool and dragged a horizontal rectangle across the middle of the image, keeping the bottom of the rectangle just above the railing of the deck. I selected Edit, Copy Merged to copy the selection, and then pasted the copy back into the composite as its own layer. Then I flipped the copied rectangle (Edit, Transform, Flip Vertical) and dragged it to the bottom of the composite to create a seamless pattern (see Figure 12.9).

A New Orientation

The stripes were interesting, but the horizontal orientation was not working. Thinking that a vertical orientation would be more effective, I selected Image, Rotate Canvas, 90° CCW. Then I added a Hue/Saturation adjustment layer (Layer, New Adjustment Layer, Hue/Saturation) with the following settings: Hue +96, Saturation −29, and Lightness −7. This change shifted the color from red to green, which seemed somewhat arbitrary, given that the image was still functioning as a backdrop. The vertical orientation did give the image more movement, which I emphasized further by adding a gradient transition from green to red. I created the transition by adding a layer mask with a black-to-white vertical gradient (see Figure 12.10). To do this, I high-

lighted the mask thumbnail in the Hue/Saturation adjustment layer and selected the Gradient tool from the toolbox. In the Options bar, I clicked on the Gradient Picker and selected the black-to-white gradient. Then I dragged the gradient from top to bottom in the image to create the vertical mask. With the mask still selected, I opened the Curves dialog box (Image, Adjustments, Curves) and tweaked the midpoint of the curve, which changed the break from black to white within the gradient mask.

Adding the Landscape

At this point, I was pretty sure that I wanted to place a landscape im-

age at the top of the composite, adding a horizon to give the image some context. After placing a few different images, I settled on the winter landscape because it created strong contrast and allowed the background to take on a subterranean feel.

I added the tricycle image at the bottom and silhouetted it using the Extract filter. I selected Edit, Free Transform and reduced the size of the tricycle by Shift+dragging the corner handle of the bounding box. Clicking and dragging inside the box allowed me to drag the tricycle into position (see Figure 12.11).

12

THE SPACE BETWEEN

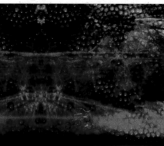

1. Open the Red Deck image.

2. Open the Curves dialog box (Image, Adjustments, Curves). Set the black point and white point.

3. Copy and paste the Corn image into the Red Deck image to begin the composite.

4. Choose Edit, Free Transform and Shift+drag the lower handle of the bounding box to reduce the size of the Corn image.

5. Choose Filter, Extract to launch the Extract dialog box.

6. From the Extract dialog box, select the Edge Highlighter tool, enable the Smart Highlighter check box, and zoom in to 100%.

7. Place the cursor on the edge of the corn and paint the highlight all around the object.

8. Select the Eraser from the extract dialog box and touch up any mistakes. Redraw the edge again with the Edge Highlighter tool.

9. Fill the image and click OK to extract the image.

10. Choose Layer, New, Layer to create a new layer. The textures you are going to clone will appear in this new layer.

11. Select the Clone Stamp tool, enable the Use All Layers check box in the Options bar, position the mouse pointer in the kernel texture, and Option+click (Mac users) or Alt+click (Windows users) to set the reference point.

12. Move the mouse pointer to the edge of the corn image and paint to extend the kernel texture.

13. Reset the reference point (Option+click or Alt+click in a new area within the original corn image to reset the reference point) and continue painting to create a varied texture area.

14. Adjust the Opacity slider in the Options bar to 45% and continue using the Clone Stamp tool to create some semi-transparent texture areas.

15. In the Layers palette, click and hold the Adjustment Layer icon and select Curves from the pop-up menu that appears.

16. Adjust the points of the curves as follows: For the Blue channel, move the point from Input=139 to Output=199. For the Green channel, move the point from Input=0 to Output=14. For the Red channel, move the point from Input=0 to Output=23.

17. Select the Rectangular Marquee tool and drag a horizontal selection through the middle of the image. Press ⌘+Shift+C (Mac users) or Ctrl+Shift+C (Windows users) to copy merge the selection. Then press ⌘+V or Ctrl+V to paste the selection to a new layer.

18. Choose Edit, Transform, Flip Vertical to flip the copied layer; drag the layer to the bottom of the composite to align the edges with the original selection.

19. Choose Image, Rotate Canvas, 90° CCW to change the orientation of the composite.

20. Click and hold the Adjustment Layer icon in the Layers palette and select Hue/Saturation from the pop-up menu that appears.

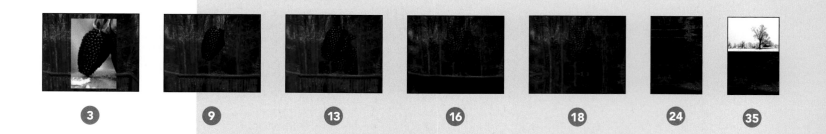

3   9   13   16   18   24   35

21. In the Hue/Saturation dialog box, set the Hue slider to +96, the Saturation slider to −29, and the Lightness slider to −7.

22. In the Layers palette, highlight the mask thumbnail for the Hue/Saturation adjustment layer you just created. Select the Gradient tool from the toolbox and select the black-to-white gradient from the Gradient Picker in the Options bar.

23. Drag from top to bottom in the image to create the gradient mask.

24. Choose Image, Adjustments, Curves to create a Curves adjustment layer. Raise the midpoint of the curve from Input=126 to Output=139.

25. Paste the Winterscape image into the composite and drag it into position at the top of the canvas.

26. Paste the Tricycle image into the composite.

27. With the Tricycle layer still selected, choose Filter, Extract to launch the Extract dialog box.

28. From the Extract dialog box, select the Edge Highlighter tool, enable the Smart Highlighter check box, and zoom to 100%.

29. Position the mouse pointer on the edge of the tricycle and paint the highlight all around the object.

30. Fill the image and click OK to extract the image.

31. Choose Edit, Free Transform and Shift+drag the lower handle of the bounding box to reduce the size of the tricycle image.

32. In the Layers palette, click the Add Layer Mask icon.

33. Set the foreground color to 50% gray and select the Paint Bucket from the toolbox.

34. Click in the image to fill the mask with gray.

35. Set the foreground color to white, select a feathered paintbrush, and paint back the handlebar of the tricycle to make it fully visible.

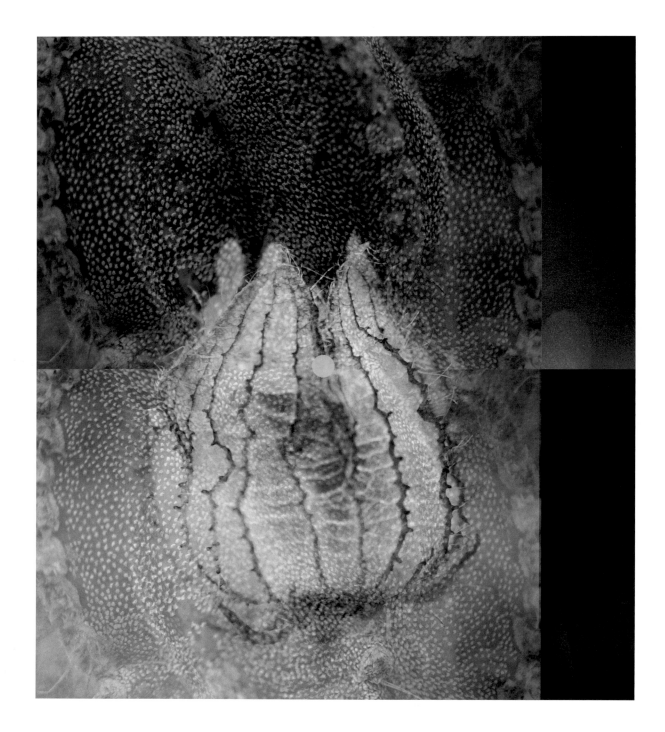

Image 13
Ominous Botanicus | ©2002 Daniel Giordan

CHAPTER 13

UNDERSTANDING THE BLENDING MODES

Ominous Botanicus operates on a tactile level that engages a range of our senses. It is sharp, abrasive, and self-sufficient, even as it beckons and compels the viewer to draw closer.

The image is constructed on an off-centered grid that serves as a backdrop for the central image of a seed pod. Although mostly monochrome, the blue color cast and bright cyan dot create a cool and sophisticated atmosphere.

The prevalent design component is the texture. The image is covered with textured dots that blanket the image in an organic patchwork. (The dots are actually the close-up surface texture from a small cactus that was duplicated and tiled vertically.) Variations in opacity and color create a visual depth that defines the parameters of the space. The visual complexity in the background is enhanced by the ribs of larger dots that echo the ribbing structure in the seed pod.

The seed pod itself stands as the focal point, covered with small hairs and a translucent membrane that hints at a mysterious interior, perhaps suggesting the darker side of nature or the inherent fear that comes with encountering the unknown.

The tonality in the image is interesting in that the midtones are carried completely by the texture area while the highlights and shadows are supplied by geometric shapes. The dark rectangle on the right is recessive, pushing the rest of the image forward. The highlight is a single blue dot in the center of the image. The dot comes across as a beacon—inherently hopeful and perhaps a bit reassuring that the ominous alien seed pod is as harmless and natural as the weeds scattered in a garden.

●

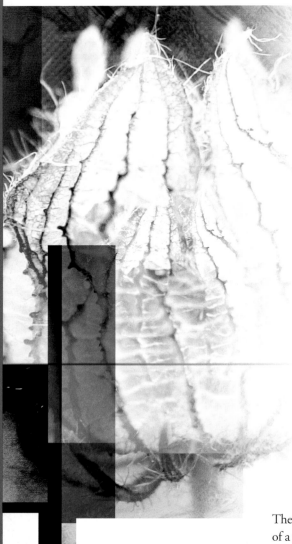

Normal ✓
Dissolve
Behind
Clear

Darken
Multiply
Color Burn
Linear Burn

Lighten
Screen
Color Dodge
Linear Dodge

Overlay
Soft Light
Hard Light
Vivid Light
Linear Light
Pin Light
Hard Mix

Difference
Exclusion

Hue
Saturation
Color
Luminosity

BLENDING MODES

In the real world, most people take an experimental approach to blending modes, trying different ones until they find the look they're after. In this chapter, I will provide enough information for you to get comfortable with blending modes and then set you loose to explore them for yourself.

Introduction to Blending Modes

Photoshop's blending modes operate on the basis of comparison. Specifically, they compare the value of one pixel to that of another pixel, and then they make a sort of value judgment. Depending on the blending mode you've selected, it may determine whether the pixel is lighter, darker, or a different color, or it may add or subtract the value of the two pixels.

The comparison looks at the value of a pixel before and after it is modified, or at the value of the pixel in relationship to adjacent layers in a layer stack. The base pixel value is that of the existing pixels in the image; the second pixel value is one that is applied in some way. In this explanation, I will call the second pixel the *blend value.*

For example, if you paint over a photo with red, you have the initial value of the photo and the red blending value. As Photoshop compares these values, it considers whether the blending value is lighter, darker, more luminous,

and so on, and then it creates the blending mode result based on these relationships.

Blending Mode Categories

It is often easier to understand each blending option by the general effect it delivers rather than be distracted by how the mode actually works. Blending mode effects can be broken into general categories that can help you anticipate how a mode is going to operate.

The blending mode categories are Darken, Lighten, Light Effect, Difference, and Color Components. Breaking it down further, the Photoshop blending mode options are Normal, Dissolve, Darken, Multiply, Color Burn, Linear Burn, Lighten, Screen, Color Dodge, Linear Dodge, Overlay, Soft Light, Hard Light, Vivid Light, Linear Light, Pin Light, Hard Mix, Difference, Exclusion, Hue, Saturation, Color, and Luminosity.

At first, the results can be hard to get a handle on because the blend and base values are constantly in

flux, and the overall logic of a particular mode is sometimes veiled. To keep things straight, remember that the blend value and the base value can be anything from a paint color to a layer to a filter result. Ask the simple question of what was there first, and you have the base value. Ask what was added second, and you have the blend value. If you are working with an existing image, that image will almost always be the base value. When you paint with a brush or apply a filter, the brush strokes or filter result is the blend value, and the previous or original state of the image is the base. With layers, the current active layer is the blend value; any layers beneath it constitute the base value. Be patient as you try to figure out what's going on, and keep your spirit of exploration open as you experiment.

Accessing the Blending Modes

Now that you have a basic understanding of which blending modes are out there, the next step is to know where to find them.

Photoshop allows access to the blending modes in the following situations:

- **Layers:** The most common use of blending modes is probably in the Layers palette. From this location, it is easy to apply the contents of a selected layer (as the blend value) with the layers beneath it in the Layers palette (as the base value).

- **Paint Tools:** Select any of Photoshop's paint tools, and the blending modes appear in the Options bar. Note that no blending modes are available for the Dodge and Burn tools, and that a limited set of blending modes is available for the Sharpen, Blur, Heal, and Patch tools.

- **Fade Command:** When you apply a filter or command, you can soften the result with the Fade command (Edit, Fade). In addition to lightening the effect with Fade, you can also access a blending mode menu that applies the new effect (as the blend value) to the previous state (as the base value).

- **Fills:** The Fill command (Edit, Fill) allows you to fill a layer or selection with a solid color, pattern, or history state. Blending modes are available with the Fill command to control how the fill is applied, using the fill as the blend value and the current image as the base value.

The Blending Modes Menu

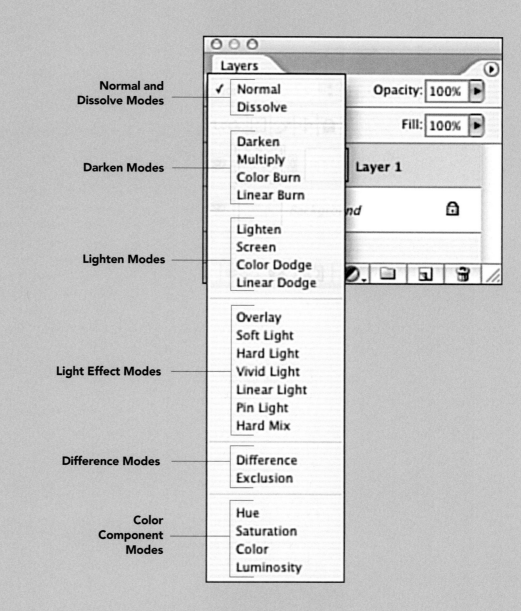

At first glance, 22 blending modes can be pretty intimidating. This may be why most people just click down the list looking for something they like. However, it helps to think of the blending modes as falling into five general categories, which could suggest a basic strategy. The five categories are listed here, with a further description of the effect each blending mode creates. Note that the Normal mode is the default; it leaves things unchanged. The Dissolve mode is based on transparency rather than on base and blend values; it is not discussed in the following sections.

Darken Blending Modes

The Darken group of blending modes compares the two pixel values and reveals the pixels with the lowest brightness value. In addition, higher saturation values also determine visibility, and colors with 100 percent saturation are always visible in some way. The Darken modes are the linear opposite of the Lighten modes

Lighten Blending Modes

The Lighten group of blending modes compares the two pixel values and reveals the pixels with the highest brightness value. In addition, higher saturation values also determine visibility, and colors with 100 percent saturation are always visible in some way. The Lighten modes are the linear opposite of the Darken modes.

Light Effects Blending Modes

Not to be confused with the Lighting Effects *filter,* the Light Effects *blending modes* create a luminous result. In Adobe's literature, these modes are referred to as having an effect like "shining a spotlight on an image." I prefer to describe them as light projections. All these modes produce a result that looks as if two slide projectors were shining their images on the same screen.

Difference and Exclusion Blending Modes

The Difference mode is the most dramatic blending mode; it frequently results in brightly saturated colors, inverted images, and other surprises. Although this mode is fun to play with, be careful not to overuse it because the Difference mode has a signature look that is easy to recognize. The Difference mode looks for the brighter pixel value between the blend and base values and subtracts the lower pixel value. White as a base color inverts the blend values, while blending with black produces no change. The Exclusion blending mode is a low-contrast version of the Difference mode

Color Component Blending Modes

The final four blending modes create effects based on a specific color variable. These modes are perhaps the most straightforward and predictable of the blending modes.

Base

Base

Base

Base

Blend

Blend

Blend

Blend

Darken Result

Multiply Result

Color Burn Result

Linear Burn Result

Darken

The Darken mode looks at the base and blend values and subtracts their brightness values to create a darker result. Think of it as a competition: If the base value is darker, it wins; if it's lighter, it loses. White and lighter base values drop out completely, letting the blend colors show through.

Multiply

The Multiply mode always darkens the image, unless white is selected as the new value, in which case there is no change in base value (that is, if you apply white as a blend value, the base is revealed at 100 percent). As it darkens, the Multiply mode also desaturates and tones down the color.

Color Burn

The Color Burn mode creates exaggerated color saturation effects when combined with black and darker tones. Pure white as a blend color always reveals the base with the Color Burn mode. The only exception is when black and pure colors with 100 percent saturation are in the base; in these cases, the pure colors are always visible.

Linear Burn

The Linear Burn mode creates a result that is similar to that of the Multiply mode. The difference is that the Linear Burn mode creates more intense color saturation. With the Linear Burn mode, a black blend color always covers the base. This is a good option for darkening the image without blowing out color.

Base

Base

Base

Base

Blend

Blend

Blend

Blend

Lighten Result

Screen Result

Color Dodge Result

Linear Dodge Result

Lighten

The Lighten mode looks at the base and blend values and combines their brightness values to create an even brighter result, in a cumulative effect. Darker base values drop out completely, letting the blend values show through.

Screen

The Screen mode always lightens the image unless black is the blend value, in which case there is no change in base value (that is, if you apply black as a blend value, the base is revealed at 100 percent). In general, the Screen mode tends to wash out everything, creating an underexposed, or bleached effect. Saturation is softened, and hue relationships are unchanged.

Color Dodge

The Color Dodge mode creates exaggerated color saturation effects when combined with white and light tones. Pure white as a blend always conceals the base with the Color Dodge mode. The only exception is when black and pure colors with 100 percent saturation are in the base, in which case the pure colors are always visible.

Linear Dodge

The Linear Dodge blending mode creates a result that is similar to the Screen blending mode. The difference is that the Linear Dodge mode creates more intense color saturation. With Linear Dodge, a white blend color always covers the base. This is a good option for lightening the image without blowing out the color.

Base

Base

Base

Base

Blend

Blend

Blend

Blend

Overlay Result

Soft Light Result

Hard Light Result

Vivid Light Result

Overlay

The Overlay mode combines the blend and base values equally, and it generally creates a darker result. The basic effect is a saturated image with strong color, although the results tend to get a bit dark. Blacks, whites, and pure colors in the base are visible at all times.

Soft Light

The Soft Light mode combines the blend and base values so that the base is dominant, and the blend is soft and subtle. It's almost as if you'd reduced the opacity on the blending values and added saturation on the base image. Blacks, whites, and pure colors in the base are visible at all times.

Hard Light

The Hard Light mode combines the blend and base values so that the blend values dominate, and the base is soft and subtle. Although the tonality of the blend values are maintained, highly saturated colors in the base still show through. Blacks, whites, and pure colors in the base are visible at all times.

Vivid Light

The Vivid Light mode creates a highly saturated result that is similar to that produced by the Color Burn blending mode. The main difference is that the result of Vivid Light is not as dark as the result of Color Burn; Vivid Light lets the tonality in the blend value show through and preserves the whites from the base.

Base

Base

Base

Base

Blend

Blend

Blend

Blend

Linear Light Result

Pin Light Result

Difference Result

Exclusion Result

Linear Light

The Linear Light mode preserves the tonality of the blend layer while mixing in the color from the base. The result is similar to that of the Hue blending mode except that instead of the blend value coloring the base, it's the base color that dominates.

Pin Light

The Pin Light mode preserves the lighter tones and highlights of the blend value; it allows the 3/4 tones and shadows of the base to come through. Light colors in the base are tinted with the hue from the blend value.

Hard Mix

The Hard Mix mode creates a posterized effect. If the upper layer is brighter than 50% gray, the resulting posterization is also brightened. Inversely, an upper layer darker than 50% gray creates a darker posterized effect. The posterization effect is minimized as the opacity of the upper layer is increased.

Difference

The Difference mode is the most dramatic blending mode; it frequently results in brightly saturated colors, inverted images, and other surprises.

Base

Blend

Exclusion

The Exclusion blending mode is a low-contrast version of the Difference mode

Hard Mix Result

Base

Base

Base

Base

Blend

Blend

Blend

Blend

Hue Result

Saturation Result

Color Result

Luminosity Result

Hue

The Hue mode maintains the luminance and saturation of the base color and the hue of the blend color. Thus, if the blend color is green, just green is applied to the bottom image, leaving the tonality and saturation of the base.

Saturation

The Saturation mode maintains the luminance and hue of the base, while changing saturation levels based on the blend values. Whatever is saturated in the blend is saturated in the final result. Color and tonality in the base are unchanged.

Color

The Color mode creates a result with the luminance of the base color and the hue and saturation of the blend color. Because the grayscale data in the base is untouched, this is a great option for creating hand-colored effects.

Luminosity

The Luminosity mode creates a result with the hue and saturation of the base color and the luminance of the blend color. In short, the tonal values in the blend are combined with the color and saturation of the base.

WORKING WITH BLENDING MODES

Although it's helpful to understand what the blending modes do, it's even more important to have a sense of how to use them. In addition to the experimentation you will do with these features, the following blending mode strategies can assist you in moving from theory to application.

 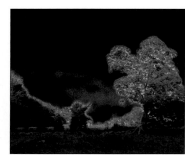 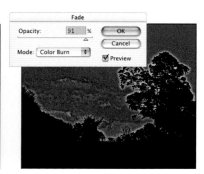

Original Image

After Applying the Diffuse Glow Filter

After Applying the Color Burn Blending Mode

Figure 13.1
After applying the Diffuse Glow filter to the original image, the final image shows the result of the Color Burn blending mode using the Fade command.

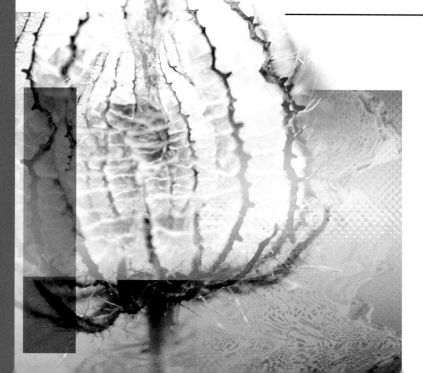

Using the Fade Command

The Fade command allows you to attach a blending mode to just about any Photoshop command that doesn't offer one naturally. Such commands include any of the Adjustment commands such as Posterize or Replace Color. You can achieve some very interesting effects by using the Fade command with Liquify, Distort, or just about any other filter option.

To use the Fade command, apply any Photoshop command and immediately select Edit, Fade <command name>. In the dialog box that appears, you can access the Blending Modes menu, which considers the original image to be the base value and the filter effect to be the blend value (see Figure 13.1). You can also modify the Opacity slider to lighten the effect.

Figure 13.2

Inversion: The upper-right background is inverted using a paintbrush set to the Difference blending mode with white as the foreground color.

Figure 13.3

Desaturation: The background is desaturated using a paintbrush set to the Color blending mode with white as the foreground color.

Figure 13.4

Hand Coloring: A hand-colored effect is applied to the figure using a brush set to the Color blending mode.

Brush Inversion Effects

By combining the brush, a white foreground color, and the Difference blending mode, it's possible to create your own custom Invert brush. To do this, select any brush type, choose white as a foreground color, and select the Difference blending mode from the Options bar. When you paint into the image with these options, the base pixels are inverted to a negative image (see Figure 13.2).

Varying the Opacity setting of the brush results in a bright, multicolored abstraction that still follows the inverted base image to some degree. If you select a color other than white, the selected color is pushed into the shadows and dark areas of the image.

Brush Desaturation

With white as the foreground color, the Color blending mode desaturates the image as you paint, inverting it to black and white (see Figure 13.3). This can be very effective if you want to emphasize one area or object, while pushing everything else back to grayscale.

Brush Hand Coloring

Another useful application of the Color blending mode is to selec- tively colorize areas of an image. As you saw in the last section, the Color blending mode leaves the tonality of the image alone, chang- ing only the color and saturation. This means that any selected color will paint over the tonality of the base image, similar to the way you would hand color a black-and- white photo (see Figure 13.4)

Seed Pod

Cactus Dots

Shoulder

BUILDING THE IMAGE: *OMINOUS BOTANICUS*

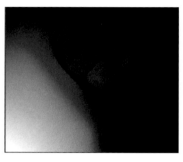

Figure 13.5
The Shoulder image is darkened with Lighting Effects and cropped.

Figure 13.6
The Seed Pod image is positioned, and the Hard Light blending mode is selected in the Layers palette.

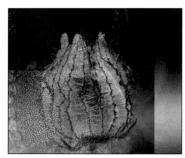

Figure 13.7
The Cactus Dots image is duplicated and merged to one layer.

The Hidden Shoulder

This image began with a photograph that is almost completely obscured in the final image. Although its subject can't be recognized, the Shoulder photo still creates a distinct tonal pattern and provides a sense of completeness to the final image.

The picture of the sleeping child was a good starting point. The slight abstraction caused by the strong light on the shoulder created an image that felt more like a landscape than a figure. After cropping and optimizing the initial photo, I modified the image with the Lighting Effects filter by casting a single light on the shoulder, darkening the remainder of the image (see Figure 13.5).

Enter the Seed Pod

Next I opened the Seed Pod image and dragged it to the Shoulder image. After positioning it against the left side of the Shoulder image, I selected Hard Light as a layer blending mode.

I trimmed away a column on the right of the Seed Pod layer by deleting a rectangular selection. I selected the portion of the Shoulder image that was showing through and lightened it using the Curves dialog box. I set the curve input/output values as follows: from Input: 0 to Output: 60 and from Input: 200 to Output: 178. This resulted in a low-contrast section that would set up the completion of the image (see Figure 13.6).

Building the Texture

The overall dot texture began as a close-up image of the surface of a cactus. After opening the image, I desaturated it to black and white and dragged it into the composite. I scaled the dots using the Free Transform command, which reduced the size of the image and positioned it in the top portion of the design.

Then I duplicated the texture layer to a separate layer by selecting Duplicate Layer from the Layers palette menu and clicking OK in the dialog box that appeared. I selected the Move tool from the toolbox and dragged the duplicate layer straight down. Holding the Shift key while I dragged ensured that the layer stayed in alignment. Then I reduced the opacity in the

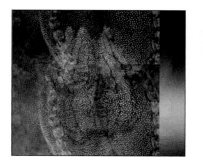

Figure 13.8

The Cactus Dots layer is duplicated and flipped.

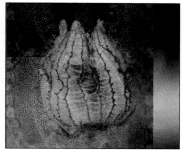

Figure 13.9

The texture layers are added to a layer set, and a mask is applied to the set.

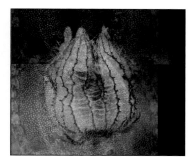

Figure 13.10

The dark rectangle is added.

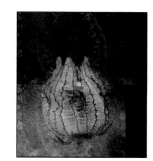

Figure 13.11

The addition of the light blue dot creates the final image.

lower layer to 62 percent to enhance readability of the main subject (see Figure 13.7).

I merged the two texture layers into a single layer by linking them in the Layers palette and selecting Merge Layers from the palette menu. The resulting single layer was duplicated again and flipped horizontally by selecting Edit, Transform, Flip Horizontal (see Figure 13.8).

At this point, the Seed Pod was becoming obscured by all the dots. To bring back the Seed Pod, I linked the two texture layers again and added them to a layer group by selecting New Group From Layers from the Layers palette menu. Then I added a layer mask to the entire group by selecting the group in the Layers palette and clicking the Add Layer Mask icon.

I selected a brush with a 300-pixel brush size and 30 percent opacity and created the mask, revealing the Seed Pod image once again (see Figure 13.9).

Finishing with Graphics Layers

The dark rectangle in the lower-right corner was added by creating a new layer, selecting the shape with the marquee tool, and filling it with a dark brown foreground color. I further modified the layer using the Luminosity blending mode to create the deep blue color (see Figure 13.10).

At this point, the image was still pretty flat because of the lack of any real highlights. Rather than try to integrate them by introducing a new image, I decided to add another graphic component. I added the circle by making a

circular selection (select the Oval selection tool and Shift+drag to create a perfect circle) and filled it with a saturated cyan color. The effect was completed by setting the layer opacity to 72 percent and applying the Linear Dodge blending mode from the Layers palette (see Figure 13.11).

13

OMINOUS BOTANICUS

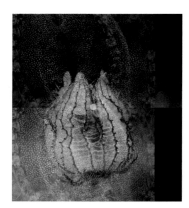

1. Open the Shoulder image.

2. Open the Curves dialog box (Image, Adjustments, Curves). Set the black point and the white point.

3. Select Filter, Render, Lighting Effects. Click in the preview window to add a single spotlight. Drag the handles to point to the shoulder area, leave the other settings at their defaults, and click OK.

4. Select the Crop tool from the toolbox and crop tightly to the head and shoulders.

5. Open the Seed Pod image and drag it to the composite.

6. With the Seed Pod layer still active, select Hard Light from the Layers palette Blending Modes menu.

7. Use the Rectangular Marquee tool to select the right column of the Seed Pod layer and delete the selection contents.

8. With the selection still active, activate the Shoulder layer and modify it with the Curves dialog box (Image, Adjustments, Curves). Change the input value 0 to an output value of 60, and the input value of 200 to an output value of 178.

9. Open the Cactus Dots image.

10. Select Image, Adjustments, Hue/Saturation. Lower the Saturation slider to −100 to reduce the colors to a black and white image.

11. Drag the Cactus Dots image to the composite. Select Edit, Free Transform and Shift+drag the corner of the Cactus Dots image until it fits the dimensions of the Seed Pod layer.

Double-click inside the layer to apply the transformation.

12. Select Duplicate Layer from the Layers palette menu to duplicate the layer.

13. Choose the Move tool and Shift+drag the duplicate layer straight down to create a mirror image.

14. Link the two Cactus Dot texture layers and select Merge Layers from the Layers palette menu to combine the layers.

15. Select Duplicate Layer from the palette menu to duplicate the combined layer.

16. Select Edit, Transform, Flip Horizontal to flip the texture layer.

17. In the Layers palette, link the two combined texture layers.

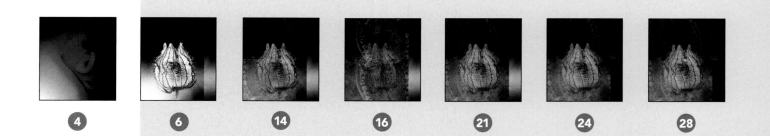

18. Select New Layer Group From Layers in the Layers palette menu to create a new layer set containing the linked layers.

19. Highlight the new layer group in the Layers palette.

20. Click the Layer Mask icon in the Layers palette.

21. Select the Brush tool with a 300-pixel brush and black as the foreground color. Paint a layer mask to reveal the Seed Pod image.

22. Click the New Layer icon in the Layers palette to create a new layer.

23. Use the Rectangular Marquee tool to select a rectangle on the lower-right side of the image. Fill the rectangular selection with a dark-brown fill color.

24. From the Blending Modes menu in the Layers palette, select the Luminosity blending mode for the rectangle layer.

25. Click the New Layer icon in the Layers palette to create a new layer.

26. Click the Elliptical Marquee tool and Shift+drag to create a small circular selection.

27. Fill the selection with a saturated cyan color.

28. Set the circle layer to 72 percent opacity and apply a Linear Dodge blending mode.

CONTENTS

Chapter 14
Painting and Custom Brushes: *Trilogy*
210

Chapter 15
Using Distort Filters: *Tree House*
232

Chapter 16
Mastering the Photoshop Patterns: *Earthly Delights*
250

Chapter 17
Using Gradients and Gradient Maps: *FreeFall*
260

Chapter 18
Using the Liquify Filter: *Birch Trees*
270

Chapter 19
Working with Lighting Effects: *On the Edge*
282

PART FOUR

SPECIAL EFFECTS

CHAPTER 14

PAINTING AND CUSTOM BRUSHES

Trilogy echoes the Three Graces theme that has been artistically explored throughout history. In mythology, Aglaia (Radiance), Euphrosyne (Joy), and Thalia (Fruitfulness) presided over all beauty and charm in nature and humanity. The three sisters have been depicted entwined in a voluptuous dance by Hellenistic Greek sculptors as well as by Rubens, Raphael, and present-day artists. Although many of these depictions have been sensual and erotic in nature, the best versions present a delicate balance and compositional strength.

The three leaves in *Trilogy* are richly colored and, although they share the same stem, they appear to be very different. The leaf on the right is obscured by the darkly textured hibiscus in the background, although the angle and volume of the leaf can still be felt. The center leaf is balanced and centered and, although it maintains an inner glow, it too seems to be fading into the background. The left leaf is unique in its clarity, size,

and placement. It breaks out of the green abyss with both its size and angle. The tip of the leaf meets a group of textured brush strokes in a tactile gesture, as the aggressive white background pushes over the leaf's edge.

And yet all the leaves seem centered by (perhaps even focused on) the halo that floats above them. The drawn circle sits on top of the green, defies gravity, and aligns itself with the white brush strokes in the upper-left corner of the image. The halo is precise, clean, and articulate—in some ways even self-sufficient in comparison with its surroundings. The leaves dance and entwine, grasping at the charms they are supposed to depict while a vision of true grace condescends to share their space and entice their aspirations, until such joy their ambition finds.

PHOTOSHOP PAINTING BASICS

There was a time not too long ago when a discussion on painting in Photoshop was a brief conversation. It began and ended with a quick overview on setting brush size, feather options, and color selection. You made these few selections and did your best with the tools at your disposal.

The new painting tools in Photoshop CS2 have changed all that. Adobe has built in advanced support for drawing tablets, organic brush and texture effects, and an intuitive painting interface—all of which add up to extensive control and power in generating convincing painting effects.

Understanding the Painting Variables

Wrapping your arms around all the new painting options in Photoshop CS2 can be a daunting task. You can poke and tweak various sliders and controls, but it's hard to feel that you have a cohesive lay of the land. Therefore, the first things you need to understand are the basic painting variables.

The Brush Options Bar Settings

Even casual Photoshop users should be familiar with the settings in the paint tools Options bar. Select the Brush, Pencil, Clone Stamp, Eraser, or any other brush-based tool (not a pen tool), and the Options bar presents you

with the Brush Presets Picker, Blending Modes menu, and Opacity slider. Other options may appear and disappear, but these three settings remain constant.

The Presets Picker features a dynamic brush size slider along with an extensive menu of brush presets. The presets are primarily variations in size and edge sharpness, with a few scatter effects thrown in for good measure.

The Opacity slider specifies the maximum amount of paint coverage applied by the Brush, Pencil, Clone Stamp, Pattern Stamp, History Brush, Art History Brush, Gradient, and Paint Bucket tools. When present, the Flow slider operates similar to Opacity—the

difference is that Flow allows you to build on top of each stroke to increase the amount of color. The Strength slider specifies the strength of strokes applied by the Smudge, Blur, Sharpen, and Sponge tools. The Exposure setting specifies the amount of exposure used by the Dodge and Burn tools.

Brush Shape Controls

If you want to push beyond the Options bar and the brush, you'll have to dig into the Brushes palette, which can be launched by selecting Window, Brushes, or by clicking the Brushes Palette icon in the Options bar. The Brushes palette controls the following brush attributes:

- *Size and Angle*
  Control pixel dimensions, angle, hardness, and spacing.
- *Brush Shape Dynamics*
  Refer to options for creating variation in the brush stroke during the act of painting. Size, angle, and roundness can be controlled as can pen pressure, angle, and other user-defined input options.
- *Scattering*
  Randomly scatters the brush marks vertically and/or horizontally across the path of the stroke. Also controls the frequency of marks and the degree of randomness.
- *Texture*
  Allows you to select a texture from the Texture Presets

palette and apply it to the brush stroke.

- *Dual Brush Capabilities*
  Allow you to specify a primary and secondary brush setting. The primary brush shape acts like a mask, which defines the stroke shape. The secondary brush attributes are applied within the boundaries of the primary shape.

- *Color Dynamics (variation)*
  Create random color variation throughout the stroke. Color variables include Foreground/Background variation, Hue, Saturation, and Brightness settings.

- *Other Dynamics (variation and check boxes)*
  This category is for everything that's left over, including opacity and flow, noise, and smoothing.

Using Drawing Tablets

Adobe takes full advantage of pressure-sensitive drawing tablets, allowing you to vary the size and shape of a brush stroke based on the stylus's pressure or angle. A wide array of brush stroke options—such as size, scattering, and opacity—can be controlled by pressure, pen angle, and stroke direction. These individual stroke attributes can be activated from the control pop-up menus in the Stroke Adjustment section of the Brushes palette.

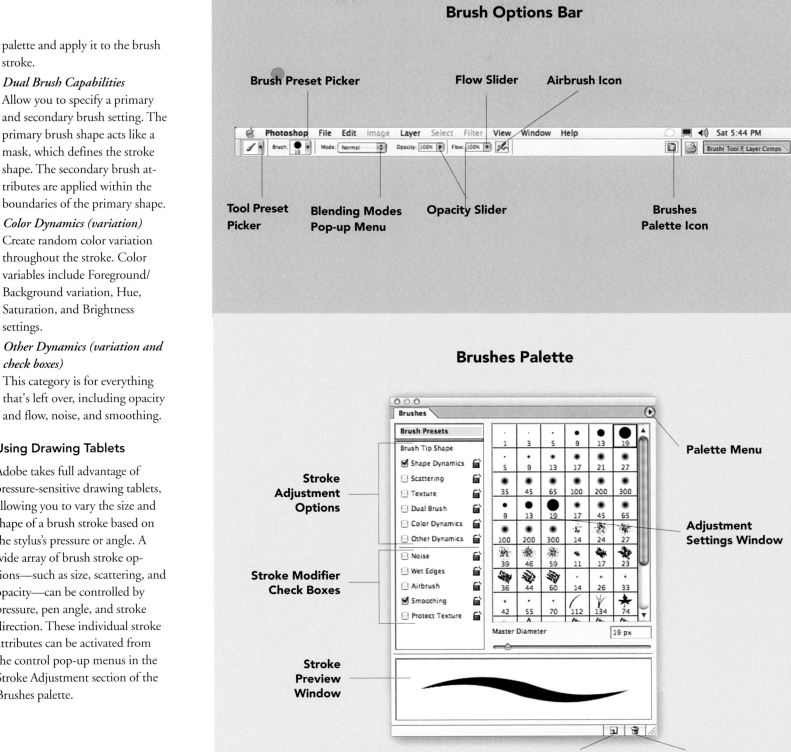

Brush Options Bar

Brush Preset Picker

Flow Slider

Airbrush Icon

Tool Preset Picker

Blending Modes Pop-up Menu

Opacity Slider

Brushes Palette Icon

Brushes Palette

Stroke Adjustment Options

Stroke Modifier Check Boxes

Stroke Preview Window

Palette Menu

Adjustment Settings Window

New Brush Icon

Delete Brush Icon

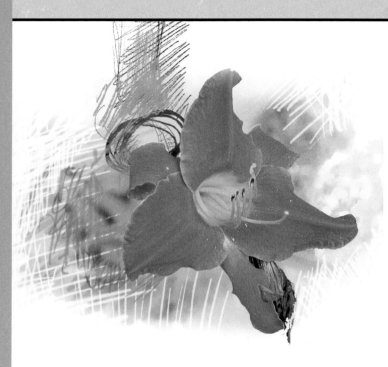

BUILDING A CUSTOM BRUSH

Much of the power in Photoshop's painting controls lies in their capability of simulating a wide array of brush types and styles. The painting controls allow you to create a wide variety of textures and painting effects, ranging from loose expressionism to tight precision.

To master the art of brush building, you must understand each of the stroke variables at your disposal, as well as how these variables can be combined and controlled. When you appreciate these controls, you will have at your fingertips an endless array of realistic effects that deliver the look and feel of real painting.

Brush Stroke Variables

Each brush stroke variable is listed in the Stroke Adjustments Options list in the Brushes palette. Click the variable name to activate the controls for that section and select its adjacent check box. After setting the controls for a variable, you can deselect the check box for each variable, toggling the variable's effects on and off in the Stroke Preview window.

Before defining the variables to customize a brush, we should define our terms. A *brush* refers to a set of characteristics that controls how pixels are applied by Photoshop's paint tools. The brush *tip* is the single point of contact that creates the marks and is defined by size, angle, roundness, and opacity.

A brush *mark* refers to the individual pixels (solid or in clumps) that are created by the brush tip. These marks are repeated to create a directional sequence referred to as a *stroke*. The Spacing control in the Brush Tip Shape section controls how frequently the marks are created during the stroke.

In the process of creating a brush, you can activate or emphasize certain stroke characteristics. The control options are None, Fade, Pen Pressure, Pen Tilt, and Stylus Wheel. (The Initial Direction and Direction options are also available for the Angle Jitter control in the Shape Dynamics section.) The Fade control fades the effect out over a specified number of pixels as the stroke is drawn. Enter the pixel length for the Fade effect in

the field to the right of the menu. The Pen Pressure, Pen Tilt, and Stylus Wheel options refer to the control characteristics for various drawing tablets.

The Brush Presets

Although not technically a brush variable, the Brush Presets Picker is a good place to start when creating a custom brush (see Figure 14.1). If a brush that's similar to the brush you want to create already exists, you may find that a few simple tweaks to the existing brush complete the process.

Brush Tip Shape

The Size and Angle section of the Brush Tip Shape settings may be familiar to many veteran Photoshop users because it was once the

only set of controls for modifying brush attributes (see Figure 14.2). In addition to another appearance by the Brush Preset Picker, the main controls for the Brush Tip Shape settings are the Diameter slider, Angle control, Roundness control, Hardness slider, and Spacing slider (which controls the flow of the brush marks).

Although you can enter a numeric Angle setting and Roundness percentage, it is easier to drag the Angle and Roundness icon to the right of these two entry fields. Click anywhere in the white square to set the angle; click and drag the dot handles to change the roundness of the brush tip. These two settings allow you to create a chiseled, calligraphic brush stroke effect.

Figure 14.9

The Stroke Modifiers section of the Brushes palette.

SAVING CUSTOM BRUSHES

After creating a brush effect, use this process to create a brush preset that you can save to access in the future.

1. Choose Window, Brushes to launch the Brushes palette.

2. Set the brush parameters. Then paint with the brush in a document to confirm the desired results.

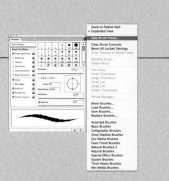

3. Select New Brush Preset from the Brushes palette menu.

4. In the dialog box that appears, name the new brush and click OK.

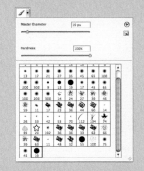

the Opacity Jitter slider in a range up to the current Opacity value specified in the Options bar. In the same manner, the range of the Flow Jitter slider is determined by the Flow setting in the Options bar (see Figure 14.8).

Stroke Modifiers

The final section in the Brushes palette features a list of check boxes that add global modifications to the current settings (see Figure 14.9). In addition to self-explanatory settings such as Noise, Wet Edges, and Airbrush, there are lesser-known controls such as Smoothing and Protect Texture.

The Smoothing option creates a softer, more rounded effect when the brush stroke you draw creates a curved shape. This option is especially effective when you're drawing quickly using a drawing tablet. The Protect Texture option applies a single, consistent texture effect to all brush strokes, creating a uniform effect that simulates a single-textured surface such as a canvas.

5. Open the Brush Preset Manager from the Brush tool Options bar or from the Brushes palette. Hold the mouse pointer over the thumbnail of the new brush shape to see the brush's name in a ToolTip pop-up.

6. Select the desired brush and paint the image.

WHY BUILD A CUSTOM BRUSH?

The previous pages outlined the vast array of controls for building a custom brush. Because the task of creating a custom brush can be daunting when viewed out of context, we'll now look at the process from a different perspective: suggesting specific instances where a custom brush might be necessary. The following pages also provide a concise list of steps that can help you organize an approach to the brush-creation variables at your disposal.

The first step to painting in Photoshop is to select a brush preset and set the color, opacity, and paint flow. This process is sufficient for most instances, but there are times when a simple soft or hard round brush just doesn't get the job done. The following sections look at some of the most common reasons you'll want to reach for the Brushes palette.

You Want to Paint into a Custom Space

A common painting mistake is to attempt to seamlessly paint a large area with a brush that's too small. This approach results in uneven, blotchy brush strokes that look anything but seamless. The best answer for this situation is to select a large brush that covers the area with just a mouse click or two. But what do you do when the area is a noncircular shape, such as an oval or something organic? This is the perfect time to access the settings in the Brush Tip Shape section of the Brushes palette. Adjust the Roundness setting to create an oval shape that matches the overall proportions of the space you want to paint. If the space you want to fill is angular, you can use the Angle setting to specify a directional axis to fit the space. Finally, set the brush diameter to the proper size (see Figure 14.10).

You're Looking for an Organic Effect

Custom brushes are great for generating random, organic painting effects. Any brush control that features the word *Jitter* is a good choice for creating an organic effect. Focus on the Shape Dynamics, Scattering, and Dual Brush sections of the Brushes palette to control the spread and distribution of the marks along the stroke. As you do this, remember that the marks themselves are controlled by the settings in Brush Tip Shape section. By combining Size, Angle, and Roundness settings with random mark generation, you can create a tremendous array of organic painting effects. In addition to mark distribution, you can also create an organic effect with the color and stroke transparency settings. Deciding on a subtle or extreme color variation is the first step, followed by tweaking the saturation and brightness settings. Finally, remember that random color variation can be enhanced with blending modes,

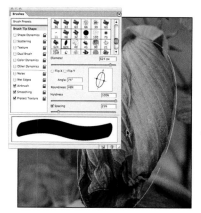

Figure 14.10
This custom brush was built to match the size and angle of the flower.

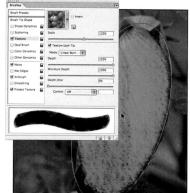

Figure 14.11
Adding texture to a brush stroke.

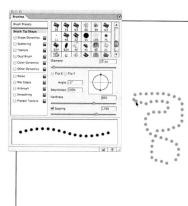

Figure 14.12
A patterned line effect.

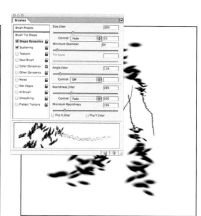

Figure 14.13
Results of a brush stroke fade effect.

which integrate the paint effect with the lower layers in the image.

You Want to Simulate a Texture

In some ways, the term *texture* is too general for the example shown here, given that many of the organic effects described in the previous section qualify as texture. Using the Protect Texture check box in the Brushes palette allows you to follow and replicate a texture consistently for all the strokes in an image (see Figure 14.11).

Without this option, each brush stroke has its own specific texture. As strokes overlap and accumulate, these individual textures don't always align and match up. The Protect Texture option implies that

there is a surface texture that covers the entire image, and it ensures that the textures from each brush stroke align and work together.

You Want a Custom Line Effect

Many people jump over to Adobe Illustrator to create dashed or dotted lines rather than create a custom brush in Photoshop to do the job. Adjust the Spacing slider in the Brush Tip Shape section of the Brushes palette to increase the intervals between the marks, creating dashes, dot sequences, and other patterned line effects.

To apply a patterned brush effect as a controlled line, create a path in the shape of the line and add a stroke to it. After selecting the

Brush tool and customizing the settings, select the Pen tool and draw the desired path of the line. From the Paths palette menu, select Stroke Path, make sure that the Brush tool is active in the dialog box that appears, and click OK. The patterned stroke effect will be painted along the path shape (see Figure 14.12).

You Want to Fade a Brush Stroke

I used to think that the Fade effect was cool when it was confined to the basic hard and feathered brushes of past versions of Photoshop. Combining the Fade effect with the various Jitter options of Photoshop 7 makes the Fade control downright amazing. You can set each Jitter effect to fade by

a specific number of pixels. You can set multiple Jitter effects to different fade rates. Thus, you can create a scatter effect that fades to a flat line that varies in size until it balances into a hard, straight line. This effect can be replicated and combined with other strokes for a unique and compelling overall effect (see Figure 14.13).

PAINTING STRATEGIES: TINTING A B&W IMAGE

Emily | ©2002 Daniel Giordan

Large color areas are defined.

The hair colors are painted in using multiple layers.

Multiple layers of crosshatched lines add detail to the face.

The Color blending mode allows you to add color over an image without disturbing the tonality of the image. This blending mode opens a world of painting possibilities because it allows you to add transparent color while maintaining the tones, shadows, and structure of an underlying photograph.

The result can range from a hand-colored photo effect to a painted image that loses touch with all but a remnant of the original image. In the example of *Emily* shown here, a color photograph was converted to black and white, and a series of layers helped me manage the build-up of the painting effect. One last note about using layers: If you want a layer to colorize the contents below it, leave the brush blending mode set to Normal and set the blending mode for that layer in the Layers palette to Color.

The initial layers of the *Emily* image defined the basic color divisions, similar to the way a watercolor artist would lay in the initial composition. Subsequent layers

pushed the development of specific areas of the image, such as the hair and the crosshatching in the face. Because the brush strokes were on separate layers, I resorted to using the Eraser tool to break up the markings if they were too heavy or in the wrong spot. Another technique for building up a gradual effect was to use the Opacity setting when I was painting in an effect. In trying to transition from a dark to a midtone, for example, I would sample the darker color, set the brush Opacity to 45%, and begin hatching.

Brushes Used

To achieve the effect in *Emily,* I used standard round brushes of various sizes. To achieve the expressive painterly brush strokes, I varied the Size Jitter slider in the Shape Dynamics section, and used a pressure-sensitive drawing tablet.

Blocking in the Image

I created a new layer set to the Color blending mode and painted in the face and shoulder areas. I

used a large brush in this instance, with the Hardness set to 0% and Opacity set to 70%. To help with color selection, I opened a photo with similar values and used the Eyedropper tool to sample a range of skin tones and lip color.

Adding Gestural Details

I knew that the only way I was going to make the hair feel right was to hit it with a strong, loose gesture. If I had been working with traditional paints or pastels, I would have been intimidated at having only one shot to get it right. However, because I was using Photoshop's layers and correction tools, I knew I could experiment until I was satisfied with the results.

I set up two layers, one for the highlights and one for the shadows. In addition to a score of undos, I used the eraser tool extensively. It was a great solution for pulling out hair highlights from the shadows and softening a few edges to integrate the brush strokes and make them recede.

Crosshatching the Face

Although it certainly was time consuming to add the countless layers of crosshatching, it was much easier than it would have been if I were using any atom-based medium. As I mentioned previously, Photoshop's ability to sample matching colors, change colors on the fly, and lay down a mark with opacity made it much easier to create the tonal transitions I was after in the subject's face.

Another effective tool when creating a crosshatched pattern is to use the Fade command. After drawing a brush stroke, select Edit, Fade Brush to lower the stroke opacity or apply a blending mode to the stroke. This approach is probably a bit tedious if you wanted to do it for single strokes, but if you make a connected series of lines using a back-and-forth motion, you can push back a block of lines pretty easily.

PAINTING STRATEGIES: PAINTING A TEXTURED MASK

The fire image is created from two separate photos.

The second image is added, desaturated, and masked.

Semi-opaque brush strokes are added to complete the effect.

Filters that automatically create textured and painterly edges in photographs have become very popular Photoshop plug-in accessories. With Photoshop CS, you can quickly generate these mask transitions using a textured or graphic brush.

In the example of *Consumption,* a wet splatter brush was used to create a random organic effect that almost felt like the fire was burning its way through to the other image. By using the Size Jitter slider in the Shape Dynamics section of the Brushes palette, I was able to achieve the full range of texture sizes without making another trip back to the Brushes palette. Light pressure with a pressure-sensitive drawing tablet and stylus created the smaller speckles, and full pressure generated the large, soft markings.

Brushes Used

The burn-out effect used a single 105-pixel brush with the Hardness set to 0% and Spacing set to 25%. I enabled the Shape Dynamics

section of the Brushes palette and set the Size Jitter slider to 77%. From the Control menu, I selected Pen Pressure and specified a 1% minimum diameter. I also enabled the Scattering section of the Brushes palette and set the following options: Scatter slider was set to 144%, the Both Axes check box was enabled, the Count slider was set to 5, and the Count Jitter slider was set to 27%. All the Control menus in the Scattering section were set to off, meaning that the scatter effect on the stroke was constant. Finally, I enabled the Dual Brush section of the Brushes palette and set the following options: the Diameter slider was set to 7 pixels, the Spacing slider was set to 25%, the Scatter slider was set to 0, and the Count slider was set to 1.

Creating the Background

The fire background image is actually a composite of two fire images I shot while camping. Using a single shot wasn't conveying the all-over pattern effect I was after; I

guess you could say that it *looked* like I shot the photos on a camping trip. By combining two of the images, however, the combination started to feel like more of a pattern. The two images were composited as separate layers and combined with the Lighten blending mode, which brought up the flames perfectly against the dark background.

The Second Image and the Mask

The image of the dried grapevine was added next, cropped and dragged into position. To create a graphic effect in the vines, I added a Hue/Saturation adjustment layer and lowered the Saturation slider to −100, converting the image to black and white. I also added a Curves adjustment layer and lightened the image to create even more of a start effect.

I added a mask to the vine layer and selected a brush with the Wet Splatter effect, configured as described in the "Brushes Used" section. By varying the stylus

pressure, I was able to control the size of the brush stroke.

I also added a mask to the Hue/Saturation adjustment layer and painted back the color and texture on the left side of the vine. The splatter brush was perfect for simulating the texture of the bark.

Adding the Final Brush Strokes

As a final gesture, I added two paint strokes to a separate layer. After creating the layer, I sampled an orange color from the flames and painted the strokes at 60% opacity. The strokes danced between the existing elements, echoing the textures around them while creating an interesting spatial effect. They also resonated well with the orange-colored branches on the left side of the composite.

Untitled | ©2002 Daniel Giordan

Selecting the area for the brush tip.

Painting with the new brush.

A second image-based brush completes the effect.

It's been possible to create a custom brush tip from a photograph in Photoshop for quite some time. The possibilities associated with this feature have grown with the advent of the various jitter options described in this section. It's now possible to select an area of an image, define it as a brush tip, and apply the myriad list of brush controls to the custom tip.

This means that a square shape containing an object can be repeated endlessly with control over attributes such as spacing, angle, and size. The result is a brush stroke comprised of spinning, swirling composites that scale themselves over the course of the stroke. Granted, it's not an effect you'd use every day, but it's a cool effect to pull out of your pocket for just the right project.

Brushes Used

This effect used two brushes made from photos. The first brush was created from an image of the flower bud in the picture. The brush had a size of 634 pixels with the Spacing value set to 75%. I

enabled Shape Dynamics and set the Size Jitter slider to 49%, selected Pen Pressure from the Control menu and specified a 1% minimum diameter. I set the Angle Jitter slider to 52% and also controlled that setting with pen pressure. I set the Roundness slider to 100%. I also enabled the Scattering section of the Brushes palette with the following options: the Scatter slider was set to 110%, the Both Axes check box was enabled, the Control menu was set to Pen Pressure, the Count slider was set to 3, and the Count Jitter slider was set to 11%.

The second brush was created from a copied version of the entire composite, captured midway through the design. The brush was created at 1509 pixels, with the Spacing set to 151%. The brush size was modified as needed during the course of the painting.

Creating the First Brush

To create the first brush, I started by dragging a rectangular selection around the single flower shape. To convert it to a brush tip, I chose

Edit, Define Brush Preset, and named it in the dialog box that appeared. The dialog box also showed the final brush tip, which was converted to grayscale. Increasing the Spacing setting turns the brush into a form of rubber stamping tool, where a click places a perfect instance of the copied area. You can modify the color of the image or change the Master Diameter slider in the Brush Presets Picker to change the scale of the brush.

Painting with the Brush

I created a new layer that I could paint on with the newly created brush tip. After setting the parameters as listed in the "Brushes Used" section, I began painting with the stylus, varying the size and proportion of each image instance. I initially began painting with black, but I switched to white to create a negative image effect and reverse an area out of the painted background. I alternated between black and white and also varied the scale of the strokes to begin the design.

To push things further, I added a layer mask to the image layer and continued painting with the image-based brush, masking the painted layer with silhouettes of the flower image.

Building the Second Brush

The second image-based brush was created almost by accident. I inadvertently selected the entire image as I was thinking about creating a new brush tip. Because a brush tip can be as large as 2500 pixels, it was no problem to save the selection, which was a paltry 1509 pixels. I increase the spacing, reduced the brush size, and began placing a few of the brush tip images on a new layer. I was curious to see how it would look, but nothing really came together until I set the new layer's blending mode to Lighten. This step created a window that let the lower layers show through the dark areas, framing the composition and adding nuance and detail.

PAINTING STRATEGIES: CLONING WITH SCATTER

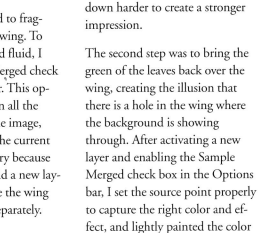

The background is cloned and abstracted.

The background is completed, and the wing is distorted.

The wing is cloned and fragmented.

This example shows how to clone an object with a scatter brush to create a duplicate object that is ethereal and fragmented. If you combine the clone tool and scatter brush with blending modes and opacity variations, a wide range of expressive effects are possible.

Brushes Used

The cloning effect used a single scatter-based brush that I varied in size and spacing to create the final effects.

The initial diameter of the brush was 160 pixels; the Angle was set to 16°, and the Roundness slider was set to 56%. The Spacing slider was set to 75%. I enabled the Shape Dynamics section of the Brushes palette and set the Size Jitter slider to 11%, controlled by Pen Pressure with a 1% minimum diameter. I also enabled the Scattering section and set the follow-

ing options: the Scatter slider was set to 191%, the Control menu was left at off, the Count slider was set to 1, and the Count Jitter slider was set to 0%.

Abstracting the Background

Knowing that I was going to abstract and pull the color out of the butterfly wing, the first step was to begin flattening out and abstracting the leafy background. I used the scatter brush described in the "Brushes Used" section but maintained firm pressure, which resulted in more consistent stroke size without too much variance. The idea was to use green pixels to cover the shadow lines, blending the areas to a solid color. I had to move the source point frequently to keep the color and tonality consistent.

Finishing the Background

I continued to work the background, cloning the leaves to create a smooth result that wasn't as distracting. I did leave the red flower on the right side to provide some measure of counterpoint and tension between the subject and the background.

At this point, I decided to fragment and dissolve the wing. To keep things flexible and fluid, I enabled the Sample Merged check box in the Options bar. This option copies the pixels in all the cumulative layers in the image, rather than from just the current layer. This was necessary because my next step was to add a new layer so that I could clone the wing and the background separately.

Dissolving the Wing

Cloning abstraction into the wing was a two-stage process. The first step was to clone the orange color of the wing over into the leaves. Because the Shape Dynamics setting was enabled, I was able to tap lightly with the stylus to create small and delicate dots, pressing down harder to create a stronger impression.

The second step was to bring the green of the leaves back over the wing, creating the illusion that there is a hole in the wing where the background is showing through. After activating a new layer and enabling the Sample Merged check box in the Options bar, I set the source point properly to capture the right color and effect, and lightly painted the color into place.

Three Leaves

Purple Hibiscus

BUILDING THE IMAGE: *TRILOGY*

Figure 14.14

A textured pattern is painted over the main image.

Figure 14.15

Conté Crayon brush strokes add depth and define shapes.

Figure 14.16

A Hue/Saturation adjustment layer shifts the color.

Painting a Photo

My initial goal with *Trilogy* was to make the image more tactile and textured. It's too simplistic to say that I wanted to make it look like a painting. What I was after was to maintain the photographic detail while adding a certain immediacy and physicality. After opening the photo and duplicating the layer, I selected the Brush tool, opened the Brushes palette, and set the brush settings as follows: In the Brush Tip Shape section, I set the Diameter to 62 pixels and the Spacing to 12%. In the Shape Dynamics section, I set the Size Jitter slider to 28%, the Control menu to Pen Pressure, and the Minimum Diameter slider to 1%. In the Scattering section, I set the Scatter slider to 225% and enabled the Both Axes check box. In the Dual Brush section, I set the Diameter to 36 pixels, the Spacing to 43%, the Scatter to 77%, and the Count to 2.

With the new brush defined, I painted over the flat areas in the image. I used the Option key (Alt in Windows) to sample the colors in the immediate area where I was painting, covering most of the image with a brush-texture patina (see Figure 14.14).

I then pasted a second copy of the three leaves image, adjusted the opacity in the Layers palette to 34%, set the blending mode in the Layers palette to Hard Light, and used the Move tool to offset the layer to the lower right. I then added a layer mask and masked out the primary leaf shapes leaving only the background and some of the leaf edges. With the 35% opacity setting, this created a subtle coloration effect that added more of an organic feel.

Crayon Marks and Tonality

The next step was to create a new brush that resembled a Conté

Crayon and begin painting and making marks in the image. To do this, I selected the brush named Conté Pastel on Bumpy Surface from the Brush Preset Picker. Because this is an 8-pixel brush, I had to increase the brush size with the Diameter slider in the Brushes palette. I also enabled the Texture check box in the Stroke Adjustment section and selected the Stone preset from the Texture Picker.

I created a new layer and began drawing into the image, around the left leaf and in the lower-right corner. Then I created a Hue/Saturation layer that I used primarily to darken the image by moving the Lightness slider setting to −37. I restricted this darkness to only the center and lower-right corner of the image by adding a layer mask and hiding all the other areas.

Figure 14.17
Texture from the original image is painted back.

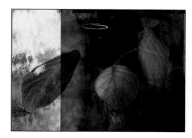

Figure 14.18
The leaves are emphasized as contrast is increased.

Figure 14.19
The hibiscus image is added and the halo is drawn.

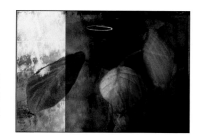

Figure 14.20
To complete the image, I selected the entire design, copied it, and pasted it as a separate layer.

I pasted another copy of the Three Leaves image into the composite and brightened it with the Curves control, adding a single curve point that I raised from Input= 130 to Output=233. Then I reduced the opacity of the very bright image result to 59% and hid it by selecting Layer, Layer Mask, Hide All. I selected the Conté Crayon brush tip again and erased the mask over the center leaf, creating a lightened effect that resembled a tombstone rubbing (see Figure 14.15).

Temporary Color Shift

I tinted the overall color of the image a cool blue by adding a Hue/Saturation adjustment layer, setting Hue to +180, Saturation to −19, and Lightness to −24 (see Figure 14.16).

I tempered this color shift by adding back the hues from the original image. The interesting thing with this application was that although the tonality matched the main image, the strokes were so abstract that they looked random and purely textural. To achieve this effect, I pasted another copy of the Three leaves image and hid it completely with a layer mask. I used a large, loose brush to erase the mask, revealing the image data in loose, abstract strokes (see Figure 14.17).

More Painting Strokes

Although the texture was getting complex and interesting, the image still lacked a solid tonal structure. As a remedy, I added a new layer and began painting to define strong areas of dark and light. White strokes covered the left side, while a dark area anchored the center and the edges of the right leaf. To accent these changes, I used a small, hard, textured brush to paint the left and center leaves.

Restating the Leaves

The back-and-forth act of obliterating and restating the leaves continued with the next step. I pasted yet another copy of the Three Leaves image and hid it with a mask. I erased the mask in only the leaf areas without obscuring the brush strokes at the edges (see Figure 14.18).

Hibiscus, Halo, and Highlights

Next I added the purple hibiscus image to the composition and dragged it into position with the Move tool. Setting the blending mode in the Layers palette to Multiply created a deep green effect over the center of the composition. I used a mask to hide the green coloration in the center, allowing the center leaf to show through.

To add the floating halo, I created another new layer and selected white as the foreground color. I used a drawing tablet and stylus to draw the halo. It took six or seven tries to get the gesture and size to feel right, but it finally went in with a clean, aggressive stroke. Although I did use a tablet for most of this design, I probably could have used a mouse to do the work. This halo shape is the exception however. I don't believe there is any way I could have achieved this exact effect using a mouse (see Figure 14.19).

To complete the image, I selected the entire design, copied it, and pasted it as a separate layer. Then I chose the Dodge Tool with a 300 pixel brush and brightened the center leaf (see Figure 14.20).

TRILOGY

1. Open the Three Leaves image.

2. Choose Image, Adjustments, Curves to open the Curves dialog box. Select the black and white eyedropper icons and set the white and black points for the image.

3. Select the Brush tool from the toolbox and click the Brushes icon in the Options bar to open the Brushes palette.

4. Set the brush settings as follows: In the Brush Tip Shape section, set the Diameter to 62 pixels and the Spacing to 12%. In the Shape Dynamics section, set the Size Jitter slider to 28%, the Control menu to Pen Pressure, and the Minimum Diameter slider to 1%. In the Scattering section, set the Scatter slider to 225% and enable the Both Axes check box. In the Dual Brush section, set the Diameter to 36 pixels, the Spacing to 43%, the Scatter to 77%, and the Count to 2.

5. Option+click (Alt+click for Windows users) below the area to be painted to sample a color and then paint over the sampled area. Adjust the Opacity slider in the Options bar to vary opacity as desired.

6. Paste another copy of the Three Leaves image into the composite.

7. Reduce the opacity for the new layer to 34%, set the blending mode in the Layers palette to Hard Light, and drag the new layer to the lower-right of the composite to offset it from the original image.

8. Click the Add Layer Mask icon, select a brush with black as the foreground, and paint the mask to hide all unwanted areas of the image, leaving only the edges of the leaf objects visible.

9. From the Layers palette menu, choose New Layer to create a blank new layer on which you can draw.

10. Select Conté Pastel on Bumpy Surface from the Brush Presets section of the Brushes palette. (Hold the mouse pointer over the brush thumbnails to show the brush names.)

11. In the Shape Dynamics section of the Brushes palette, adjust the Size Jitter slider to 78%; in the Dual Brush section, deselect all the options.

12. Select black as the foreground color and draw around the left leaf.

13. Select white as the foreground color and draw lightly around the center leaf.

14. Make additional marks with coral and green paint colors on the tip of the left leaf and in the lower-right corner.

15. Click and hold the Adjustment Layer icon in the Layers palette and select Hue/Saturation from the pop-up menu that appears. Move the Lightness slider to −37 and click OK.

16. Paste another copy of the Three Leaves image into the composite.

17. Choose Image, Adjustments, Curves to add a Curves adjustment layer to the new copy of the leaves. Click a single point on the curve and raise the value from Input=130 to Output=223.

18. Choose Layer, Layer Mask, Hide All to mask the entire layer.

5 15 23 26 34 41 45

19. Select the Fuzzball brush from the Brush Preset section of the Brushes palette. (Hold the mouse pointer over the brush thumbnails to show the brush names.) Disable all the options in the Color Dynamics section.

20. Select white as the foreground color and erase the mask around the center leaf.

21. Click and hold the Adjustment Layer icon in the Layers palette and select Hue/Saturation from the pop-up menu that appears. Move the Hue slider to +180, move the Saturation slider to −19, move the Lightness slider to −24, and click OK.

22. Choose Layer, Layer Mask, Reveal All.

23. With the Fuzzball brush still selected, paint in the mask over a portion of the center leaf to obscure the adjustment layer effect.

24. Paste another copy of the Three Leaves image into the composite.

25. Choose Layer, Layer Mask, Hide All. Select the Brush tool with white as the foreground. From the Brushes palette, select the brush you created in step 4.

26. Paint the original photograph back into the composite using the textured brush.

27. Choose New Layer from the Layers palette menu.

28. With the brush from step 4 still selected, choose white as the foreground color and paint the upper-right corner of the image.

29. Select the Fuzzball brush from the Brush Presets section of the Brushes palette. (Hold the mouse pointer over the brush thumbnails to show the brush names.) Deselect all options in the Color Dynamics section.

30. Select black as the foreground color and paint the upper-center of image. Adjust transparency as necessary.

31. Create a new brush in the Brushes palette. Specify the following brush settings: In the Brush Tip Shape section, set the Diameter to 9 pixels, the Roundness to 32%, the Hardness to 100%, and the Spacing to 375%. In the Shape Dynamics section, set the Angle Jitter to 13% and set the Control menu to Off. In the Scattering section, set Scatter to 449%, enable the Both Axes check box, and set Count to 4.

32. Select black as the foreground color and paint around the edges of all the leaves.

33. Paste another copy of the Three Leaves image into the composite.

34. Select Layer, Layer Mask, Hide All. Select the Brush tool with white as the foreground and specify a standard 65-pixel round brush. Paint the leaves back into composite.

35. Drag the Purple Hibiscus image into the composite. In the Layers palette, set the blending mode to Multiply and the opacity to 92%.

36. Choose Layer, Layer Mask, Reveal All. Select the Brush tool with black as the foreground and select a standard 65-pixel round brush. Erase the layer to allow the center leaf to show through.

37. From the Layers palette menu, choose New Layer to add a new layer.

38. Select the Conté Pastel on Bumpy Surface brush from the Brush Presets section of the Brushes palette.

39. In the Shape Dynamics section, adjust the Size Jitter slider to 78%. Deselect all the options in the Dual Brush section.

40. Select white as foreground color and draw the oval shape.

41. Select the Move tool and drag the halo to adjust its position as needed.

42. Choose Select, All to select the entire image.

43. Choose Edit, Copy Merged to copy the composite; then choose Edit, Paste to paste a copy of the entire image as a separate layer.

44. Select the Dodge tool from the toolbox, set the Range menu in the Options bar to Midtones, and set the Exposure to 18%.

45. Select a 300-pixel brush and lightly click the center leaf to lighten the area and complete the design.

Image 15
Tree House | ©2002 Daniel Giordan

CHAPTER 15

MASTERING THE DISTORT FILTERS

While working on *Tree House,* I found myself compelled to do the unexpected and push against the anticipated next step. The image itself is a surreal juxtaposition of a house in a tree with what could easily be mistaken for a flaming baby. At first glance, this unexpected combination seems to fit in well with the melting clocks and flaming giraffes of the surrealists.

The background is a jumble of tree branches that bend, twist, and almost melt as they wrap around the frame of a traditional white clapboard house. The sun breaks through the tree branches, and the entire image is steeped in a warm, soothing green.

In the middle of everything is the glowing putto figure, slightly distorted and sitting uncomfortably on a branch. The lines of the figure play off the geometry created in the background, to the point that the vertical leg anchors the entire lower half of the image.

Tree House is a study of created and denied symmetry—which makes it slightly unsettling. The tree background began as a mirror image before a well-placed crop reestablished the organic sensibility. The distorted branches go even further in keeping things off balance. And although the house looks centered, a closer look reveals that it's just off to the side. The figure is just off to the other side.

In the end, although it may have visual pointers towards surrealism, the image resists even that classification. For all of the metaphorical references, the image presents itself as a series of off-balance decisions, merged into a delicate and cohesive similarity.

UNDERSTANDING THE DISTORT FILTERS

As a component of the Photoshop CS Filter Gallery, the Photoshop Distort filter set delivers a wide range of imaging effects—from subtle lighting effects to complex textures and wild, chaotic distortions. Because the Distort filters create such a strong transformation in an image, many Photoshop users have shied away from understanding what they offer and how they work. The results of the Distort filters are thought of as radical departures and not something that can be used from day to day.

This chapter provides an overview of the range of effects you can achieve using the Distort submenu; the chapter also provides ideas about how to put the filters to use in all kinds of projects—even those with a more conservative aesthetic.

Distort Filter Overview

The Distort filters are very powerful, and their controls are often more complex than those for a standard filter. The controls can make the filters intimidating to say the least, especially if you're used to a simple one-step approach to a special effect. The reality is that these filters can be used effectively with just a few adjustments, and it's easy enough to experiment to see what the different settings can accomplish.

The Distort effects can be broken into two general categories: texture and warp effects. Texture effects tend to maintain the overall structure of the image while creating a texture pattern. These patterns can be enlarged or reduced for dramatic effect or subtle nuance. Warp effects create global shifts in the structure of the image, shifting, twisting, and bending the image often beyond recognition. The difference between the texture and warp Distort effects is like looking at someone through frosted glass and then seeing that person in a funhouse mirror.

The Texture Effects

The texture effects are Diffuse Glow, Glass, Ocean Ripple, and Ripple. These Distort filters create an interesting effect without obliterating the entire image. In other words, you may not be able to identify the person in the image, but you'll know it's a person.

An important decision when applying a Distort texture filter is deciding the relative size of the texture. If the effect is larger, more detail is lost. A smaller effect preserves detail but can get lost in a high-resolution image or can make the image look blurry or of poor quality.

The Warp Effects

The warp effects are Pinch, Polar Coordinates, Shear, Spherize, Twirl, Lens Correction, and Wave. The Distort warp effects divide the image into a grid or coordinates that are then modified according to the specific filter. The Twirl filter twists the grid, while Shear offsets the grid on just the horizontal axis. Based on this definition, the Liquify filter also qualifies as a distort filter for the way it allows you to distort the image grid, although it does go one step further by letting you do it manually. Liquify is discussed in detail in Chapter 18, "Using the Liquify Filter."

The Lens Correction tool is a new addition with CS2 that corrects common lens distortion problems

such as barrel or pincushion distortion and chromatic aberration. It's a great tool to correct architectural distortions or to compensate for extreme camera angles (where you may have had to point the camera directly upwards). This new feature is somewhat unique in that it actually corrects an existing distortion rather than creating a new, divergent reality.

The Exception

It seems that every time you try to classify filter or tool types in Photoshop, there's one example that defies categorization. In the case of the Distort filters, the honor goes to the Displace filter, which applies a distortion based on the grayscale values of another file. The second image must be a Photoshop image with a reasonable tonal range. Photoshop distorts the image by moving the pixels along a vertical and horizontal axis based on the values in the reference image. A neutral gray does not move the pixels at all, while a black value moves them in the maximum negative direction, and a white value moves the pixels in the maximum positive direction.

The Distort Filters Submenu

Filter	⌘F
...act...	⌥⌘X
...er Gallery...	
...ify...	⇧⌘X
...ern Maker...	⌥⇧⌘X
...ishing Point...	⌥⌘V
...stic	▶
	▶
...sh Strokes	▶
...tort	▶
...ve	▶
...elate	▶
...der	▶
...rpen	▶
...tch	▶
...ize	▶
...xture	▶
...eo	▶
...her...	▶
...gimarc	▶

Diffuse Glow...
Displace...
Glass...
Lens Correction...
Ocean Ripple...
Pinch...
Polar Coordinates...
Ripple...
Shear...
Spherize...
Twirl...
Wave...
ZigZag...

Texture Effects:
Diffuse Glow
Glass
Ocean Ripple
Ripple

The Displace Filter

Warp Effects:
Lens Correction
Pinch
Polar Coordinates
Shear
Spherize
Twirl
Wave

THE TEXTURE AND WARP FILTERS

Some of the Distort filters are easy to understand and apply while others take some getting used to. The key is to get beyond the technical confusion and look at how they can work with the design process. This section looks at the texture and warp categories in greater detail in an effort to explore the creative possibilities offered by the Distort filters.

Distorting Textures

The texture-based Distort filters create distortion waves in the image that repeat over the surface. You have control over the size and frequency of the waves—and, in some cases, over the density or focus of the wave.

The Glass, Ocean Ripple, and Ripple filters are remarkably similar, so much so that it can be hard to tell the results apart. But a closer look reveals that there are differences (see Figure 15.1):

- **Ripple** is the simplest effect. The filter uses a single slider and pop-up menu to control the degree of distortion and the size of the effect.

- **Ocean Ripple** is more complex than Ripple. This filter offers a slider to control the size of the ripples. It also creates a result that is more complex and granular, without the "lava-lamp" cellular shapes of the Ripple filter.

- **Glass** is the most powerful of the texture filters, offering a wide range of effects. A major difference between the Glass filter and the two Ripple filters is that the Glass filter tends to be more pattern based and less organic in the way it generates patterns. The Glass filter even

Ripple   Ocean Ripple   Glass

Figure 15.1
The results of the Ripple, Ocean Ripple, and Glass filters (Glass is set to the Tiny Lens texture).

allows you to import your own .psd file to use as a pattern, as described in the "Creating a Custom Texture for the Glass Filter" steps on this page.

The remaining texture filter is Diffuse Glow (see Figure 15.2). This filter creates a hazy graphic effect that combines high contrast, gritty, and bleached image

effects into a unique result. When working in the Diffuse Glow dialog box, it can be hard to tell exactly how the effect will be applied to the image, regardless of how much you reposition the preview window. The best approach is to apply an approximate setting and use the Fade controls (Edit, Fade Diffuse Glow) to adjust the effect.

Figure 15.2

The results of Diffuse Glow filter.

CREATING A CUSTOM TEXTURE FOR THE GLASS FILTER

These steps show how to use a .psd file as a texture source for the Glass filter.

1. Choose Filter, Distort, Glass to launch the Glass filter.

2. Select Load Texture from the Texture pop-up menu.

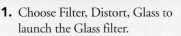

3. In the Open dialog box, navigate to the .psd file that will serve as the texture source for the image and click Open.

4. Set the Distortion and Smoothness sliders as desired.

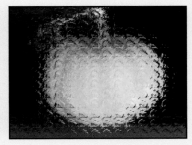

5. Drag the Scaling slider to control the size of the texture mapping. Texture files that are smaller than the target image will be tiled. Click OK.

6. If necessary, select Edit, Fade and lower the Opacity slider to minimize the effect.

Simple Warp Distortions

The options in the warp category are sometimes referred to as the "single-slider" distortion filters. These filters allow you to apply an effect with a single slider that controls the offset or intensity of the distortion. The filter dialog box may contain other modifier boxes or pop-up menus for some effects, but the central control is the slider. The simple slider effects are Pinch, Polar Coordinates, Spherize, Twirl, and ZigZag (see Figure 15.3).

ZigZag

Spherize

Figure 15.3

The results of the Pinch, Polar Coordinates, Spherize, Twirl, and ZigZag Distort filters.

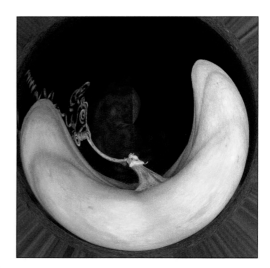

Polar Coordinates

Pinch

Twirl

CREATING A SEAMLESS TILE WITH THE SHEAR FILTER

This is a great technique for creating abstract graphic backgrounds that are completely seamless.

1. Select the Rectangular Marquee tool and drag a rectangular selection the source for the seamless tile.

2. Select Filter, Distort, Shear to open the Shear dialog box.

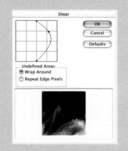

3. Click and drag the vertical line in the grid to distort the image.

4. Click repeatedly on the vertical line to add other points, positioning them as desired. Enable the Wrap Around check box and click OK.

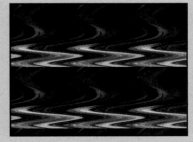

5. Choose Edit, Define Pattern to save the pattern effect.

6. Deactivate the selection (Select, Deselect). Choose Edit, Fill and then choose Pattern from the Use menu. Click OK to fill the image with the pattern.

THE SHEAR AND WAVE FILTERS

The final two Distort filters (Wave and Shear) are more complex, at least in the number of sliders and controls they put at your disposal. Approach these filters with a spirit of exploration, paying close attention to how a single variable impacts the overall result.

Figure 15.4
The original image, the Shear dialog box, and the final result.

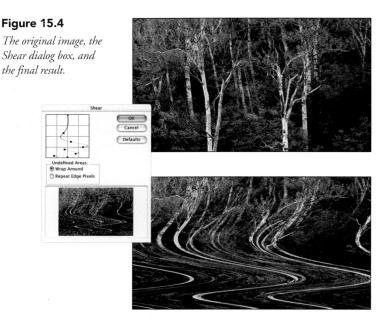

Figure 15.5
The original image, the Wave dialog box, and the final result.

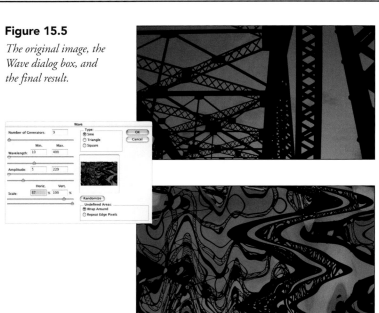

Using the Shear Filter

The Shear filter lets you apply a complex horizontal distortion to an image, shifting, twisting, and wrapping the results (see Figure 15.4). The grid in the upper-left corner of the Shear dialog box resembles the Curves control grid. Just as with Curves, Shear allows you to click the vertical line to create a point and then drag that point right or left to create a horizontal distortion. You can add as many "handles" as you want, with each handle adding another level of complexity to the shear effect.

The preview section at the bottom of the dialog box updates the results quickly, and the whole experience of twisting and turning your image is really spellbinding.

Using the Wave Filter

The Wave filter creates a distorted wave pattern that converts an image to abstract, algorithmic patterns (see Figure 15.5). The Wave filter allows you to specify the number of wave generators (which control the overall complexity of the effect), the Min/Max Wavelength, and the image Amplitude. Wavelength and Amplitude define

minimum and maximum values used to plot the horizontal and vertical characteristics of the wave shape. As the Wavelength Max value goes higher, the wave effect gets longer and smoother because the horizontal distance between wave crests is increased. As the Wavelength Max value goes shorter, the waves are repeated with more frequency. The Amplitude values control the height of the wave. The Amplitude determines whether the wave will be high and choppy, or low and smooth. The other controls in the dialog box determine the shape of the wave patterns generated and the percent-

age of vertical or horizontal distortion; a Randomize button creates random wave patterns. When in doubt, click Randomize and see whether you get anything you like.

Wave Filter Results Chart

The following chart shows how the Amplitude and Wavelength sliders in the Wave dialog box impact the final result of the Wave filter. Wavelength increases left to right across the chart; Amplitude increases top to bottom.

Wavelength (Distsnce Beween Wave Crests

Amplitude (Wave and Height)

Wavelength 1-1, Amplitude 1-10

Wavelength 1-100, Amplitude 1-10

Wavelength 1-200, Amplitude 1-10

Wavelength 1-500, Amplitude 1-10

Wavelength 1-999, Amplitude 1-10

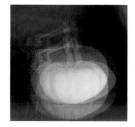

Wavelength 1-1, Amplitude 1-50

Wavelength 1-100, Amplitude 1-50

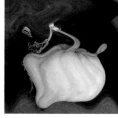

Wavelength 1-200, Amplitude 1-50

Wavelength 1-500, Amplitude 1-50

Wavelength 1-999, Amplitude 1-50

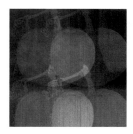

Wavelength 1-1, Amplitude 1-200

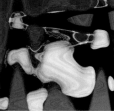

Wavelength 1-100, Amplitude 1-200

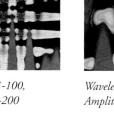

Wavelength 1-200, Amplitude 1-200

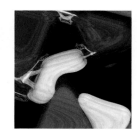

Wavelength 1-500, Amplitude 1-200

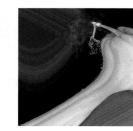

Wavelength 1-999, Amplitude 1-200

Wavelength 1-1, Amplitude 1-999

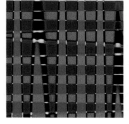

Wavelength 1-100, Amplitude 1-999

Wavelength 1-200, Amplitude 1-999

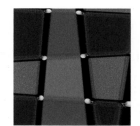

Wavelength 1-500, Amplitude 1-999

Wavelength 1-999, Amplitude 1-999

MASTERING THE DISPLACE FILTER

Although the Displace filter is very powerful, it is seldom used because it resists a one-click result. If you just open the dialog box and apply the filter, you get nothing back; the image pixels shift a bit, but the change is minimal. The Displace filter requires a little forethought and analysis; hopefully, this section will lay the groundwork for further exploration.

The Displace Filter Process

The Displace filter allows you to wrap an image or texture around a target image as though the texture were projected onto the object. Therefore, the target image you use should show dimensional volume, such as a face or ball. The examples here use a small pumpkin as the target image, which has smooth graduated tones into the shadows. The texture image itself should be detailed enough to follow and describe the contours of the target image (the object being mapped to).

After you have a target object and a texture, you will need to prepare a displacement map. The *displacement map* should be created from the target image because the tones in that image are what dictate the distortion effect.

A white value in the displacement map shifts the mapped pixels (from the texture image) in one direction, and a black value in the displacement map shifts them in the opposite direction. Gray does not move the pixels at all. Because color has no effect on the result, the displacement map should always be grayscale, allowing you to see the tonal relations clearly.

After you've decided on the target image and the texture image, the process for using the displace filter is as follows:

1. Create the displacement map.
2. Wrap the texture.
3. Tweak the results.

Create the Displacement Map

1. Open the target image and convert it to grayscale (Image, Adjustments, Desaturate).
2. Apply a slight Gaussian Blur of 3 to 4 pixels (Filter, Blur, Gaussian Blur).
3. Use Curves to adjust the tonality for the proper distortion effect (Image, Adjustments, Curves).
4. Choose File, Save As and save the target image as a separate .psd file (see Figure 15.6).

Wrap the Texture

1. Re-open the original target image (not the grayscale displacement map file you made from the target image in the last section).
2. Drag or paste the texture image into the target image as a new layer.
3. Lower the Opacity slider in the Layers palette for the texture layer and drag the texture layer to align the texture with the target object image to optimize the wrapping effect. Return the opacity of the texture layer to 100%.
4. Use the selection tools to select the background of the object in the target image. Choose Select, Save Selection. In the dialog box that appears, name the selection as desired and click OK.
5. Select the texture layer in the Layers palette and open the Displace dialog box (Filter, Distort, Displace).
6. In the Displace dialog box, type percentage values for the horizontal and vertical offset, enable the Stretch To Fit option, and click OK. (See the Displace Filter Results chart later in this chapter for percentage and image map options.)
7. To load the selection saved from step 4, choose Select, Load Selection, pick the selection name from the Channel pop-up menu, and click OK. Press the Delete key to erase the background from the texture layer (see Figure 15.7).

Tweak the Results

1. Choose a blending mode from the Layers palette to better inte-

Figure 15.6

The displacement map is made from the target image.

Figure 15.7

The initial application of the Displace filter.

Figure 15.8

The final result.

grate the texture and the object. The Multiply and Hard Light blending modes are often good places to start.

2. Lower the Opacity slider in the Layers palette for the texture layer as desired.

3. If necessary, add a layer mask to the texture layer (Layer, Layer Mask, Reveal All), select a feathered brush with black as the foreground, and hide the texture in the shadow areas to reestablish areas of the target object (in Figure 15.8, I masked the texture so that the pumpkin's stem and vines were once again visible).

Controlling the Variables

By now, it should be obvious that the Displace filter is not a "one-size-fits-all" application. Care must be taken at several steps along the way to ensure that everything turns out as expected. Here are the keys to getting the effect right:

• ***Choosing the right object and texture.*** Choose a target object with volume and a wide tonal range. The texture image should have linear elements, edges, or other components that will articulate the wrapping effect.

• ***Creating the proper tones in the displacement map.*** Gray areas of the displacement map will not be changed. Add gray to the areas you want to preserve. Recall that white areas in the displacement map will displace pixels in the texture image in one direction, and black in another. You may want to exclude black or white from the map if you want all the distortions to wrap in the same direction.

• ***Setting the optimum offset percentages in the Displace dialog box.*** The default offset percentage is 10% in each direction. This value is usually too timid for this effect. Try a higher number and then adjust downward if it's too much. Also remember that the horizontal and vertical offsets can be different values.

Displace Filter Results Chart

The following chart shows the effect of incremental changes to the values of the displacement map, and the results created by the specified offset percentages. The displacement map images that appear in the top row of the chart were created by modifying the tonal curve in the Curves dialog box to shift the highlights, midpoint, and shadows. The Highlight to Gray map was created by lowering the highlights to the midtone values and raising the midpoint of the curve to white. See Chapter 6, "Mastering Curves" for details on how to use curves to adjust tonal values.

Standard Map

Inverted Map

Standard Map: 10% Offset

Inverted Map: 10% Offset

Standard Map: 30% Offset

Inverted Map: 30% Offset

Standard Map: 60% Offset

Inverted Map: 60% Offset

Standard Map: 90% Offset

Inverted Map: 90% Offset

*Gray/Black
Map*

*White/Gray
Map*

*Highlight to
Gray Map*

*Gray/Black
Map:
10% Offset*

*White/Gray
Map:
10% Offset*

*Highlight to
Gray Map:
10% Offset*

*Gray/Black
Map:
30% Offset*

*White/Gray
Map:
30% Offset*

*Highlight to
Gray Map:
30% Offset*

*Gray/Black
Map:
60% Offset*

*White/Gray
Map:
60% Offset*

*Highlight to
Gray Map:
60% Offset*

*Gray/Black
Map: 90%
Offset*

*White/Gray
Map: 90%
Offset*

*Highlight to
Gray Map:
90% Offset*

Vermont House

Abstract Trees 2

Putto

BUILDING THE IMAGE: *TREE HOUSE*

Figure 15.9
Abstract Trees 2 is rotated 90° CCW to start the design.

Figure 15.10
The Abstract Trees pattern is flipped, aligned, and cropped.

Figure 15.11
The Vermont House image is added using the Overlay blending mode.

Building the Background Texture

I suppose that it should come as no surprise that an image called Tree House should start with a picture of some trees. Abstract Trees 2 was compelling for its overall branch pattern as well as for the intensity of light as the sun shone through the branches.

After I rotated the image 90° counterclockwise (see Figure 15.9), I enlarged the canvas to accommodate the mirror effect I was planning. I made the canvas square and flipped the image horizontally to mirror it.

After aligning the edges of the two layer, I was pleased to see the intricate lace pattern that was beginning to emerge. The main issue I had with this result was that it was too symmetrical and predictable. To address this, I cropped the design to eliminate a few of the branches on the right and the top in an effort to counteract the mirroring effect. To complete this stage of the design, I selected Merge Visible from the Layers palette menu, which combined the two layers into one (see Figure 15.10).

Placing the House

After placing the house, I began to experiment with the blending modes, settling on the Overlay mode for the way it pushed the green of the grass behind the branches, creating a colorized effect for the background.

The next step was to extend the grass so that the green would cover more of the background. With the house layer selected, I used the Marquee tool to drag a horizontal selection across the lower grass area. I selected Edit, Free Transform and dragged the bottom center handle of the selection to the bottom of the composite to extend the grass color and texture. Because the Overlay blending mode was reducing everything to a color, the distortion in the stretched grass area wasn't visible. The remaining areas of green were filled in using the Clone Stamp tool with a large feathered brush set to 100%. The grass area was

Figure 15.12

A second house layer is added with a layer mask.

Figure 15.13

The Abstract Trees pattern is duplicated and distorted using the Wave filter.

Figure 15.14

The Putto figure is added.

Figure 15.15

The flare is added to the Putto figure to complete the image.

sampled and used to fill the open areas of the rectangle (see Figure 15.11).

With the background in place, the next step was to reinforce the house which was all but invisible because of the Overlay blending mode. I duplicated the house layer and created a mask that hid the entire layer. Then I painted the house back in, carefully fading the mask out on the left side to let the branches show through the house (see Figure 15.12).

Adding the Distortion

The image needed more complexity in the background. After duplicating the trees layer, I selected Filter, Distort, Wave to open the

Wave dialog box. Knowing that I wanted an all-over distortion effect, I adjusted the wave filter to create a balanced wave shape without creating too much height in the waveforms.

I left the Horizontal and Vertical Scale values in the Wave dialog box at the default of 100% and changed the Type to Triangle. I enabled the Repeat Edge Pixels option in the Undefined Area section, which repeats edge pixel values for any open areas near the edge that may have been created by the distortion.

Because it was on its own layer, I was able to blend the original trees pattern with the distorted one. To do this, I left the distorted layer

above the original trees layer and applied the Darken blending mode. This blending mode allowed the darker branches to show through against the lighter background without changing the other background values (see Figure 15.13).

Adding the Glowing Figure

The Putto figure is a detail from the plaster model of Rodin's *The Gates of Hell*, hence his distortion and general sense of torment. I opened the Putto image file and silhouetted the figure of the boy using a layer mask. Then I scaled the boy to fit with the house. The unique challenge was that the Putto was somewhat distorted and deformed and presented in stark

silhouette. I tried softening some of the edges and making it blend, but out of the context of Rodin's sculpture, the little guy just looked strange.

To add a bit of mystery and visual interest, I duplicated the Putto layer and applied a motion blur. (see Figure 15.14). I generated the glow around the figure using a Curves adjustment layer and a layer mask. Once again, I selected Layer, Layer Mask, Hide All to create a mask that hid the entire layer. With white as the foreground color, I lightly painted in the glow to complete the design (see Figure 15.15).

15

TREE HOUSE

1. Open the Abstract Trees 2 image.

2. Choose Image, Adjustments, Curves. In the Curves dialog box, select the black and white eyedropper icons and set the white and black points.

3. Choose Image, Rotate Canvas, 90° CCW to rotate the image.

4. Choose Image, Canvas Size. In the New Size section, double the Width value, set the anchor value to the upper-left corner of the grid, and click OK.

5. Double-click the Abstract Trees 2 layer in the Layers palette and click OK in the dialog box that appears to change the layer from a background layer to a standard layer.

6. Choose Duplicate Layer from the Layers palette menu to duplicate the trees layer.

7. Choose Edit, Transform, Flip Horizontal to flip the copied layer of the trees so that it mirrors the original trees layer.

8. Select the Move tool from the toolbox and drag the duplicate layer to the right, aligning its edges with the edges of the original layer.

9. Select the Crop tool from the toolbox. Drag a marquee around the image, trimming the left side and the top. Double-click inside the selection to apply the crop.

10. Drag the Vermont House image into the composite as a separate layer.

11. Choose Image, Adjustments, Curves. In the Curves dialog box, select the black and white eyedropper icons and set the white and black points for the Vermont House image.

12. Select Overlay from the Blending Modes pop-up menu in the Layers palette to blend the house and tree images.

13. Select the Rectangular Marquee tool from the toolbox and drag a horizontal selection from the bottom of the house layer to the bottom edge of the house (you are selecting the grass).

14. Choose Edit, Free Transform. Click the lower-center handle of the selection and drag it to the bottom of the composite image to stretch the grass to fill the bottom area of the composite.

15. Select the Clone Stamp tool from the toolbox and specify a 300-pixel brush and 100% opacity. Option+click (Mac users) or Alt+click (Windows users) to set the source point in the green area of the house layer. Click to paint in any gaps in the background color.

16. With the Vermont House layer still selected, choose Duplicate Layer from the Layers palette menu.

17. Choose Layer, Layer Mask, Hide All to hide the new layer behind a mask.

18. Select the Brush tool with white as the foreground. In the Options bar, specify 22% opacity and a 150-pixel feathered brush.

19. Paint lightly into the image to reveal the white house.

20. Select the Abstract Trees 2 background layer in the Layers palette. Choose Duplicate Layer from the Layers palette menu.

21. Choose Filter, Distort, Wave to open the Wave dialog box.

3   **9**   **15**   **19**   **23**   **26**   **32**

22. Set the Generators slider to 7. Set the Wavelength Min and Max values to 10 and 346 respectively. Set the Amplitude Min and Max values to 1 and 124. Set the Horizontal and Vertical Scale values at 100%, enable the Repeat Edge Pixels option, and click OK to create the effect.

23. In the Layers palette, choose Darken from the Blending Mode menu.

24. Drag the Putto image into the composite.

25. Choose Layer, Layer Mask, Hide All. Select the Brush tool with white as the foreground color. In the Options bar, specify 22% opacity and a 64-pixel feathered brush.

26. Paint lightly into the image to reveal the figure.

27. With the figure layer still active, select Duplicate Layer from the Layers palette menu.

28. Choose Filter, Blur, Motion Blur. In the Motion Blur dialog box, specify an Angle of −21°, and a Distance of 38.

29. Click and hold the Adjustment Layer icon and select the Curves option from the pop-out menu.

30. Set the curves to RGB Input=179/Output=76, Red Input=61/Output=171, Green Input=114/Output=184.

31. Select the layer mask on the adjustment layer. Select the Brush tool with white as the foreground color. In the Options bar, specify a 22% opacity and a 30-pixel feathered brush.

32. Paint lightly into the image to reveal the glow effect.

Image 16
Earthly Delights | ©2002 Daniel Giordan

CHAPTER 16

MAKING PHOTOSHOP PATTERNS

The upper section of *Earthly Delights* is an organic water texture that ripples and cascades over the central painted image. The lower half of the image is darkness and shadow that is slightly disorienting because of its lack of structure and detail. The grass, leaves, and water present a textural tapestry that dictates the overall feel of the composition.

The center is dominated by Raphael's painting of Adam and Eve being tempted by the serpent. This ceiling panel shows Eve's encouragement of Adam towards his fatal indulgence. Her frontal, naked pose suggests that she has already yielded to sin, in contrast to Adam's dark silhouette, which suggests his indecision and confusion. His lower body is turned away, even as his upper body turns toward his stygian demise.

And yet, those who read the title and the overt subject matter as being just another story of original sin are jumping to conclusions. The organic backdrop is a brilliant patterning of texture and color. It presents itself in a spectacular sense, with a divine beauty that stands as a counterpoint to the godless transaction occurring in the center. The water and leaves break into the boundaries of the painting, irresistible and compelling, washing away the artificial and sinful constructs.

Rising from the center is a trio of leaves that seems to echo the figures, connected to the figures by stems and a center leaf that becomes the focal point. The right leaf leans in as if echoing Adam's posture; the left leaf stands upright over Eve, mimicking her stance and covering some of her nakedness. The center leaf is the hub of the image. It echoes the hierarchical beauty of the background, provides context for the color in the painting, and connects and unifies the other leaves.

INTRODUCTION TO PHOTOSHOP PATTERNS

Patterns are an effective way of developing special effects and backgrounds for a wide range of design projects. They can create a distinctive presentation background, set off a central subject, or work as a ground for complex montage treatments.

The primary tool for creating patterns in Photoshop is the Pattern Maker filter, which generates random pattern tiles that can be applied to the image or saved as a preset. This chapter focuses primarily on using the Pattern Maker filter, although it will also consider other tools and techniques for creating seamless tile effects, fills, and repeating designs.

Introduction to the Pattern Maker Controls

The Pattern Maker filter is similar to the Extract and Liquify tools in that it is a self-contained set of controls in its own interface window. These controls allow you to create a wide range of patterned tiles, which are randomly generated based on the parameters you specify.

As with the Extract and Liquify filters, Pattern Maker features a set of tools on the left side of the dialog box; you use these tools to manipulate the preview image. The difference between Pattern Maker and the Extract and Liquify dialog boxes is that Pattern Maker doesn't have many tools to speak of. Standard Marquee, Zoom, and Hand tools allow for basic selection, magnification, and dragging of the image. The image is pre-

viewed in the center of the dialog box. The right side of the window features the main control areas for Pattern Maker; here you can specify tile parameters and preview options as well as browse for the tile examples previously created.

Making a Pattern

When Pattern Maker is launched, the Marquee tool is selected and the current layer is displayed in the preview area of the dialog box. Drag the Marquee tool over the preview image and click the Generate button; the preview area will fill with a randomly generated tile effect. After the first tile is generated, the Generate button changes to read Generate Again. Click this button repeatedly to view a history sequence of 20 generated patterns. Click the OK button when you find the desired effect to apply it to the current image or image layer.

Sampling Multiple Layers

The basic approach for creating patterns works well for flat images, or when the pattern data is contained within the active layer. If pattern data is spread across several layers, the solution is to select the desired area and choose Edit, Copy Merged before launching the Pattern Maker. When the Pattern Maker dialog box opens, enable the Use Clipboard as Sample check box in the Tile Generation section and click Generate to create a pattern based on the copied section of the original image.

Adjusting Tile Size and Alignment

By default, Pattern Maker creates a tile that is 132x132 pixels. To create tiles of different proportions, click and hold the Width or Height slider to set the desired tile

size. These sliders control how the pattern repeats. To further control how the tiles repeat, you can offset the tile alignment vertically or horizontally by selecting options from the Offset pop-up menu. The Amount slider just beneath the Offset menu controls the percentage of vertical or horizontal shift.

The last set of controls in the Tile Generation section of the dialog box affect the Smoothness and Sample Detail of the pattern tile. Smoothness refers to the prominent edge contrast that can create an obvious repeated effect. Increasing the Smoothness setting to 2 or 3 results in smoother tile transitions. The Sample Detail field specifies the size of the sample used to create the tile. A higher sample detail setting makes any objects within the pattern more recognizable. This field is less effective on larger images or image samples because the largest sample point in Pattern Maker is just 21 pixels.

Controlling Previews

The Preview controls section of the Pattern Maker dialog box allows you to set the preview to the generated tile or to the original image layer (the image layer you started with). This section also has a check box you can use to turn on and off the tile boundaries and a color sample control to specify the color of the boundary grid.

Browsing the Tile History

The Tile History section of the dialog box holds up to 20 separate tile effects, presented in a thumbnail window with forward and back controls you can use to view the thumbnails in sequence. In addition to the back and forward buttons, options include buttons to go to the first and last tiles, a trash can icon to delete unwanted tiles, and a diskette icon to save the current tile as a pattern preset. After saving a preset, you can click Cancel to exit the dialog box and leave the file unchanged, while still saving the pattern to the Preset Manager.

The Pattern Maker Dialog Box

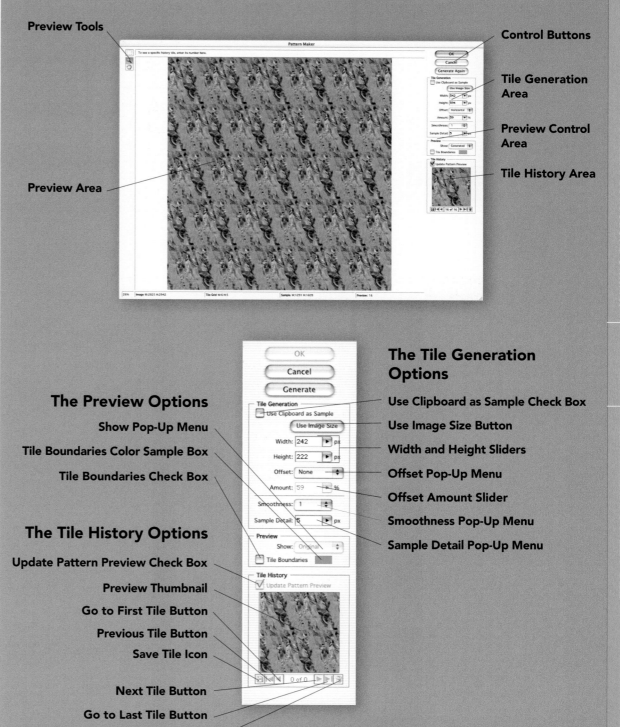

Preview Tools

Preview Area

Control Buttons

Tile Generation Area

Preview Control Area

Tile History Area

The Preview Options

Show Pop-Up Menu

Tile Boundaries Color Sample Box

Tile Boundaries Check Box

The Tile History Options

Update Pattern Preview Check Box

Preview Thumbnail

Go to First Tile Button

Previous Tile Button

Save Tile Icon

Next Tile Button

Go to Last Tile Button

Delete Tile Icon

The Tile Generation Options

Use Clipboard as Sample Check Box

Use Image Size Button

Width and Height Sliders

Offset Pop-Up Menu

Offset Amount Slider

Smoothness Pop-Up Menu

Sample Detail Pop-Up Menu

CREATING A PATTERN

1. In the Layers palette, select the target layer you want to use to generate and receive the pattern.

2. Choose Filter, Pattern Maker to open the Pattern Maker dialog box.

3. Drag a marquee in the preview area to create a sample area for the pattern.

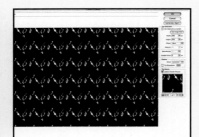

4. Click the Generate button to create a pattern.

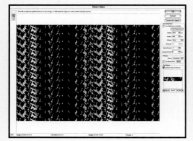

5. Revise the tile generation parameters and click Generate Again to create more patterns as desired.

6. Use the Next and Previous buttons to browse all of the patterns created. Click OK to apply the pattern to the selected layer.

PATTERN STRATEGIES

The Pattern Maker filter can be confusing at first in that the results are hard to predict. As a result, many people get frustrated or confused and never go beyond casual tinkering with this powerful new tool. The examples and suggestions listed here can smooth the rough edges of your experimentation to help deliver better results and manage your expectations.

High-Contrast Sample Areas

Sample areas that are high in contrast usually deliver high-contrast results. Figure 16.1 shows that the small, high-contrast section of a butterfly wing results in a complex repeated pattern that maintains its clarity and definition.

Text Samples

Sampling sections of letterforms can create graphic pattern results with strong visual interest. These patterns maintain many of the characteristics of the font style, but in a highly repeatable, stylized result (see Figure 16.2).

To sample a font or letter for a pattern, you must first convert the font layer to a graphic by highlighting the text layer in the Layers palette and choosing Layer, Rasterize, Type. From there, follow the standard instructions for using the Pattern Maker. An advantage to using text as your pattern base is that the rasterized type layer will be transparent in the non-text areas, resulting in a pattern with a high degree of transparency. This makes it easier to blend the pattern with underlying layers.

Pattern Maker with Distort Filters

The Distort filters are extremely useful tools for creating and modifying the way a pattern repeats. There are many cases in which the pattern created by Pattern Maker looks like a bunch of square tiles rather than a smooth, seamless pattern. To overcome this, you can use the Wave or Shear filters to distort the tile pattern and create an all-over look. The key is to enable the Wrap Edge Pixels option, which picks up the pixels from one side of the tile and repeats them on the other, creating an

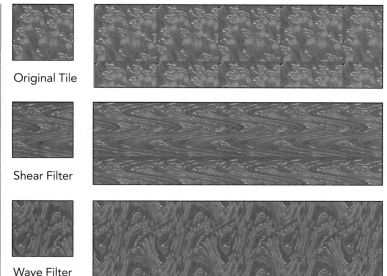

Original Tile

Shear Filter

Wave Filter

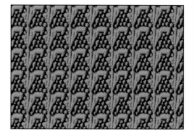

Figure 16.1

The high-contrast sample of the butterfly wing creates a high-contrast repeating pattern

Figure 16.2

The sampled portion of text, the resulting pattern, and its application over an image layer, using a layer mask and the Linear Light blending mode.

Figure 16.3

The original Pattern Maker tile result does not create a seamless pattern. The Shear filter creates a seamless horizontal distortion, while the Wave filter creates a seamless distortion in all directions.

invisible transition (see Figure 16.3). The difference between the Shear and Wave filters is that Shear works only horizontally, while Wave works in all directions. For details on the Distort filters, refer to Chapter 15, "Mastering the Distort Filters." You can select a portion of an image and apply these filters directly, or you can use the filters to touch up tiles created by Pattern Maker.

If you have already created a pattern with Pattern Maker, you can select a single tile in the pattern, copy it, and paste it into a new document. From there you can apply the Wave or Shear filter with the Repeat Edge Pixels check box enabled in the filter's dialog box. When the tile distortion is complete, choose Edit, Define Pattern, name the new pattern, and click OK. This action makes the new

pattern accessible from any Photoshop document by choosing Edit, Fill, selecting Pattern from the Use pop-up menu, and selecting the pattern sample from the Custom Pattern pop-up menu.

Pond Ripples

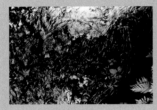

Riverbank

Tapestry

Droplet

Three Leaves

BUILDING THE IMAGE: *EARTHLY DELIGHTS*

Figure 16.4
The Riverbank image is placed against a black background.

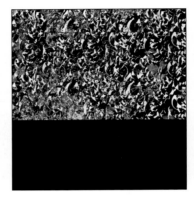

Figure 16.5
A text-based abstract pattern is added.

Figure 16.6
The image is cropped and a mask hides part of the texture.

Building a Watery Backdrop

Before it acquired its saturated palette and renaissance imagery, *Earthly Delights* began as an exploration of monochromatic water images, patterns, and texture. The Riverbank image is a black-and-white image shot at high speed, looking down at where a stream meets the grassy shore. I shot it from a footbridge, positioned directly over the rushing water. After opening the Riverbank image, I pasted it into the design composite. I drew a marquee underneath the Riverbank image, selected black as the foreground color, and filled the selection using the Paint Bucket tool (see Figure 16.4).

Because the image was highly modeled and textural, I decided to add a pattern to emphasize this effect even further. I began by selecting the Text tool and typing a capital "W" in the Edwardian Script typeface. Before I could use the type layer with the Pattern Maker filter, I had to rasterize it, converting it from a text character into a bitmap graphic. To do this, I chose Layer, Rasterize, Type.

With the font layer now converted to a bitmap, I chose Filter, Pattern Maker to launch the Pattern Maker dialog box. Following the instructions outlined elsewhere in this chapter, I drew a selection over the type and generated a series of pattern samples, which I browsed, selected, and applied to the type layer. While the pattern layer was still active, I selected the Difference blending mode from the Layers palette to blend the pattern with the underlying Riverbank image (see Figure 16.5).

At this point, I pasted the Pond Ripples image into the composite and set the blending mode to Hard Light. Then I created a new layer and filled it with black using the Paint Bucket tool. My plan was to mask the layer everywhere except the lower edge, integrating the flat black background with the complex texture area. To do this, I selected the Add Layer Mask icon from the Layers palette, set the foreground color to black, and painted the mask in with a large feathered brush. To complete the

Figure 16.7
The figures are added and integrated with the background.

Figure 16.8
Color saturation is increased...

Figure 16.9
The Three Leaves image is added to the composite.

Figure 16.10
Saturation in the leaves is increased and a drop shadow completes the effect.

background, I cropped the image, focusing in on the details of the water while eliminating some of the black background in the lower area (see Figure 16.6).

Adding the Figures

I'm not sure exactly why I chose this painting of Adam and Eve, except that it does feature prominent foliage and has strong color and an interesting composition. The fact that it's painted by Raphael didn't hurt either.

After placing the image, I selected the Add Layer Mask icon and began painting a mask. I completely hid the right side of the painting (the area next to Eve) to allow the foliage to come right up to her figure, overlapping it in some places.

Other subtle tweaks at this stage were to enlarge the canvas and add additional background texture. To do this, I drew a selection marquee 100 pixels high across the top of the image and copy/pasted it to its own layer. After enlarging the canvas by 100 pixels, I flipped the new layer vertically by choosing Edit, Transform, Flip Vertical, and dragged the layer into position (see Figure 16.7).

Polishing the Apple

Okay, so there's no apple, but I couldn't resist the pun, given the present imagery. Polishing the image involved masking out the palm leaves in the lower-right corner of the image and bumping up the saturation in the red section of the painting. To do this, I placed

the Droplet image, which is predominantly a saturated blue backdrop, in the lower-right corner of the Raphael painting. By selecting the Saturation blending mode for the Droplet layer, I created a saturated color effect in the area where that layer was positioned (see Figure 16.8).

The Three Leaves

After looking at more images than I care to count, I settled on the Three Leaves image as the element that would complete the design. I tried numerous images and discarded one after another in an attempt to find the right design element. After pasting Three Leaves into the composite, I was amazed at how the leaves mirrored the gestures of the figures in the

painting so perfectly. The "Adam leaf" is leaning into the composition, the center leaf features a vertical ripple that picks up the movement of the tree, and the right leaf feels like a standing figure (see Figure 16.9). After silhouetting the leaves, I chose Image, Adjustments, Hue/Saturation and increased the Saturation slider to +73 to bump up the color in the leaves. To complete the effect, I clicked the Add Layer Style icon and selected Drop Shadow from the pop-up menu. I set the Distance slider to 49 pixels and set the Size slider to 46 pixels to further enhance the leaves and complete the effect (see Figure 16.10).

16

EARTHLY DELIGHTS

1. Open the Riverbank image.

2. Choose Image, Adjustments, Curves, select the black and white eyedropper icons, and set the white and black points to optimize the image.

3. Select the Rectangular Marquee tool and draw a rectangular selection 1150 pixels high, spanning the full width of the Riverbank image.

4. Select black as the foreground color, choose the Paint Bucket tool, and click within the selection to fill it with black.

5. Select the Type tool from the toolbox and click to place the cursor.

6. With black as the foreground color, select Edwardian Script from the Font menu in the Options bar and type a capital *W*.

7. Select Layer, Rasterize, Type to rasterize the type layer.

8. Select Filter, Pattern Maker and draw a rectangular selection around a portion of the letter you typed in step 7.

9. In the Tile Generation section of the dialog box, enter a Width value of 242 and a Height value of 222. Click Generate to create a pattern.

10. Click Generate Again repeatedly to create multiple patterns.

11. Click the Previous and Next buttons in the Tile History section of the dialog box to browse through the created patterns. Navigate to the thumbnail of the pattern you want to use and click OK.

12. In the Layers palette, select the pattern layer you just created and select the Difference blending mode.

13. Paste the Pond Ripples image into the composite.

14. In the Layers palette, set the blending mode to Hard Light.

15. From the Layers palette menu, choose New Layer and select black as the foreground color. Choose the Paint Bucket tool from the toolbox and click to fill the new layer with solid black.

16. Choose Layer, Layer Mask, Hide All.

17. Choose the Brush tool from the toolbox and select a large feathered brush with white as the foreground color.

18. Click to paint the mask, revealing the black layer in the lower-right corner of the image.

19. Paste the Tapestry image into the composite.

20. Click the Add Layer Mask icon in the Layers palette. Select the Brush from the toolbox and specify black as the foreground color.

21. Paint to add the mask to allow the background to show through the Tapestry layer.

22. Paste the Droplet image into the composite.

23. Drag the Droplet image to the lower-left corner of the composite image and set the blending mode in the Layers palette to Saturation.

24. Select the Rectangular Marquee tool and draw a selection across the full width of the upper portion of the design, 100 pixels deep.

25. Choose Edit, Copy Merged to copy all the layers in the area you selected in step 24.

26. Choose Edit, Paste to paste the copied area onto a new layer.

 4   12   18   21   31   36   39

27. Choose Edit, Transform, Flip Vertical to flip the new layer. Select the Move tool from the toolbox and align the new layer with the edge of the composite.

28. Select New Layer from the Layers palette menu

29. Select the Rectangular Marquee tool and draw a selection across the pasted layer.

30. Select the Paint Bucket tool with white as the foreground color and fill the selection.

31. Choose the Move tool and drag the white box layer to cover a portion of the pasted strip from step 27. This leaves a strip of the pasted layer visible.

32. Paste the Three Leaves image into the composite.

33. Choose Filter, Extract to launch the Extract dialog box.

34. Select the Edge Highlighter tool and highlight the edges of the leaves. Choose the Fill tool to fill the shape and click Preview. Click OK to extract the image.

35. Click the Add Layer Mask icon in the Layers palette, select the Brush tool from the toolbox, and specify black as the foreground color.

36. Paint to add the mask to the leaf on the right to blend it into the figure of Eve.

37. Choose Image, Adjustments, Hue/Saturation. Move the Saturation slider to +73 and click OK.

38. Click and hold the Add Layer Style icon in the Layers palette, and select Drop Shadow from the pop-up menu.

39. Set the Distance slider to 49 pixels; set the Size slider to 46 pixels. Click OK to apply the drop shadow.

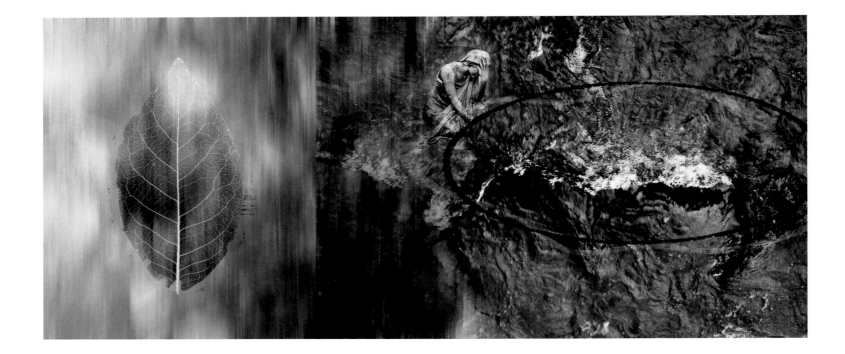

Image 17
FreeFall | ©2002 Daniel Giordan

CHAPTER 17

USING GRADIENTS
AND GRADIENT MAPS

A voyeuristic undercurrent runs through the *FreeFall* image that is both subtle and pervasive. The pictographic narrative seems to be telling us a story about a significant event or tragedy, recounting various aspects of the incident as we read from left to right.

The green leaf on the left side of the image seems to represent the central figure in the account, given its frontal presentation and the fact that it is the only spot of color in the entire composition. Although the background seems to rush past the leaf in a blur, the subject itself is tack sharp. This implies that either the leaf is not a part of the action, or that we are falling at the same rate of speed as the leaf. Is the movement up or down?

Moving towards the center of the image, we encounter a despondent figure, head in hand, overcome with grief. The figure is kneeling next to a circular shape that seems to mark an area of significance. The position of the figure—and the underlying fact that it is actually a cemetery statue—implies that perhaps this is a grave site or place of remembrance. Is the memory of a person or an event?

The division of the image—and the contrast between the two sides—is an interesting point to ponder. The left side seems to reside within the moment as the mysterious event is unfolding. We meet the central subject and sense that something is happening. The right side is an examination of the after effects. Everything is in sharp focus, all movement has ceased, and specific areas have even been singled out. The immediacy of the moment and the permanence of its consequence are combined in a single space, leaving us to consider the missing details and the nature of cause and effect.

CREATING AND USING GRADIENTS

Photoshop defines gradient as the gradual, linear progression between colors. Simple gradients have two colors that act like polar opposites, as one fades into the other. More complex gradients feature a wide array of colors and can include transparent areas that let the underlying design show through.

Gradient color transitions can be applied globally to the entire image or into a selected area. They are applied with the Gradient tool, using a click and a drag to define the beginning and end of the gradient. It's usually a good idea to apply gradients to a separate layer so that you can make further adjustments and fine-tune the interaction between the gradient and any lower layers in the image.

Gradient Shapes

When you select the Gradient tool, the Options bar changes to reveal the gradient options immediately available. One of the most prominent areas of the Gradient Options bar is the Gradient Shapes area, which includes buttons for linear, radial, angled, reflected, and diamond gradients. These gradient shapes are created in relation to the direction and length of the line drawn by the Gradient tool.

The most common gradient shape is linear, which presents bands of color that run perpendicular to the line drawn by the Gradient tool. The radial gradient creates a circular shape that emanates from the starting point of the line drawn by the Gradient tool, creating a concentric target shape as it describes the color transitions. The angled

gradient shape is also circular, wrapping the gradient transitions in a linear sweep around the center point. The reflected gradient shape creates a mirror-image effect, presented in perpendicular, linear bands. The diamond gradient creates concentric diamond-shaped bands, emanating from the center point.

Components of a Gradient

The other prominent area in the Gradient Options bar is the Gradient color bar or swatch. The color bar represents the color of the gradient that will be created when the Gradient tool is used. Click and hold the arrow on the right end of the color swatch to display the gradient picker, where you can double-click to select a new gradient. The gradient picker also has an options menu, which you can access by clicking the arrow at the

upper-right of the gradient picker window. At the bottom the menu are eight sets of presets you can load if you need more gradient presets. The problem here is that the presets are seldom useful for most purposes, especially if you're looking to integrate a gradient with an existing image or design. To do this, you really need to create your own custom gradient.

To create a custom gradient, click the Gradient color swatch in the Options bar to launch the Gradient Editor. The top of the Editor window is filled with the presets and the preset options menu. Under the presets is a field in which you can name and create your new gradient, and a Gradient Type area where you can define the characteristics of your new gradient. The Gradient Type menu offers options of solid or noise gradients;

you can use the Smoothness slider to fine-tune the type of gradient you select. You will usually leave the Gradient Type menu at Solid and the Smoothness slider at 100%, although the noise type options are discussed as special effects later in this chapter.

Beneath these settings is the gradient bar, where you can define and modify the color and transparency variables for the gradient you are creating. The basic approach for defining a gradient is to define the value and distribution of the variables, and then click the New button to save it to the Presets palette.

Adding Stops

Transition points for new color or transparency settings are defined by stops, which are positioned along the gradient bar as boxes with arrows pointing to a spot on the bar. The stops at the top of the gradient bar define transparency; the stops beneath the bar define specific colors in the gradient. By default, there is a stop at each end for color and transparency, and the overall gradient settings reflect the gradient that was active when the Gradient Editor was launched.

Click above or below the gradient bar to add a new transparency or color stop; click an existing stop to activate it for further editing. As you do, the Stops section of the Gradient Editor becomes available, allowing you to select the desired levels of color or transparency, as well as to specify the precise position of the stop along the gradient bar. You can modify the values in the Stops section, or you can drag the stops into position along the gradient bar. To delete a stop, select it and press the Delete key, or simply drag the stop off the bar.

Adjusting Midpoints

When a stop is active, a small diamond appears along the gradient bar, midway between the active stop and adjacent stops. These diamond symbols represent the midpoint between the stop values. Drag the midpoint diamond to adjust the center of the color or transparency transition, compressing or extending the distribution.

The Gradient Tool

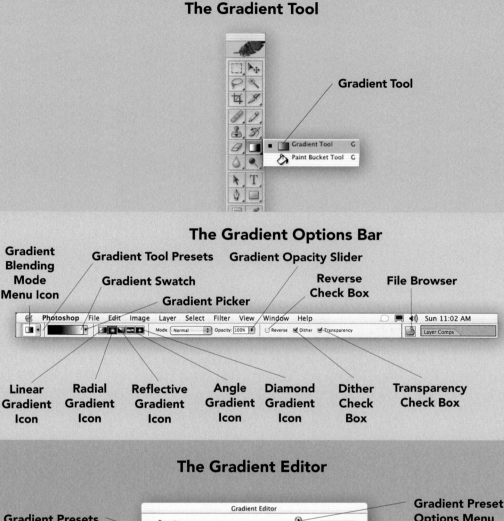

Gradient Tool

The Gradient Options Bar

Gradient Blending Mode Menu Icon · Gradient Tool Presets · Gradient Opacity Slider · Gradient Swatch · Reverse Check Box · File Browser · Gradient Picker

Linear Gradient Icon · Radial Gradient Icon · Reflective Gradient Icon · Angle Gradient Icon · Diamond Gradient Icon · Dither Check Box · Transparency Check Box

The Gradient Editor

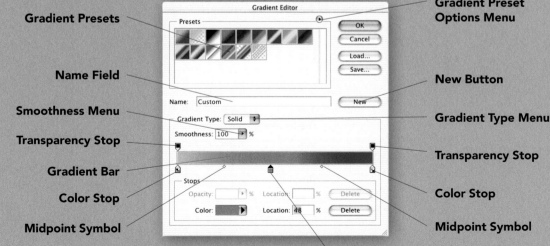

Gradient Presets · Gradient Preset Options Menu · Name Field · New Button · Smoothness Menu · Gradient Type Menu · Transparency Stop · Transparency Stop · Gradient Bar · Color Stop · Color Stop · Midpoint Symbol · Midpoint Symbol · Color Stop

CREATING A CUSTOM GRADIENT

This technique outlines how to specify colors, color breaks, and transparency for a custom gradient.

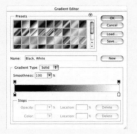 

1. Select the Gradient tool from the toolbox and click the Gradient color swatch in the Options bar to launch the Gradient Editor.

2. Select the first color stop and click the Color swatch in the Stops section to launch the Color Picker. Select a new color and click OK. Repeat for the other color stops.

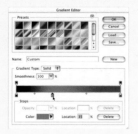 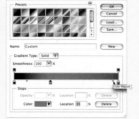

3. Click just underneath the gradient bar to add additional color stops. Drag the stop to the desired position and select the color for that portion of the gradient as described in step 2.

4. For each set of stops, adjust the midpoint diamond to control the color transition between the stops.

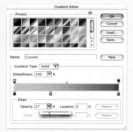 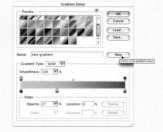

5. Select the first transparency stop and click the Opacity slider in the Stops section. Adjust the slider to set the transparency percentage. Repeat for the other transparency stops.

6. Type the name for the new gradient in the Name field and click the New button to save the gradient as a preset.

GRADIENT SPECIAL EFFECTS

Although using and creating gradients may seem pretty straightforward, there are a few things you can do to push the envelope further. Photoshop features a Gradient Map command that maps a gradient to an image or channel. This is a great way to simulate duotones and other graphic effects. In addition, you can also break away from the traditional smooth gradient transition and create a noise gradient, which randomly distributes bands of color within a predefined color range.

Noise Gradients

Noise gradients generate random stripes of color within a specified range of colors. They are called noise gradients because of this random quality, even though they do not create the stipple effect found in other noise filters and commands.

Noise gradients are created in the Gradient Editor by selecting Noise from the Gradient Type menu. When you select this option, the gradient bar changes to a series of stripes, and the Roughness slider defaults to 50%. A low Roughness setting will create subtle banding effects in a restricted color range, while a higher Roughness setting will create a more chaotic array of lines and colors.

The Color Model section (that replaces the Stops section of the Gradient Editor window when working with noise gradients) determines the range of colors used in the noise gradient. From the Color Model menu, you can select RGB, HSB, or Lab color; the sliders in the Color Model section change to reflect your choice. As you move the slider triangles to adjust the color, remember that only the colors between the triangles will be present in the noise gradient. Move the two triangles to the same spot to eliminate a color completely.

Finish creating your noise gradient by tweaking the Options section. Enable the Restrict Colors check box to reduce the highlights and restrict the tonal range; enable the Add Transparency check box to create random transparent gradient areas. Finally, click the Randomize button to generate random noise results within your current color settings; keep clicking the Randomize button until you get something you like (see Figure 17.1).

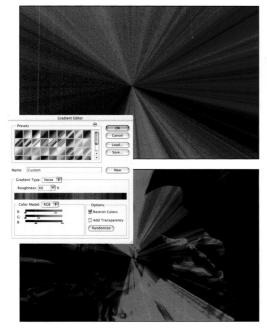

Figure 17.1

The first noise gradient is applied using the Angle shape to create a starburst effect. The second example shows the same starburst gradient applied with the Linear Light blending mode over a flower image.

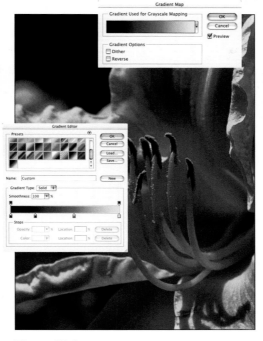

Figure 17.2

Four colors are mapped to the tonal range of this flower, simulating a quadtone effect.

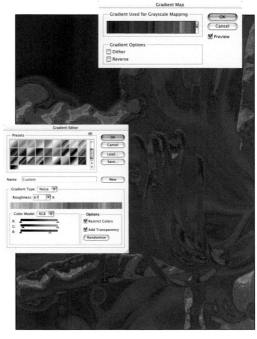

Figure 17.3

A random Noise gradient is used as a Gradient Map, creating an abstract result.

Gradient Maps

The Gradient Map command allows you to create a gradient and apply it to an image; the result is based on the image's grayscale tonal range. The color stop positioned at 0% is mapped to the blacks in the image, and the color stop at 100% is mapped to the whites. (The color stop location percentage is listed in the Stops section of the Gradient Editor.)

Thus, if your gradient is bright orange at the 0% (or far left) position, the darks in the image will change to orange. The relationship holds across the tonal range so that a color in the middle, at 50% will replace the midtones. When mapping a gradient, you should remember to use the midpoint diamond to control how color fades from one area to another. Positioning the midpoint diamond is an effective way to restrict the color in the gradient from certain areas in the image.

To launch the Gradient Map dialog box, choose Image, Adjustment, Gradient Map. The dialog box is simple; it features a gradient bar and buttons to dither the gradient and reverse the gradient direction. Click the gradient bar to launch the Gradient Editor window and revise the gradient. The great thing about this process is that as you apply colors to the gradient, they are automatically updated in the image itself. In this way, you can add colors and adjust midpoint breaks with real-time feedback on the final results. Figure 17.2 shows an example of a gradient map application, along with the Gradient Editor and Gradient Map dialog boxes. Figure 17.3 shows the same image after using a random noise gradient to create an abstract color mapping effect.

Leaf Web

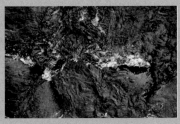

Wake

Backlit Leaf

Cemetery

BUILDING THE IMAGE: *FREEFALL*

Figure 17.4
Canvas is added and the Leaf Web image is modified with the Glass and Liquify filters.

Figure 17.5
The Motion Blur filter is applied to the Leaf Web layer, and the Wake image is added.

Figure 17.6
Hue/Saturation adjustment layers convert the image to grayscale.

Starting with a Gradient

FreeFall began as an exploration of gradient map effects, with overt attempts to push a complex gradient into various leaves and branch patterns. I settled on the Leaf Web image for these experiments, and although none of the gradient maps worked, I did use it to start the design.

After optimizing the white and black points for the Leaf Web image, I applied the Glass filter (Filter, Distort, Glass) to create an overall distortion effect. I set the controls to Distortion=10, Smoothness=9, Scale=198%, and selected the Frosted Glass option. The rippling result looked as if the leaves and branches were frozen beneath a thin sheet of ice. Knowing that I was going to contrast this image with the watery Wake image, I used the Liquify filter (Filter, Liquify) to distort the

edges so that the two images would blend (see Figure 17.4).

I found it difficult to make the Leaf Web and Wake images work together because their sharp textures were so similar. To change this fact, I applied the Motion Blur filter (Filter, Blur, Motion Blur) to the Leaf Web side of the composite. In the Motion Blur dialog box, I set Angle to −90° and Distance to 241 (see Figure 17.5).

Going Monochrome

The movement and texture caused by the Motion Blur effect were interesting,. But the color felt arbitrary. I decided to push the design to black and white to emphasize the tone and texture even further. I selected Image, Adjustment, Gradient Map, clicked the gradient sample in the dialog box that

appeared, and tweaked a black-to-white gradient to get the desired result (see Figure 17.6).

Adding the Cast

Now that I had a pretty interesting background, it was time to populate my stage with some actors. I started with the Backlit Leaf image as the anchor for the right side. After placing the image and scaling it with the Free Transform command (Edit, Free Transform), I used the Extract command to silhouette the object (Filter, Extract). I intentionally kept the extract results rough, in contrast with the smooth, blurred background. I set the blending mode to Overlay and the Opacity to 82%.

I used another gradient map to set the green color in the leaf. I created a new gradient with white and black at the ends and a single color stop of sap green set at a location

Figure 17.7
The Leaf and Cemetery images are added and silhouetted.

Figure 17.8
The oval is drawn on a separate layer.

Figure 17.9
The oval is duplicated and distorted using the Wave filter.

Figure 17.10
Final contrast adjustments are made with Hue/Saturation adjustment layers.

of 39%. This adjustment layer was attached to the leaf layer with a clipping mask.

To add the lamenting figure, I placed the cemetery image and then scaled it and dragged it into rough position. I selected the Add Layer Mask icon, a large brush, and a black foreground color to paint out everything in the cemetery except the figure. I zoomed in a few times to get the detail right, and then used the Move tool and the arrow keys to nudge the figure into final position (see Figure 17.7).

Drawing the Oval

To support the textured oval shape, I created a new layer. I clicked on the Elliptical Marquee tool from the toolbox and dragged an oval over the composite that was 280 pixels taller than what I intended the final result to be. I added a stroke to the selection

(that is, I made the selection a visible line) by selecting Edit, Stroke, setting the width to 30, choosing black as the color, and clicking the Inside Location option. I reduced the height of the oval by selecting Edit, Free Transform and dragging down the top center handle to compress the shape. To add texture to the shape, I selected Filter, Sketch, Conté Crayon and set the Foreground, Background, and Relief levels very high. I settled on Sandstone for the texture type at a Scaling value of 170%. In the Layers palette, I selected the Multiply blending mode to complete the effect (see Figure 17.8).

Nuance and Detail

The next step was to select and duplicate the oval layer. To accomplish this, I selected Filter, Distort, Wave, and moved the Wavelength control from 10 to 464, the Amplitude control from 5 to 35, and enabled the Repeat Edge Pixels

check box. I left all the other controls at their defaults. Finally, I inverted the layer (Image, Adjustments, Invert) and set the layer opacity to 20%. This created a subtle, wavy shape that visually held the space between the oval and the waves in the background (see Figure 17.9).

The randomness in the blurred side of the composite took a lot more experimentation and exploration to figure out. I finally arrived at the desired result by duplicating the Leaf Web layer and lightening it with curves (Image, Adjustment, Curves). I moved the first point from Input=0 to Output=130 and the second point from Input=46 to Output=142. I created a layer mask for the new layer and used a horizontal gradient to control visibility. The gradient I used had white at both ends and black in the middle and was drawn horizontally from right to left.

The final touch was to add a Hue/Saturation adjustment layer beneath the new Leaf Web layer; in the Hue/Saturation dialog box, I enabled the Colorize check box and set Hue to 356, Saturation to 68, and Lightness to −21. Because this colored adjustment layer was positioned beneath the grayscale gradient created earlier, no color shows through, although the layer does adjust the tonality of the image. Things get darker towards the center where the mask was positioned, and the image stays light on the right side, reflecting the lighter layer we just created (see Figure 17.10).

FREEFALL

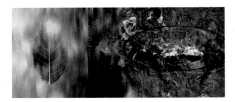

1. Open the Leaf Web image.

2. Select Image, Adjustments, Curves; select the black and white eyedropper icons and set the white and black points for the image.

3. Select Image, Canvas Size, type 3105 pixels in the Width field to make room for the Wake image. Set the anchor point to the center right and click OK.

4. Choose Filter, Distort, Glass to apply the Glass filter to the Leaf Web image. Set the filter options as follows: Distortion=10, Smoothness=9, Texture=Frosted, and Scaling=198%.

5. Paste the Wake image into the composite and drag it to the right side of the canvas.

6. Click the Leaf Web layer in the Layers palette to highlight that layer.

7. Choose Filter, Liquify and apply the filter to the Leaf Web layer. Enable the Backdrop check box in the Liquify dialog box, select All Layers from the Layers pop-up menu, and specify an Opacity of 75%. From the toolbox, select the Warp tool with a 64-pixel

brush and distort the edges of the Leaf Web image to blend it into the watery Wake image.

8. With the Leaf Web layer still selected, select Duplicate Layer from the Layers palette menu.

9. Choose Filter, Blur, Motion Blur. Set the Blur Angle to −90° and the Distance to 241 pixels.

10. Click and hold the Adjustment Layer icon in the Layers palette and select Gradient Map from the pop-up menu that appears.

11. Click the gradient swatch and choose the black-to-white gradient from the gradient Presets section of the Gradient Editor.

12. Click and hold the Adjustment Layer icon in the Layers palette and select Curves from the pop-up menu that appears.

13. In the Curves dialog box, set the Channels pop-up menu to Composite, and change the input/output values from Input=103 to Output=50. Then set the Channels pop-up menu to Red, and change the input/output values from Input=179 to Output=193.

14. Paste the Backlit Leaf image into the composite.

15. Choose Edit, Free Transform. Resize the leaf and center it vertically in the composite. Drag the image to the left side and double-click inside its bounding box to apply the transformation.

16. Choose Filter, Extract. Select the Edge Highlighter tool from the dialog box and outline the edges of the leaf. Fill the shape using the Fill tool and click OK.

17. Using the options at the top of the Layers palette, set the blending mode for the Backlit Leaf image to Overlay and set the Opacity to 82%.

18. Click and hold the Adjustment Layer icon in the Layers palette and select Gradient Map from the pop-up menu that appears.

19. Click the gradient swatch; in the Gradient Editor that appears, create a custom gradient with three color stops. Sequentially set the stop colors to white, sap green (R167, G177, B15), and black.

4   9   13   23

20. Paste the Cemetery image into the composite.

21. Click the Add Layer Mask icon in the Layers palette, select the paintbrush from the toolbox, and select black as the foreground color.

22. Paint out the background of the Cemetery image, leaving only the main statue.

23. Select the Move tool from the toolbox and drag the masked layer into position just to the right of center.

24. Choose New Layer from the Layers palette menu.

25. Select the Elliptical Marquee tool from the toolbox and drag an oval selection over the Wake image.

26. Choose Edit, Stroke; set the Width to 30, choose black as the color, and enable the Inside Location button. Click OK to apply stroke.

27. With the oval selection active, select Edit, Free Transform and drag the top center handle down to compress the oval shape.

28. Choose Filter, Sketch, Conté Crayon and set the Foreground to 11, the Background

to 7, and the Relief to 14. Select Sandstone from the Texture menu and set Scaling to 170%.

29. In the Layers palette, set the blending mode for the oval layer to Multiply.

30. With the oval layer still selected, choose Duplicate Layer from the Layers palette menu.

31. Choose Filter, Distort, Wave and set the controls as follows: Number of Generators 5, Wavelength Min 10, Wavelength Max 464, Amplitude Min 5, Amplitude Max 35, Type Sine. Also set Undefined Areas to Repeat Edge Pixels. Leave all the other settings at their defaults.

32. In the Layers palette, set the blending mode to Linear Dodge and the Opacity to 20%.

33. In the Layers palette, drag the distorted oval layer so that it is positioned beneath the original oval layer.

34. In the Layers palette, select the second Leaf Web Layer (the one created in step 8).

35. Choose Image, Adjustments, Curves. Change the RGB composite values from In-

put=0 to Output=130 and from Input=46 to Output= 142.

36. Click the Add Layer Mask icon in the Layers palette and select the Gradient tool from the toolbox.

37. Click the gradient swatch in the Options bar to launch the Gradient Editor. Select the black-to-white gradient from the Presets area of the Gradient Editor window.

38. In the gradient sample at the bottom of the Gradient Editor, drag the black color stop to the center of the gradient and click underneath the gradient bar to add a replacement color stop.

39. Click the Color swatch in the Stops section and select white as the color of the new color stop, completing a white/ black/white gradient.

40. Select the Gradient tool from the toolbox, position the cursor at the left side of the composite image, and drag horizontally to the start of the oval to apply the gradient to the layer mask.

41. Choose Image, Adjustments, Curves. Choose Composite

from the Channels pop-up menu and adjust the values to control the visibility of the layer based on the break in the curve. In this case, move the curve point from Input=130 to Output=167.

42. In the Layers palette, select the second Leaf Web layer (the one created in step 8).

43. Click and hold the Adjustment Layer icon in the Layers palette and select Hue/Saturation from the pop-up menu that appears.

44. Set the Hue/Saturation values as follows: Hue 356, Saturation 68, and Lightness −21.

29   32   44

Image 18
Birch Trees | ©2002 Daniel Giordan

CHAPTER 18

USING THE LIQUIFY FILTER

There's something primal and somehow foreboding about looking into the woods. Our eyes try to see past the impeding branches and into the dark shadows and recesses of the brush. In the process, the tangled branches, colors, and textures create a layered patchwork that can be beautiful, yet elusive.

It's elusive in the sense that the intricate and vibrant layers of line and shape are heavily dependent on the weather, light direction, and the time of day. One minute you're presented with a beautiful and delicate matrix of line and color, then the sun goes behind a cloud and all is lost in muddy shadows.

I've shot hundreds of photographs this way, peering into the woods, waiting for the right light and definition, and missing many more than I've hit. In **Birch Trees,** I took matters into my own hands a bit, pursuing this elusive scenario. The branches of the trees overlay and intertwine, creating an impenetrable web that almost seems to move of its own accord. This impression is heightened by the way the color fades to black and white as your eye goes to the top.

The result is similar to the feeling one has when looking at the paintings of Jackson Pollack. Although many critics focus on the throwing and splattering of paint, it's really the impenetrable buildup of layers that is compelling and frustrating. In this image, no matter how hard you try, the birch trees are not going to let you pass. They reduce the entire image to surface and line, forcing you to sit back, admire the lines, and feel the space from a distance.

INTRODUCTION TO LIQUIFY

When people encounter the Liquify filter for the first time, they are amazed at the responsiveness of the controls. This elegant and intuitive tool allows you to modify pixels with such deftness that it feels as if you're digitally finger painting.

Introduction to the Liquify Interface

The Liquify filter is similar to the Extract and Pattern Maker tools in that it is a self-contained set of controls in its own interface window. The controls allow you to create a wide range of distortions that twist and twirl the image as though it were melting.

As with the Extract and Pattern Maker filters, Liquify features a set of tools on the left side of the dialog box that you can use to manipulate the preview image. The right side of the dialog box contains the main control areas, which allow you to specify tool settings and masking and preview options.

Behind the Scenes

Liquify works its magic by imposing a grid over the image; it distorts the grid along with the underlying pixels. The grid, which looks like ordinary graph paper, is called a mesh; it is the mesh that dictates how the distortion is applied to the image. To view the mesh, enable the Mesh check box in the View Options area of the Liquify dialog box. When you can see the mesh, you can more easily determine where any distortions have been applied.

As you use the paint tools to manipulate the filter effects, the intersection points in the mesh are displaced based on the brush size, pressure, and overall brush action. These points pull the connecting lines along with them, creating the warped grid that drives the distortion. The mesh is so central to the Liquify effect that it can even be saved like a Curves setting and applied to another image; use the Save Mesh and Load Mesh buttons in the upper-left corner of the Liquify dialog box. (This technique is covered later in this chapter.)

The Tool Set

You use the Liquify tools like standard brushes, with the exception that the Liquify tools move the mesh and the image in a slightly different way than do standard tools. The Warp tool operates like the Smudge tool in that it pulls and smears the pixels as you paint. The Turbulence tool offsets the mesh coordinates (and the associated pixels) in a random direction without moving them far from their points of origin. The Twirl tools spin the mesh in circles, creating brushed-in effects similar to the Twirl filter located in the Distort submenu of the Filters menu. The Pucker and Bloat tools expand the pixels in or out from the center of the brush as you paint.

The Shift Pixels tool moves pixels perpendicular to the stroke direction. Drag to move pixels to the left; Option+drag (Mac users) or Alt+drag (Windows users) to move pixels to the right.

The Reflection tool copies and stretches adjacent pixels into the brush area. The default settings shift pixels from the left on a downward stroke, and from the right on an upward stroke; the pixels are shifted above on a stroke that moves to the left, and below on a stroke that moves to the right. Option+drag (Mac users) or Alt+drag (Windows users) to reverse the directions.

The Reconstruct, Freeze, and Thaw tools allow you to revert to previous states, mask areas to protect from distortion, and erase the mask, respectively. The Reconstruct tool works like a gradual undo that slowly reverts a distortion to its previous states, all the way back to the original if desired. The Freeze and Thaw tools paint and erase a mask that locks the mesh in place and prevents any change to the coordinates. The Zoom and Hand tools magnify and move the image placement.

Tool Options Controls

The Tool Options section of the Liquify dialog box controls the size, pressure, and jitter of the brush. The Brush Pressure setting controls how fast the effect is applied. The Turbulent Jitter option is active when the Turbulence tool is selected. Enable the Stylus Pressure check box to control these variables when using a pressure-sensitive drawing tablet.

Reconstruction and Freeze Area Controls

The Reconstruction controls allow you to step backward to various states in the distort process. The Reconstruct button restores all un-frozen areas, while the Revert button restores all areas, frozen or not. To restore a portion of the image, select the Revert option from the Mode menu in this area of the dialog box, choose the Recon-struct brush from the left side of the dialog box, and paint out the changes. We will look at other reconstruction options later in this chapter.

The Freeze Area settings control the parameters around the protec-tive mask created by the Freeze tool. These controls allow you to erase ("thaw") the entire mask or invert the mask to switch between frozen and active areas.

View Options Controls

You can use check boxes in the View Options area of the Liquify dialog box to toggle frozen areas, image, and mesh on and off, as well as control the appearance of the mesh and frozen mask. Finally, the Backdrop check box allows you to view the layer being distorted against one or all of the other layers in the file.

Liquify Dialog Box

Painting Tools

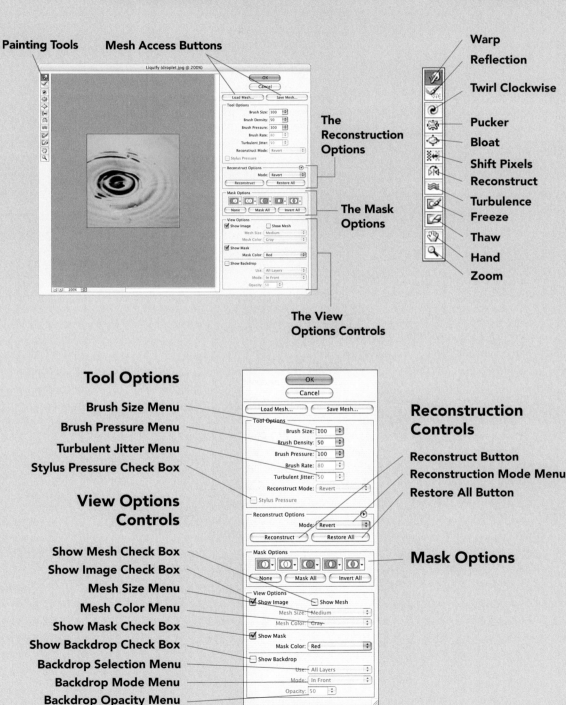

Painting Tools   Mesh Access Buttons

The Reconstruction Options

The Mask Options

The View Options Controls

Warp
Reflection
Twirl Clockwise
Pucker
Bloat
Shift Pixels
Reconstruct
Turbulence
Freeze
Thaw
Hand
Zoom

Tool Options

Brush Size Menu
Brush Pressure Menu
Turbulent Jitter Menu
Stylus Pressure Check Box

View Options Controls

Show Mesh Check Box
Show Image Check Box
Mesh Size Menu
Mesh Color Menu
Show Mask Check Box
Show Backdrop Check Box
Backdrop Selection Menu
Backdrop Mode Menu
Backdrop Opacity Menu

Reconstruction Controls

Reconstruct Button
Reconstruction Mode Menu
Restore All Button

Mask Options

USING CHANNELS AS LIQUIFY MASKS

The Liquify filter operates on the basic, painterly level of pushing color around with a brush. On the surface, this interface is easy and accessible, but there are nuances you can explore and exploit. This section looks at Liquify's capability of simulating a water reflection.

Figure 18.1
The first figure shows the original image; the second shows the result of the copy-and-paste mirror effect.

rendering program delivers the convincing results of Liquify. (Besides, the Liquify effect will take you maybe half an hour to apply to your image, compared with the more elaborate and time-consuming 3D options.)

Setting Up the Reflection

Obviously, the first step in reflecting an image is to duplicate the area to be reflected, flip it, and move it into place. In the example shown in Figure 18.1, the lower area of the tree image was selected,

copied, and pasted as a separate layer. I then chose Edit, Transform, Flip Vertical to flip the new layer upside down. With the Move tool, I dragged the flipped layer into position, aligning the edges to create a mirrored effect. At this point, the reflected layer is ready to be distorted to simulate the ripple effects of water.

Using an Alpha Channel to Freeze

The key to getting the "water" to look right is to create a Freeze mask that locks in a part of the image as you distort other parts. Specifically, the idea is to create the ripples on the water with a

series of bands created in a separate channel.

The thing to remember about channels is that they act like masks: They define an area of the image you can recall for selections or other effects. For example, when you save a selection (Select, Save Selection), Photoshop creates an alpha channel of the selection. As in other masking options, white signifies an active area (an area that is selected, visible), and black signifies a passive area (an area that is deselected, hidden).

Creating a separate channel is as easy as opening the Channels palette (Window, Channels),

Creating Water Reflections

What better use for the Liquify filter than to simulate liquid? There have been various tutorials that attempt to simulate this effect, but nothing short of a 3D

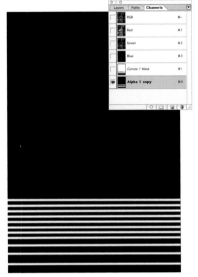

Figure 18.2

Painting horizontal lines in the alpha channel.

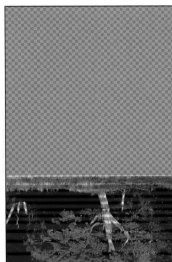

Figure 18.3

Choose the alpha channel in the Liquify dialog box to freeze the black channel areas

Figure 18.4

The result of applying the Liquify filter.

Figure 18.5

The final image.

selecting New Channel from the palette menu, and naming the channel in the dialog box that appears. The screen will turn black, showing the current state of the channel. I selected a 70-pixel feathered brush and created horizontal bands across the bottom of the channel, corresponding to the reflected water area. Hint: Hold down the Shift key as you paint to restrict the stroke to a straight line—very helpful in this application. I spaced the strokes further apart toward the bottom of the image to simulate the visual compression of perspective (see Figure 18.2).

Adding the Distortion

Having reflected the image and created the alpha channel, it's time to add the Liquify distortion. Open the Liquify dialog box (Filter, Liquify) and select the alpha channel from the pop-up menu in the Mask Options section of the dialog box. A red mask will cover the frozen areas, leaving the editable areas exposed (see Figure 18.3). I selected a large brush (300 pixels), left the Brush Pressure setting at 50, and painted across the water area in one stroke, creating a uniform distortion (see Figure 18.4).

To add to the realism, I clicked the Add Layer Style icon in the Layers palette and added a drop shadow effect to the distorted layer. For

the drop shadow, I set the Opacity control to 52%, Angle to −132, Distance to 4 pixels, Spread to 18%, and Size to 16 pixels. This treatment created an angled dark area where the water meets the shore. With this drop shadow in place, I clicked the Add Layer Mask icon to add a mask to the effect. I chose a small feathered brush and painted out part of the horizontal edge of the distortion layer, simulating an organic shoreline shape.

Making Waves

The reflection effect was shaping up, but it still looked somewhat plastic and stark. The image needed more detail in the waves. To address this, I found an image of

rippling water that I pasted into the composite and scaled to fit over the distorted layer. I set the Layer blending mode to Lighten and the Opacity to 45%. To finish off the effect, I chose Layer, New Adjustment Layer, Curves, and added the following Curve points: from Input=86 to Output=54 and from Input=204 to Output=165. In the Layers palette, I placed the cursor between the waves layer and the adjustment layer, and Option+ clicked (Alt+click for Windows users) to restrict the adjustment effect to just the lower layer, completing the effect shown in Figure 18.5.

REUSING THE LIQUIFY MESH

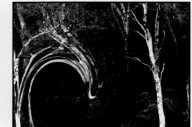

1. Open the first image and select Filter, Liquify to launch the Liquify dialog box.

2. Distort the image as desired.

3. Click the Save Mesh button; name the mesh file and select its folder location in the Save As dialog box that appears.

4. Click OK to apply the Liquify filter you just defined to the current image.

5. Open a second image and select Filter, Liquify to launch the Liquify dialog box.

6. Click the Load Mesh button and select the saved mesh from the dialog box that appears. Click OK to apply the effect.

WORKING WITH THE LIQUIFY MESH

As mentioned earlier in this chapter, the Liquify filter creates its effect based on the distortions applied to a grid-like mesh that is imposed over the image. The mesh is considered a separate set of control data, and is saved as a standalone file with a .msh suffix. This allows you to save the Liquify effect from one image

Figure 18.6

The original image in two separate layers.

Mesh File Overview

Mesh files are separate files created by the Liquify interface for the purpose of saving and restoring distorted mesh patterns to multiple files or layers. As the step-by-step instructions on this page show, it's simple to save a mesh file and load it for use on another layer or file. The mesh file always carries a .msh suffix and can be saved and loaded from any accessible directory.

When you load the mesh, it is scaled up or down depending on the proportion of the image. Because the mesh is vector based, the scaling does not degrade the smoothness of the distortion. This means that you can experiment with a low-res copy of an image, save the mesh, and apply it to the high-res version of the image when you've finalized the distortion effect.

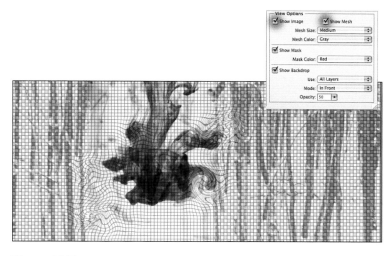

and apply it to a second image, not unlike a saved Curves dialog box or a paintbrush preset. This section reviews the various options and techniques for creating, saving, and loading a Liquify mesh.

Figure 18.7
The results of the Liquify distortion and the visible mesh.

Figure 18.8
The final result of the Liquify filter, with the mesh applied to the lower layer.

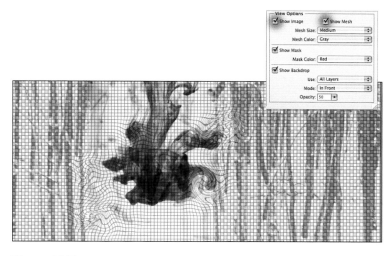

Reusing a Saved Mesh

Although the Liquify effect is restricted to a single layer, it's possible to apply a mesh distortion to multiple layers or images. In the example shown in Figure 18.6, an image of billowing liquid is in a separate layer over a group of birch trees.

After highlighting the Liquid layer, I opened the Liquify dialog box and used a variety of distort tools

to paint the distortions, extending the billowing edges of the Liquid image even further. Figure 18.7 shows a portion of the Liquify dialog box and the way the mesh looks with the distortions. (Note that the Mesh check box was enabled in the View Options area of the dialog box, making the gridlines of the mesh visible.) In addition, the Backdrop check box was also enabled, making both

layers visible in the preview area. Before applying the effect, I saved the mesh by clicking the Save Mesh button and naming the mesh file.

After I applied the Liquify effect to the Liquid layer, I selected the Background layer (the layer containing the trees) and relaunched the Liquify filter. I clicked the Load Mesh button and selected

the saved file. I made a few minor corrections to the mesh to localize the distortion effect to the trees image and reapplied the distortion. The result is a distortion that works seamlessly between multiple layers (see Figure 18.8).

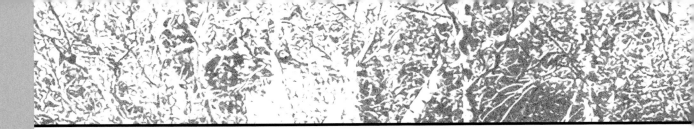

BUILDING THE IMAGE: *BIRCH TREES*

Figure 18.9
The Birch Trees image is optimized.

Figure 18.10
A Hue/Saturation adjustment layer removes the color.

Figure 18.11
A Curves adjustment layer increases the contrast.

Focusing on the Image

The Birch Trees image walks a fine line between digital distortion effects and straightforward photography. Each time I started opening things up with the Liquify filter and abstract treatments, I felt compelled to calm things down and keep the effects subtle and understated. As usual, these decisions are driven by the starting image, and in this case, I wanted to get out of the way and let the image speak for itself.

I began working with the original Birch Trees image by applying basic image optimization. I opened the Curves dialog box and set the white point and black point to ensure a solid tonal range. I also applied an Unsharp Mask filter to make sure that the starting image was crisp and clean (see Figure 18.9).

The first big decision had to do with the color. The color in the original image was somewhat flat and lifeless. There was nothing very directional or dramatic, and the foliage was a uniform green. I decided to see whether I could create a more dramatic black-and-white effect instead. I added a Hue/Saturation adjustment layer and set the Saturation slider to −100 and the Lightness slider to −24 (see Figure 18.10). Although these settings created a somewhat dark overall result, it positioned the shadow areas right where I wanted them.

To bring up the highlights, I added a Curves adjustment layer. I created a basic "S" curve to bring up the highlights and create more contrast in the midtones. I moved the first curve point from Input=160 to Output=227. The second point remained stationary, with Input and Output values

equal to 56 (see Figure 18.11). In the process of brightening the highlights, the Curves adjustment layer flattened the shadows, sacrificing details in the bushes. Loss of shadow and highlight detail is a common occurrence with an "S" curve, where contrast at the two ends of the spectrum is sacrificed for extra contrast in the midtones. Graphically, this is evident in the fact that tonal contrast is connected with a steeper curve shape; a lack of contrast makes the curve flatten. Thus, the steepness of the curve in the middle and the flatness at the ends foreshadows the final result.

Rather than try to remedy the situation within a single dialog box, I accepted the initial curve settings and added a second Curves adjustment layer to add detail back to the shadows. I moved the second curve point from Input=108 to Output=229. The

Figure 18.12

A second Curves adjustment layer brings out the detail in the foliage.

Figure 18.13

A layer mask is used to add color back into the image.

Figure 18.14

The image is distorted with the Liquify filter.

Figure 18.15

The distortion is softened and the center branch is erased.

only problem was that lightening the shadow values blew out the details in the rest of the image. To get around this, I decided to use a layer mask that would apply the second curve settings only in the shadow areas, leaving the rest of the image untouched. I added the mask and painted the effect of the second Curves adjustment layer into the foliage at the bottom of the image (see Figure 18.12).

Adding Back Some Color

Although the black-and-white coloration was working, the image was beginning to feel like the thousands of other black-and-white birch tree images that have been created over the years. I decided to add some of the color back in: I duplicated the original image layer and dragged it to the top of the stack. I added another layer mask and painted it into the tops of the trees with a large feath-

ered brush, revealing the black-and-white effect from the lower layers (see Figure 18.13).

Distorting the Image

One of the things that drew me to this image was the idea of using the Liquify filter to create twirl effects within the tree trunks. I was going for a Van Gogh Starry Night effect within the trees. I tried to achieve this several times with less-than-spectacular results. In the end, I wound up covering over the distortion effects and making the result far more subdued than what I had originally envisioned.

After launching the Liquify dialog box, I started with the Warp tool, a large brush, and a light pressure of around 23. I painted across the tops of the tree branches, creating an all-over distortion effect. Then I chose the Twirl Clockwise tool and held down the Option key (Alt for

Windows) to swirl counterclockwise and began painting a twirl into several of the tree trunks. I ultimately erased most of the twirl effects with the Restore tool, although I allowed one twirl in the center foreground to remain.

Continuing my trend of adding an effect and then erasing it, I added another layer mask and began painting to conceal the Liquify distortions. The Liquify filter is experimental in nature and seductive in application. You tend to try many different ways, applying various effects and tools. The filter is also a lot of fun to use, so I tend to go overboard. Thus, I leave a safety net as I did here, go crazy with effects, and pare them back later. In this case, I restored most of the image to normal with the exception of the tree branches and a portion of a tree trunk on the right side of the image (see Figure 18.14).

Finishing Touches

Finishing the image was the hardest part of the process because I had to strike the right balance between the polarities I had set up. What was the proper color-to-monochrome ratio? How about the distortion-to-clarity balance? I punched things back and forth a bit until the image seemed to lock in. In the process, I decided that the branch on the lower left side of the central tree was a distraction and had to be eliminated. Rather than try to figure out which layer held the branch, I selected the entire image, chose Copy Merged, and then pasted the copy in as a separate layer. I then used the Clone Stamp tool to cover the branch with foliage and complete the effect (see Figure 18.15).

18

BIRCH TREES

1. Open the Birch Trees image.

2. Choose Image, Adjustments, Curves, select the black and white eyedropper icons, and set the white and black points.

3. Click the Adjustment Layer icon in the Layers palette and select Hue/Saturation from the pop-up list that appears.

4. Set the Saturation slider to −100 and the Lightness slider to −24. Click OK to create the adjustment layer that creates a monochrome image.

5. Click the Adjustment Layer icon in the Layers palette again and select Curves from the pop-up list that appears.

6. Set the Channel pop-up menu to RGB and add a curve point with the values Input=160, Output=227. Add a second point with the values Input=56, Output=56. Click OK to create the second adjustment layer.

7. Click the Adjustment Layer icon in the Layers palette a third time and select Curves from the pop-up list that appears.

8. Set the Channel pop-up menu to RGB and add a curve point with the values Input=108, Output=229. Click OK to create the third adjustment layer (the second Curves adjustment layer).

9. Choose Layer, Layer Mask, Hide All.

10. Select the Brush tool from the toolbox and specify a large feathered brush with white as the foreground color.

11. Click to paint the mask, increasing the visibility in the foliage at the bottom of the image.

12. Highlight the Background layer in the Layers palette and select Duplicate Layer from the palette menu.

13. Drag the duplicated layer to the top of the layer stack.

14. Choose Layer, Layer Mask, Reveal All.

15. Select the Brush tool from the toolbox and specify a large feathered brush with black as the foreground color.

16. Click and drag to paint the mask into the treetops area, creating a soft transition from color to monochrome.

17. Choose Select, All to select the entire image.

18. Chose Edit, Copy Merged to copy all the layers.

19. Choose Edit, Paste to paste the merged layers as a single layer back into the image.

20. Choose Filter, Liquify to launch the Liquify dialog box.

21. Select the Warp tool with a brush size of 309 pixels and a brush pressure of 23. Paint across the top of the trees to offset and blur the branches slightly.

22. Increase the brush pressure to 45 and make the brush size smaller (to 223 pixels). Paint across the tree trunks in the background to create a more extreme distortion than what you did in the branches.

23. Select the Twirl Clockwise tool, hold down the Option key (Alt for Windows) to twirl counterclockwise, and click on the foreground tree trunks to create a twirl distortion there.

2   4   6   8   11   27   34

24. Select the Turbulence tool and set the Turbulent Jitter slider to 70.

25. Paint the tree trunk in the right foreground to create a pinched distortion effect.

26. Lower the brush size to 130 and paint within the twirl distortion created in step 23 to create the white bubble effect.

27. Click OK to apply the Liquify effects.

28. Choose Layer, Layer Mask, Reveal All.

29. Select the Brush tool from the toolbox and specify a large feathered brush with black as the foreground color.

30. Experiment with the mask, adding and subtracting the distortions until you achieve the desired effect. When I worked with the layer mask, this experimentation resulted in a mask that revealed the distortion layer in the upper-left tree tops and in the tree trunk on the far right.

31. Choose Select, All and then chose Edit, Copy Merged to copy all visible layers. Chose Edit, Paste to paste a copy of the entire composite in a single layer.

32. Select the Clone Stamp tool and double-click the magnifying glass to zoom the image to 100%.

33. With the branch on the lower-left side of the center tree visible, hold down the Option key (the Alt key for Windows users) and click in the foliage to set the reference point for the tool.

34. Paint out the center branch with the Clone Stamp tool, changing the reference point as needed to achieve a seamless effect.

Image 19
On the Edge ©2002 Daniel Giordan

CHAPTER 19

WORKING WITH LIGHTING EFFECTS

On the Edge is an unsettling walk in the woods where things are not quite as they seem. It almost feels as if the landscape itself conspires against us. The image starts off as a black-and-white photo of pine trees after a recent snow. The snow on the branches creates stark staccato accents to the strong upward pull of the tree trunks.

Color also plays a key role. In addition to the green tint that pervades the left side, the edges of the trees and branches feature vibrant traces of orange, blue, and violet. An interesting thing about the color is that it is not confined to an edge or object. It flows through the image creating a subtle patchwork.

The lower-right corner is simplified and open, inviting us to enter the landscape and walk down the path that runs down the center of the image. As we move forward, however, we can't help but feel a bit unsettled by the left side of the frame. It's dark and murky, with ominous shadows that are almost palpable, especially when viewed in contrast with the bright, simplified path on the right. The trees seem to form a border between these two areas, although it wouldn't take much to accidentally slip from the safety of the path to the uncertainty of the shadows. In fact, as we walk into the image, the trees themselves seem to tilt towards the dark corner. The path narrows, the trees tilt, and there is perceived danger.

All this emotion adds a perceptible kinetic quality to the image; the trees seem to vibrate as they corral and coerce us. The branches are sharp, and the trees lean. The primal feeling is that of being outnumbered, surrounded, and accosted from all angles. Thankfully, *On the Edge* has given us a glimpse of hope because we do see a way out. We have to move quickly, though…the path is closing and something lurks.

●

INTRODUCTION TO LIGHTING EFFECTS

With the Lighting Effects filter, Adobe has taken a basic Photoshop function and wrapped it in a clever and engaging package that is fun to use and that produces impressive results. The filter operates on the premise that you can cast an external light on any RGB image, creating hot spots, shadows, and various other effects.

You can achieve similar results by creating an adjustment layer and masking it in the shape of a spotlight, but the concise arrangement of controls in the Lighting Controls interface delivers a world of nuance and finesse—all with real-time feedback.

Introduction to the Lighting Effects Interface

To launch the Lighting Effects filter, choose Filter, Render, Lighting Effects. The basic approach to working with Lighting Effects is to add light sources to the image and then set the characteristics for the light, surface, and ambient conditions. The Lighting Effects interface groups its controls around a stage area for previews, with control sliders within sections that focus on presets, lights, surface, and texture.

The Preview Window

The Preview window shows a thumbnail of the current layer in the image you're working on. Enable the Preview check box to simulate the light that will be created by the current control settings. To add a light to the group, drag the light bulb icon located under the Preview window into the stage. You can create and combine up to 16 different light sources, each with its own custom control set.

The stage depicts the light source as a dot with a ring around it; the ring defines the area that will be cast by the light. The stage also features a line that connects the dot with the ring; this line indicates the direction in which the light is pointing (in the case of a spotlight). Enable the Preview check box to simulate how the light will be cast; notice that the preview changes as you move the light or adjust its focus or position. To move the light, click and drag the center dot. To widen or narrow the spread of light, click and drag any of the four handles on the edge of the outer ring. To change the direction of the light, drag the handle at the end of the line to rotate the light's angle. ⌘+drag (Mac users) or Ctrl+drag (Windows users) to restrict the line length and, consequently, the light's position and intensity.

Light Style and Type

The Style section of the Lighting Effects dialog box is a place to save, store, and access preset lights. Photoshop starts you off with 16 presets you can choose from the Style pop-up menu. You can also save your own settings as presets by clicking the Save button and naming the current settings as desired. After you save your lighting settings, the new preset automatically appears in the Style pop-up menu. (Note that Lighting Effects presets are stored in the Lighting Styles folder, which you can access by following the path Plug-ins, Filters, Lighting Styles.) To remove a saved style, select it from the Styles pop-up menu and click the Delete button.

The Light Type section contains controls that determine the overall type and shape of the light. Select from Spotlight, Omni, or Directional lights and adjust the sliders for Intensity and Focus. The Spotlight option casts an elliptical beam of light and allows you to control the spread, angle, and light intensity. The Directional option simulates natural sunlight in that the light is flat and even. In the stage preview, Directional lights

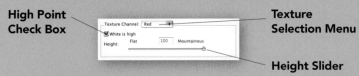

do not have an outer focus ring, although they do have the straight line that controls the closeness of the light (and therefore the light intensity). The Omni light option is supposed to simulate the stark, even light cast from a single light bulb. The big difference between the Omni and Directional options is that the light fades out outside the Omni light's focus ring and is not universally even and smooth.

After choosing the type of light, the next task is usually to choose a light color. The default is white, although you can click the Color Picker Swatch on the right side of this section to launch the default Color Picker and select a new color for the light you are casting. The Intensity slider controls the brightness of the effect, while the Focus slider dictates the width (the spread) of the light. (The Focus slider is available only with the Spotlight.) The entire effect specified for the active light can be activated or deactivated by toggling the On check box.

Light Properties

The Properties section of the Lighting Effects dialog box controls how the light you are defining will actually "reflect" off your image. The Gloss slider determines how the light reflects off the implied surface of the image. Options range from Matte to Glossy. The Material slider determines the visual dominance between the

light and the object. The Plastic end of the scale reflects more of the light's color; the Metallic end of the scale reflects the object's color. Increase the Exposure slider to brighten the effect. Decrease it to darken it. The Ambience slider combines the light effect you are defining with another ambient light source. Choose a value of 100 to use the created light source as the only light in the image (like a flashlight in a dark room); choose a value of −100 to remove the light source you are defining. To change the color of the ambient light, click the color swatch on the right side of this section and use the Color Picker that appears.

Adding Texture

The Texture Channel section of the Lighting Effects dialog box allows you to add any channel information as a texture to the effect of the light you are creating. You can use canvas or burlap textures and even the existing default RGB channels—although you should make sure that there is enough contrast to create a noticeable effect. After selecting the desired texture channel, adjust the Height slider to control the degree of the effect.

The Lighting Effects Dialog Box

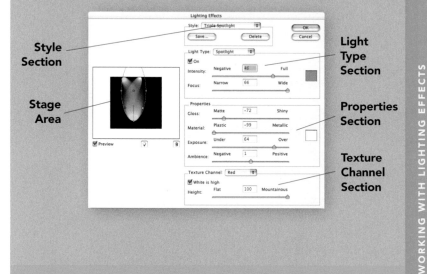

Style Section

Stage Area

Light Type Section

Properties Section

Texture Channel Section

The Light Type Section

Light Type Check Box

Focus Slider

Intensity Slider

Light Type pop-up menu

Color Picker Swatch

The Properties Section

Gloss Slider

Material Slider

Exposure Slider

Ambience Slider

Color Picker Swatch

The Texture Channel Section

High Point Check Box

Texture Selection Menu

Height Slider

CREATING EMBOSSED TEXT WITH LIGHTING EFFECTS

These steps explain how to create embossed text effects using the Lighting Effects filter.

1. With a target file open, select the Type tool and create black text as desired.

2. Choose Layer, Rasterize Type to turn the text into editable pixels.

3. Choose Flatten Image from the Layers palette menu to combine all the layers into a single image layer.

4. Choose Filter, Render, Lighting Effects to launch the Lighting Effects dialog box.

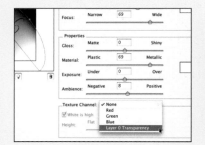

5. Select the *<layer name>* Transparency channel from the Texture Channel pop-up menu and set the Height slider to 100.

6. Add multiple spotlights in the Preview window. Click the center of each light and assign it a color. Click OK to apply the effect.

LIGHTING EFFECTS STRATEGIES

Lighting effects can transform any image by adding color, mood, and nuance. The Lighting Effects filter can also deliver a few clever tricks that are worth exploring. Here you'll learn how to create a complex emboss effect and how to make an object glow.

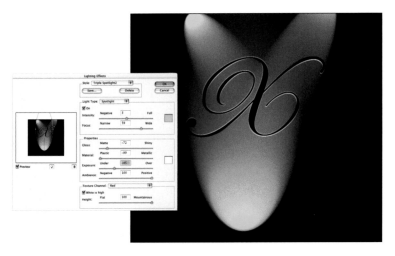

Figure 19.1
The Lighting Effects dialog box lets you create a multicolor text emboss effect using two directional lights.

Creating True Emboss Text Effects

Although you can create a simple emboss by adding the Emboss layer effect, the results of this approach are usually simple and generalized. A better solution is to use the Lighting Effects filter with a high-contrast black-and-white channel for texture. This embossing approach is especially effective for text effects, where any of the RGB channels can be used.

Figure 19.1 shows an embossed text effect that uses two light sources. This is an important point: The bevels in the emboss effect pick up the directional light, just as they would in real life. This multicolor embossing detail is not possible with a standard layer effect.

Making an Object Glow

Creating glowing effects is tricky because you really need just the

Figure 19.2

Glow effects can also be applied to landscapes.

Figure 19.3

The original seed pod image was a perfect choice for a glow effect.

Figure 19.4

A Lighting Effects spotlight adds a glow to the seed pod object.

Figure 19.5

The final glow effect, created with the Lighting Effects filter.

right type of image to pull off a convincing effect. To make an object glow, the object in your original image should be translucent, with good surface definition. Alternatively, you can add a glow in a landscape, which you can apply in a much more atmospheric way (see Figure 19.2).

The series of examples on this page shows a seed pod that was transformed into a glowing organic lantern. The starting image was

perfect for this: The light shone through the translucent surface, and the ribbing along the sides of the seed pod added definition (see Figure 19.3).

A single spotlight in the center of the pod created the initial glow effect. The challenge was to get a glow impression without darkening the rest of the image. To do this, I launched the Lighting Effects filter and dropped the Exposure slider to -46, which added

coloration and a slight brightness to the pod area. In addition, I raised the Ambient slider to 80, which lightened the surrounding image (see Figure 19.4).

To complete the image, I duplicated the background image, darkened it with the Curves dialog box settings, and added to the background with a layer mask. Finally, I added a Hue/Saturation adjustment layer, selecting the Colorize check box. I set the Hue slider to

44, the Saturation slider to 49, and the Lightness slider to +17. I applied this golden glow effect to the leaf and stem areas by using a layer mask to simulate cast lighting (see Figure 19.5).

Snow Pines

Three Leaves

BUILDING THE IMAGE: *ON THE EDGE*

Figure 19.6

The Three Leaves image is optimized.

Figure 19.7

The image is modified with the paint tools.

Figure 19.8

The canvas is enlarged to make room for the Snow Pines image.

Down Another Path

On the Edge presented me with a real dilemma. I could show you a simplified way to reconstruct it, but in the process, we would loose the sense of exploration that led to the result in the first place. I've decided to take you the long way around, showing you a few steps that never quite made it to the final design and describing some subtle nuances that may be hard to see in the thumbnail images of this book.

This design started as a variation of the *Trilogy* image that is described in Chapter 14, "Painting and Custom Brushes." I opened and optimized the Three Leaves image to begin the design (see Figure 19.6). From there, I painted the image with various colors and textures, creating the painterly effect shown in *Trilogy*. This process involved a series of adjustment layers, duplicate image layers, custom brushes, and blending modes. I used a variation of the *Trilogy* design as the point of departure for *On the Edge* (see Figure 19.7).

As I explored the *Trilogy* image, I brought in a number of other images as potential composite material. One of these images was the Snow Pines image that becomes central in *On the Edge.* Knowing that the Snow Pines image would require a square format, I chose Image, Canvas Size, and enlarged the canvas to 2000 pixels high.

When I enlarged the canvas, the foreground color swatch happened to be a dark mauve color, which found its way into the background of the base layer of the image (see Figure 19.8).

Adding the Trees

Next I pasted the Snow Pines image into the composite. After bringing it to the top of the layer stack, I started exploring various opacity and blending mode options. The exploration led me to the Linear Light blending mode, which kept the high contrast of the snow and the trees while adding a subtle color cast (see Figure 19.9). The color effect was a direct result of the colors present in the background image,

Figure 19.9

Snow Pines is added as the top layer, with the Linear Light blending mode.

Figure 19.10

A Hue/Saturation adjustment layer changes the mauve background to cool blue.

Figure 19.11

The Lighting Effects filter brightens the lower-right corner.

Figure 19.12

The final image.

especially the mauve color created when the canvas was enlarged.

Thus, by using the Linear Light blending mode, I modified the color in the lower layer and reflected those results in the main composite. Although a more direct approach would have been to modify the mauve color within its own layer, I decided instead to add a Hue/Saturation adjustment layer so that I could adjust the variables throughout the design process and continuously tweak things as the image progressed. I set the Hue/Saturation settings as follows: Hue +180, Saturation −19, and Lightness −24. These values created a cool blue cast that felt more consistent with the subject. After applying the adjustment layer, I

added a mask that retained the original color in the center leaf, which resulted in the orange glow in the center of the image.

In fact, I wanted to add some additional orange light along the right side of the center tree. To do this, I selected the background layer and painted a blue line down the edge of the tree trunk. Because of the Hue/Saturation adjustment layer, the blue was converted to a matching orange (see Figure 19.10).

Using Lighting Effects

Next I created a directional light that shone on the Snow Pines layer by using the Lighting Effects filter. I pulled a single spotlight into the Preview window and placed it outside the lower-right corner of the

image so that it pointed in towards the center. I set the Intensity slider to 46 and the Focus slider to 66. With all other sliders set to neutral, I applied the effect. The result created a high contrast graphic effect in the lower-right corner, while also providing a visual point of entry for the viewer in the lower-center (see Figure 19.11).

Final Touches

The final effect I added to the image may not even show up in the printed copy of this book, but it made a world of difference when I printed the image photographically. The black branches on the left side of the image were filling in a bit too much, forcing a loss of detail. To fix this, I created a new

layer, drew a rectangular selection on the left side, and filled it with a light version of the central orange color. I set this layer to the Overlay blending mode, which opened up the anti-aliased edges of the branches, creating a clean look and giving the image more detail (see Figure 19.12).

19

ON THE EDGE

1. Open the Three Leaves image.

2. Choose Image, Adjustments, Curves, select the white point eyedropper and set the white point. Add a Curve point with an Input value of 110 and an Output value of 95 and click OK to optimize the image.

3. Use the brush and paint tools to create a painterly effect in the image. This process is outlined in Chapter 14, "Painting and Custom Brushes."

4. Click the background color swatch; in the Color Picker that opens, set the RGB values to Red=88, Green=46, and Blue=66 to create a mauve color you'll use in step 5.

5. In anticipation of adding the Snow Pines image to the composite, choose Image, Canvas Size. Set the new height of the canvas to 2000 pixels and set the anchor point to the center top. Click OK to enlarge the canvas. Note that the color you created in step 4 fills the canvas you added.

6. Open the Snow Pines image and paste it into the composition as a separate layer.

7. Choose Linear Light from the Blending Modes menu in the Layers palette. This blending mode lets the color cast from the lower layers (the canvas) show through.

8. In the Layers palette, select the lowest layer in the stack (the layer that contains the mauve background color specified in step 4).

9. Click and hold the Add Adjustment Layer icon in the Layers palette and choose Hue/Saturation from the pop-up menu that appears.

10. Set the Hue/Saturation sliders as follows: Hue +180, Saturation −19, and Lightness −24. These values change the mauve to green (a better color for the image).

11. Choose Layer, Layer Mask, Reveal All.

12. Choose the Brush tool from the toolbox and specify a large feathered brush with black as the foreground color.

13. Click to paint the mask into the center-leaf area of the background, hiding the orange glow in the leaf.

14. In the Layers palette, select the background image.

15. Choose the Brush tool from the toolbox and specify a 45-pixel feathered brush with and blue as the foreground color.

16. Paint the right side of the center tree to create an orange highlight line in the final image (the highlight is orange and not blue because of the adjustment layer added in step 10).

17. In the Layers palette, select the Snow Pines layer.

18. Choose Filter, Render, Lighting Effects to launch the Lighting Effects filter.

19. Drag a single spotlight into the Preview window. Place it outside the lower-right corner of the image so that it points in toward the center.

20. Set the Intensity slider to 46 and the Focus slider to 66. Leave all the other sliders at their neutral midpoints and click OK.

2

3

5

7

13

20

25

INDEX

A

accessing blending modes, 194-195

active color areas, 139

Add a Mask icon, 101

Add Layer Mask icon, 172-175, 205

Add Layer Mask, Hide All command (Layer menu), 155, 179, 247

Add mode, 177

Add Noise dialog box, 99

Add Noise filter, 96-98, 178

additive color, 116

Adjustment Layer icon, 105

adjustment layers
    blending modes, 153
    clipping groups, 150
    fills, 152
    filters, 152
    layer masks, 152, 174
    layer sets, 149

Adjustments, Channel Mixer command (Image menu), 129

Adjustments, Color Balance command (Image menu), 126

Adjustments, Curves command (Image menu), 242

Adjustments, Desaturate command (Image menu), 242

Adjustments, Hue/Saturation command (Image menu), 129

Adjustments, Invert command (Image menu), 175

Adjustments, Selective Color command (Image menu), 126

Adobe Color Picker, 136-137

Align option, Clone Stamp tool, 184

All command (Select menu), 175

Amplitude value, 240-241

angle of brushes, 212, 215

angled gradient shape, 262

Apple Color Picker, 136-137

Apply Image command (Image menu), 176

Apply Image dialog box, 177

Arbitrary Map icon, 112

arbitrary mapping, 112

Arnheim, Rudolph (Entropy and Art), 109

Auto Color variable (global controls), 124

Auto Contrast variable (global controls), 124

Auto Levels variable (global controls), 124

B

B radio button, 137

backgrounds
    darkening, 105
    Extract filter, 162

base values, blending modes, 194

black-and-white images, coloring, 221

black points, 87
    setting, 89
        Curves dialog box, 88
        Levels dialog box, 88blend values, 194

blending modes, 194
    accessing, 194-195
    adjustment layers, 153
    attaching, 202
    base values, 194
    brush desaturation, 203

brush inversion effects, 203

brushes
        colorizing black-and-white images, 221
        hand color, 203

categories, 194-201

Clone Stamp tool, 186, 188

Darken, 247

Fade command, 202

Hard Light, 143, 204

layer masks, 177

layer sets, 149

Linear Dodge, 205

Luminosity, 205

operations, 194

Overlay, 246

Screen, 178

Soft Light, 178

Blending Modes menu, 202, 212

Bloat tool (Liquify filter), 272

Blur command (Filter menu), 266

Blur tool, 96, 98-99

Blur, Gaussian Blur command (Filter menu), 242

Blur, Motion Blur command (Filter menu), 179

blurring images, 99, 101

blurs

adding, 93

Gaussian Blur, 96, 98

Border command 52

breaking links, layer masks, 174

Brightness/Contrast variable (global controls), 124

browsing tile history in Pattern Maker, 253

brush inversion effects, 203

Brush Preset Picker, 212-214, 228

Brush Pressure option (Liquify filter), 272

Brush Shape Dynamics options (Brushes palette), 215

Brush tool, 60

brushes

Clone Stamp tool, 184, 187

colorizing black-and-white images, 221

customizing, 214-217

Invert brushes, creating, 203

from photos, 225

theories, 218-219

desaturation, 203

hand coloring, 203

History, 188

options, 212-217

painting

photos, 228-229

textured masks, 223

Pattern Stamp tool, 185

scatter brushes, 227

Brushes command (Window menu), 212

Burn tool, 62, 96-98, 100-102

darkening images, 99

buttons

Midtones, 126

Preview, 164

Randomize, 240

Shadows, 126

C

Cache Level value, 87

Calculations command, 176

categories, blending modes, 194, 196-201

chain icon, 174

channel color, 129

Channel drop-down menu (Extraction control option), 162

Channel Mixer, 129

Channel Mixer dialog box, 129

Channel Mixer variable (specialty controls), 125

Channel palette menu commands, Duplicate Channel, 129

Channel pop-up menu, 86

Channels, 129, 165

cloning, 186-187

creating, 163, 176

grayscale channels, 125

Liquify filter, 274-275

Channels palette, 129, 165, 175

check boxes

Colorize, 140, 154

Force Foreground, 163-165

Monochromatic, 129

Preview, 176

Smart Highlighting, 164, 166

Wrap Around, 239

cleaning images (Clone Stamp tool), 186

Cleanup tool, 162-164

clipping masks, 150

Clone Stamp tool, 184-188, 246

CMYK, 91, 117

color, 103. **See also** image color

additive, 116

brushes, 213, 216

channel color, 129

correcting with curves, 116-117

distribution of, 51

hand coloring, 203

gradients, 262

noise gradients, 264

hand coloring, 203

Lab color, 129

lighting effects, 285

previewing, 50

ranges, selecting 49

sample, 50

selecting, 50

single color, excluding, 141

subtractive, 116

variations, using Curves command, 110

Color Balance dialog box, 125-126

Color Balance slider, 126-127

Color Balance variable (component controls), 124-125

color bars, 138

Color Burn category (blending modes), 197

color casts, 126-127

Color Balance, 126-127

fluorescent lighting, 127

scans, 127

Selective Color, 126-127

Color category (blending modes), 201

Color Components category (blending modes), 194-196

color correcting with curves, 116-117

Color Dodge category (blending modes), 198

color models

CMYK, 91

Grayscale, 91

HSB, 91, 136-137

Lab color, 91

Web Color, 91

Color Picker, 61, 136-137

color range 54

Color Range command, 49-51

Color Range dialog box, 50

Color Range variable (isolation controls), 125

color ranges, 139

activating, 141

color selection options, 49

color spaces
 additive, 117
 subtractive, 117
color-based selections, 49
Colorize check box, 140, 154
 colorizing black-and-white
 images, 221
ColorSampler tool, 90
commands
 Border, 52
 Calculations, 176
 Channel palette menu,
 Duplicate Channel, 129
 Color Range, 49-50, 54
 Control menu, Pen
 Pressure, 225
 Curves, 110-111, 114, 166
 Edit menu
 Copy, 175
 Copy Merged, 189
 Define Brush, 225
 Define Pattern, 239
 Fade, 195, 202
 Fade Brush, 221
 Fade Diffuse Glow,
 237
 Fill, Pattern, 239
 Fills, 195
 Free Transform, 130,
 189, 246
 Master, 139
 Paste, 175, 179
 Transform, Flip
 Horizontal, 205
 Yellows, 139
 Expand and Contract, 52
 Feather, 52

File menu
 Distort, Shear, 239
 Save As, 242
Fill menu, Other, 162
Filter menu
 Distort, Displace,
 242
 Blur, 266
 Blur, Gaussian Blur,
 242
 Blur, Motion Blur,
 179
 Distort, Wave, 247
 Extract, 164, 166,
 188
 Pattern Maker, 256
 Render Lighting
 Effects, 284
 Sketch, 267
Free Transform, 72, 204
Grow 52
Hue/Saturation, 166
Image menu
 Adjustments,
 Channel Mixer,
 129
 Adjustments,
 Curves, 242
 Adjustments, Color
 Balance, 126
 Adjustments,
 Desaturate, 128,
 242
 Adjustments,
 Hue/Saturation,
 129
 Adjustments, Invert,
 175

Adjustments,
 Selective Color,
 126
 Apply Image, 176
 Copy Merged, 179
 Mode, Grayscale,
 128, 175
 Mode, Lab, 129
 Rotate Canvas, 189
Layer menu
 Add Layer Mask,
 Hide All, 155, 179,
 247
 All Layer Masks,
 Hide All, 155
 Duplicate Layer,
 179, 204
 Layer Set, 149
 Mask Enabled, 172
 Mask, Hide All, 179
 Merge Visible, 246
 Merged Linked, 205
 New Adjustment
 Layer, 189
 New Layer, 179
 New Set from
 Linked, 205
 Rasterize, 254
 Remove Layer
 Masks, 173
Liquify, 65
Modify, 52
Photoshop menu,
 Preferences, 136-137
Select menu
 All, 175
 Deselect, 239

Load Selection, 242
 Save Selection, 163
 Selection, 242
 Similar, 52
 Smooth, 52
 Transform, 72
 Window menu
 Brushes, 212
 Info, 126, 136
comparing pixels (blending
 modes), 194
component controls, 124-125
composite channels, 176
Constant slider, 129
contrast, increasing, 105
Control menu commands, Pen
 Pressure, 225
controls
 component controls,
 124-125
 Curves, 127
 Extraction controls,
 options, 162-163
 Fade controls, 237
 global controls, 124
 Hue/Saturation, 127
 isolation controls, 125
 specialty controls, 125
conversion options, grayscale
 optimization, 128-129
converting images to grayscale,
 175
Copy command (Edit menu),
 175
Copy Merged command
 Edit menu, 189
 Image menu, 179

copying Clone Stamp tool, 184-185

Count value, 87

creating

channels, 163, 176

custom Invert brushes, 203

displacement maps, 242

layer masks, 172-173

patterns, 252, 254-255

selections, 176

seamless tiles, 239

Crop tool, 104-105

curves, 110

adding points to, 112

basic techniques, 112-115

changing, 111

color correcting, 116-117

deep U, creating, 115

drawing, 112

inverted S, creating, 115

inverted straight, creating, 115

mid-plateau, creating, 114

S, creating, 113

Shapes, creating, 114-115

sharp rise, creating, 114

smoothing, 112

tonal direction, reversing, 111

tools, 111-113

U, creating, 115

Curves command, 110-111, 114, 166

Curves control, 127

Curves dialog box, 88, 110-113, 154-155, 189, 204, 244

Curves variable (global controls), 124

custom brushes (Clone Stamp tool), 187

custom Invert brushes, creating, 203

customizing

brushes, 214-217

from photos, 225

theories, 218-219

gradients, 262, 264

D

Darken blending mode, 247

Darken category (blending modes), 194, 196-197

darkening images, 99

Define Brush command (Edit menu), 225

Define Pattern command (Edit menu), 239

deleting layer masks, 173

Desaturate variable (global controls), 124

desaturations (brushes), 203

Deselect command (Select menu), 239

dialog boxes

Add Noise, 99

Apply Image, 177

Channel Mixer, 129

Color Balance, 125-126

Curves, 154-155, 189, 244

Diffuse Glow, 237

Displace, 242

Extract, 162, 165-166

Gaussian Blur, 99

Gradient Map, 265

Hue/Saturation, 129, 136-138, 140-141, 155

Preferences, 136-137

Replace Color, 125

Save, 163

Selective Color, 126

Shear, 239-240

Unsharp Mask, 99, 101

Variations, 129

Wave, 240, 247

Difference category (blending modes), 194, 196, 200

Diffuse Glow dialog box, 237

Diffuse Glow effect, 234, 237

Directional lighting effect option, 284

Displace dialog box, 242

Displace filter, 242

results chart, 244

displacement maps, 242, 244

Distort filters, 234

creating patterns with, 254-255

effects, 234

Distort, Displace command (Filter menu), 242

Distort, Shear command (Filter menu), 239

Distort, Wave command (Filter menu), 247

distorting textures, 236

Dodge tool, 62, 96, 98, 102

lightening images, 99

drawing tablets, 213

dual brush capabilities, 212, 216

Duplicate Channel command (Channel palette menu), 129

Duplicate Layer command (Layers palette menu), 179, 204

E

Edge Highlighter tool, 162, 164, 166

Edge Touchup tool, 162, 164

edges

darkening, 62

effects, 63

eliminating feathered effects, 63

equalizing, 63

inverting, 63

modifying, 164

posterizing, 63

rounding using Smooth command 52

sharpening, 96, 98

softening, 52, 62

Edit menu commands

Copy, 175

Define Brush, 225

Define Pattern, 239

Fade, 195, 202

Fade Brush, 221

Fade Diffuse Glow, 237

Fill, 195

Fill, Pattern, 239

Free Transform, 130, 189, 246

Master, 139

Paste, 175, 179

Reds, 141

Transform submenu, 74-75, 205

Yellows, 139

effects

Diffuse Glow, 234, 237

Distort filters, 234

Glass, 234, 236

monochrome, 104-105

Ocean Ripple, 234, 236

Pinch, 235, 238

Polar Coordinates, 235, 238

Ripple, 235-236

saturation/desaturation, 99

Shear, 235

Spherize, 238

swirl, 105

texture, 234, 236-237

textured fiber, 103

Twirl, 235, 238

warp, 235, 238

Wave, 235

wrap, 234

ZigZag, 238

embossed text, 286

Eraser tool, 162-164

Exclusion category (blending mode), 196, 200

Expand and Contract command 52

Extract command (Filter menu), 164-166, 188

Extract dialog box, 162, 165-166

Extract filter, 162-163

channels, 165

edges, modifying, 164

Force Foreground, 164

painting tools, 162

Smart Highlighting, 164

Extraction control, options, 162-163

Eyedropper tool, 165

Color Sampler tool, 90

F

Fade Brush command (Edit menu) 221

Fade command (Edit menu), 195, 202

Fade controls, 237

Fade Diffuse Glow command (Edit menu), 237

falloff color areas, 139

Feather command, 52

feathering selections, 53

fields, 177

File menu commands, Save As, 242

Fill command (Edit menu), 195

Fill menu commands, Other, 162

Fill tool, 162

Fill, Pattern command (Edit menu), 239

Fill/Adjustment Layer icon, 153

fills, adjustment layers, 152

Filter menu commands, 64-65

Blur, 266

Gaussian Blur, 242

Motion Blur, 179

Distort

Displace, 242

Shear, 239

Wave, 247

Extract, 164, 166, 188

Pattern Maker, 256

Render Lighting Effects, 284

Sketch, 267

filters. **See also** Distort filters; effects

Add Noise, 96, 98, 178

adjustment layers, 152

Displace, 235, 242

results chart, 244

editing Quickmasks, 64-65

Extract, 162-163

channels, 165

Force Foreground, 164

modifying edges, 164

painting tools, 162

Smart Highlighting, 164

Glass, 266

Lens Flare, 179

Lighting Effects, 204, 285, 288-289

strategies, 286-287

Liquify, 105, 272-273, 278-279

channels, 274-275

mesh, 276-277

Motion Blur, 64

Radial Blur, 64

Shear, 240

creating seamless tiles, 239

single-slider distortion filters, 238

Unsharp Mask, 96, 98

Wave, 240

flipping layers, 75, 205

fluorescent lighting, 127

Force Foreground, 163-165

Free Transform command (Edit menu), 72, 76, 130, 189, 246, 204

shortcuts, 77

Freeze masks (Liquify filter), 272-275

Fuzziness slider, 50

G

gamma lines, 110

Gaussian Blur, 96, 98

Gaussian Blur dialog box, 99

geometric tools, 49

Glass effect, 234, 236

Glass filter, 266

global controls, 124

Gradient Editor, 262-263

Gradient fill, 152

Gradient Map, 129

Gradient Map dialog box, 265

Gradient Map variable (specialty controls), 125

Gradient tool, 189

gradients, 266-267

color, 262

customizing, 264

gradient maps, 265

noise gradients, 264

shapes, 262

stops, 262-263

grayscale, 91

    grayscale channels, 125, 176

    grayscale masks, 173

    images, converting to, 175

    layer masks, 175

    optimizing

        conversion options, 128-129

        options to avoid, 128-129

Grow command 52

H

H radio button, 137

hand coloring, 203

Hand tool, 162, 272

Handles (Shear filter), 240

Hard Light blending mode, 143, 204

Hard Light category (blending modes), 199

hiding layer masks, 172

Highlight to Gray map, 244-245

highlights, 102

Highlights option (Color Balance dialog box), 126

Histogram window, 86-89

History brush, 188

HSB (Hue/Saturation/Brightness) color model, 91, 136-137

Hue category (blending modes), 201

Hue slider, 136, 138

Hue/Saturation dialog box, 140

Hue/Saturation, 136

    color bars, 138

    color ranges, 139

    HSB color model, 136-137

Hue/Saturation command, 166

Hue/Saturation control, 127

Hue/Saturation dialog box, 129, 136-138, 141, 155

Hue/Saturation option, 154

Hue/Saturation variable (component controls), 124-125

Hue/Saturation/Brightness. **See** HSB color model

I-J

icons

    Add Layer Mask, 172, 174-175, 205

    chain icon, 174

    Fill/Adjustment Layer, 153

    trash icon, 173

image color, 124

    component controls, 124-125

    global controls, 124

    isolation controls, 125

    specialty controls, 125

image focus, 96-102

    controlling with multiple layers, 101, 103

    sharpening, using Gaussian Blur, 96, 98

Image menu commands

    Adjustments

        Curves, 56, 106, 206, 242

        Invert, 175

        Channel Mixer, 129

        Color Balance, 126

        Desaturate, 128, 242

        Hue/Saturation, 129

        Selective Color, 126

    Apply Image, 176

    Copy Merged, 179

    Mode

        Grayscale, 128, 175

        Lab, 129

    Rotate Canvas, 189

images

    blurring, 99, 101

    darkening, 99

    grayscale images

        converting to, 175

        layer masks, 175

    lightening, 99

    optimizing, 86-87

    pasting, 55

    repairing, Clone Stamp tool, 186

    rotating, 75

    selecting, 92

    sharpening, 99-101

    smearing using Liquify command, 65

    target images, 176, 242

    tonal range, 86-87

    wrapping, 242

Impressionist option (Pattern Stamp tool), 185

Info command (Window menu), 126, 136

Info Palette, 87-91, 126, 136

    numeric values, 88

Invert brushes, creating custom, 203

Inverting layer masks, 175

Isolating single objects, 140

isolation controls, 125

Jitter Size option (brushes), 215

K-L

L channels, 129

Lab color, 91, 129

layer masks, 172

    adjustment layers, 152, 174

    blending modes, 177

    channels, 176

    creating, 172-173

    deleting, 173

    grayscale images, 175

    hiding, 172

    inverting, 175

    links, 174

    modifying, 173

    painting, 172-173

    positioning, 174

    selections, 176

    showing, 172

    target images, 176

    turning on/off, 172

Layer menu commands

    Layer Mask, Hide All, 155, 179, 247

    Layer Set, 149

    Mask, Hide All, 179

    New Adjustment Layer, 189

    Rasterize, 254

Layer Groups command (Layer palette menu), 149

layer groups, 149

layers, 103

    adjustment layers, 174

    applying perspective effects, 75

    cloning, 186-187

    creating patterns from, 252

    flipping, 75, 205

    resizing, 74

    rotating, 74-75

    scaling, 74

    skewing, 74

    transforming, 71-72, 74-77

Layers menu commands

    Duplicate Layer, 179, 204

    Mask Enabled, 172

    Merge Visible, 246

    Merged Linked, 205

    New Layer, 179

    New Group From Layers, 205

    Remove Layer Masks, 173

Layers palette, 172

    blending modes, accessing, 195

Lens Flare filter, 179

Level value, 87

Levels dialog box, 88

Levels variable (global controls), 124

Light Effect category (blending modes), 194

Light Effects category (blending modes), 196

Light slider, 136

Lighten category (blending modes), 194-198

lightening images, 99

lighting effects, 284, 288-289

    color, 285

    embossed text, 286

    fluorescent lighting, 127

    quality of light, 285

    saving preset effects, 284

    strategies, 286-287

    textures, 285

Lighting Effects command (Filter menu), 284

Lighting Effects filter, 204

Linear Burn category (blending modes), 197

Linear Dodge blending mode, 198, 205

linear gradient shape, 262

Linear Light category (blending mode), 200

links, layer masks, 174

Liquify command, 65

Liquify filter, 105, 272, 278-279

    channels, 274-275

    Freeze tool, 273

    mesh, 276-277

    Reconstruction control, 273

    viewing options, 273

Load Selection command (Select menu), 242

luminosity, 86

Luminosity blending mode, 201, 205

M

Magic Wand Options bar, toler-ance settings, 52

mapping, 112

maps

    displacement maps, 242, 244

    Gradient Map, 125, 129

    Highlight to Gray, 244-245

Marquee tool, 239, 246

Mask Enabled command (Layers menu), 172

mask thumbnails, 172

Mask, Hide All command (Layer menu), 179

masks. *See also* layer masks; Quickmasks

    grayscale masks, 173

    layer masks, adjustment layers, 152

    Liquify filter, 274-275

    textured masks, 223

Master command (Edit menu), 139

Merge Visible command (Layers palette menu), 246

Merged Linked command (Layers palette menu), 205

mesh (Liquify filter), 272, 276-277

midpoints (gradients), 263

Midtones button, 126

Mode menu (Options bar), 99

Mode, Grayscale command (Image menu), 128, 175

model. *See* color models

modes. *See also* blending modes

    Add mode, 177

    blending modes

        layer masks, 177

        Screen, 178

        Soft Light, 178

        Subtract mode, 177

Modify commands, 52

modifying

    edges, 164

    layer masks, 173

Monochromatic check box (Channel Mixer dialog box), 129

monochrome effects, creating, 104-105

Motion Blur effect, 266

Motion Blur filter, 64

Multiple category (blending modes), 197

N-O

New Adjustment Layer command (Image menu), 189

New Layer command (Layers palette menu), 179

New Group command (Layers palette menu), 205

noise gradients, 264

noise textures, adding, 105

numeric transform options, 76

Numerical Uncertainty image, 109

    creating, 118-120

objects

    scaling, 76

    single objects, isolating, 140

Ocean Ripple effect, 234, 236

Omni lighting effect option, 284

opacity, reducing, 104-105

Opacity option (Clone Stamp

tool), 186-188

Opacity slider, 212

optimizing
  grayscale, 128-129
  tonal range, 86-87, 91-92
    setting black points, 88

Options bar
  controls, 49, 72
  Mode menu, 99
  Pressure settings, 100

organic selections, 49

Other command (Fill menu), 162

Overlay category (blending modes), 199, 246

P

paintbrushes. *See* brushes

painting
  black-and-white images with color, 221
  blending modes, accessing, 195
  brush options, 212-215
  brushes, 214-217
    customizing brushes, 218-219
    scatter brushes, 227
  Clone Stamp tool, 184-185, 188
  layer masks, 172-173
  Pattern Stamp tool, 185
  photos, 228-229
  textured masks, 223

tools, 162

translucent masks, 61

palettes
  Channels, 129, 165, 175
  Info, 126, 136
  Layers palette, 172
    accessing blending modes, 195

Paste command (Edit menu), 175, 179

Pattern fill, 152

Pattern Maker, 252
  previews, 253

Pattern Maker command (Filter menu), 256

Pattern Stamp tool, 185

patterns
  creating, 252-255
  multiple layers, 252

Pen Pressure command (Control menu), 225

Percentile value, 87

photos
  customizing brushes, 225
  painting, 228-229

Photoshop menu commands, Preferences, 136-137

Pin Light category (blending mode), 200

Pinch effect, 235, 238

pixel values, 88-90
  comparing in different color models, 91
  measuring in different color models, 91
  tracking multiple areas, 90

pixels
  blend values, 194
  blending modes, 177
  comparing (blending modes), 194
  enhancing contrast between adjoining pixels, 96-98

points
  adding to curves, 112
  placing, 90

Polar Coordinates effect, 235, 238

Positioning layer masks, 174

Preferences dialog box, 136-137

Preferences, General command (Photoshop menu), 136-137

Pressure setting (Options bar), 100

Preview button, 164

Preview check box, 176

previewing
  lighting effects, 284
  patterns, 253

Puckered tool (Liquify filter), 272

Q

Quickmask Options dialog box, 61

Quickmask
  advanced features, 62
  applying effects
    patterns, 64
    sharpen/blur, 64
    textures, 64

twirl patterns, 65
wave patterns, 65

blurring, 62

changing densities of, 63

creating selections, 62

darkening, using Burn tool, 62

editing, 63

getting started, 60-61

lightening using Dodge tool, 62

options, 61

sharpening, 62

tools, 61

translucency, modifying with curves, 63

R

Radial Blur filter, 64

radial gradient shape, 262

Randomize button, 240

ranges
  color ranges, 139
    activating, 141
  tonal ranges, Color Balance dialog box, 126

Rasterize command (Layer menu), 254

Reconstruct tool (Liquify filter), 272-273

Reds command (Edit menu), 141

reference points
  activating, 72
  controlling placement of, 76

designating pixel locations, 72

designing, 72

reflected gradient shape, 262

Reflection tool (Liquify filter), 272

Remove Layer Masks (Layers menu), 173

repairing images, Clone Stamp tool, 186

Replace Color controls, 131

Replace Color dialog box, 125

Replace Color variable (isolation controls), 125

RGB, 86, 116

Ripple effect, 235-236

Rotate Canvas command (Image menu), 189

rotating layers, 74-75

S

S curves, creating, 113

S radio button, 137

Saturation category (blending modes), 201

Saturation radio button, 129

Saturation slider, 129, 136, 155

Saturation. *See* Hue/Saturation

Save As command (File menu), 242

Save dialog box, 163

Save Selection command (Select menu), 163, 242

saving

custom brushes, 217

Liquify filter meshes, 276-277

preset lighting effects, 284

Scale field, 177

scaling

objects, 76

proportionately, 76

scans, color casts, 127

scattering brush marks, 212, 215, 227

Screen blending mode, 178

Screen category (blending modes), 198

Screen Tip pop-up window, 76

seamless tiles, creating, 239

Select menu, 50

Select menu commands

All, 175

Deselect, 239

Load Selections, 242

Save Selection, 163

Selection, 242

selecting images, 92

selection modifiers, 53

selections

adding, 53

borders, isolating, 53

color-based, 49

combining, 52

complex, creating, 48

contrasting, 53

converting, paths to selections, 53

creating, 176

expanding, 53

feathering, 53

fine-tuning, 52

inverting, 53

isolating borders, 53

marquee tool, 239, 246

modifiers, 53

nudging, 53

organic, 49

selecting colors, 53

smoothing, 53

softening edges, 52

tools, 49

transforming, 72-77

Selective Color dialog box, 126

Selective Color slider, 126-127

Selective Color variable (global controls), 124

Setting white points, 88

shadows, 102

Shadows button, 126

Sharpen tool, 96, 98-100, 172

sharpening images, 99-101

sharpening effects, Threshold settings, 101

Shear dialog box, 239-240

Shear filter, 235, 240

seamless tiles, creating, 239

Shift Pixels tool (Liquify filter), 272

shortcuts

Alt+drag, 77

Command+drag, 77

Ctrl+Alt+drag, 77

Ctrl+Alt+Shift+drag, 77

Ctrl+drag, 77

to modify selections, 53

Option+Command+drag, 77

Option+Command+Shift+drag, 77

Option+drag, 77

Option+Shift+drag, 77

Shift+O, 99

Shift+R, 99

Shift+drag, 77

Shift+O, 99

Shift+R, 99

transform, 76-77

Show menu (Extraction control option), 163

showing layer masks, 172

Similar command, 52

single color, excluding, 141

single objects, isolating, 140

single-slider distortion filters. *See* warp effects

size of brushes, 212, 214

size/angle of brushes, 215

Sketch command (Filter menu), 267

skewing layers, 74

sliders

Color Balance, 126-127

Constant, 129

Hue, 136, 138

Light, 136

Saturation, 129, 136, 155

Selective Color, 126-127

Smart Highlighting, 164, 166

Smooth command, 52

Smoothing option (brushes), 217

Smudge tool, 172

Soft Light blending mode, 178

Soft Light category (blending modes), 199

Solid Color fill, 152

specialty controls, 125

Spherize effect, 235, 238

Sponge tool, 96, 98-99, 103

Spotlight lighting effect option, 284

stops (gradients), 262-263

Stretch To Fit option (Distort dialog box), 242

Stroke Adjustment options (brushes), 213-214, 228

Subtract mode, 177

subtractive color, 116

symmetry, 104-105

T

target images, 176, 242

text

creating patterns from, 254

embossed text, 286

Texture control (brushes), 216

texture effects, 234-237

textured masks, 223

textures

brushes, 217

distorting, 236

lighting, 285

wrapping, 242

Thaw tool (Liquify filter), 272

threshold, 96, 98

thumbnails, 172

tiles, Pattern Maker, 252-253

tolerance settings, 52

tonal range, 86-87

Color Balance dialog box, 126

evaluating, 90

histogram, 86-89

optimizing, 86-87, 91-92

setting black points, 88

tools for optimizing, 87

Toning tool, 172

tools

Bloat, 272

Blur, 96, 98-99

Burn, 62, 96, 98-99

Cleanup, 162, 164

Clone Stamp, 184-188, 246

Color Sampler, 90

Crop, 104-105

Curve, 111-113

Dodge, 62, 96, 98-99

Edge Highlighter, 162, 164, 166

Edge Touchup, 162, 164

Eraser, 162, 164

Eyedropper, 162, 165

Fill tool, 162

Freeze, 272

Freeze Area, 273

geometric 49

Gradient, 189

Hand, 162, 272

image focus, 99

Marquee, 239, 246

optimizing tonal range, 87

organic selections, 49

paint tools, accessing blending modes, 195

painting, 162

Pattern Stamp, 185

Puckered, 272

Reconstruct, 272-273

Reflection, 272

Selection, 49

Screen Tip pop-up window, 76

Sharpen, 96, 98-99, 172

Shift Pixels, 272

Smudge tool, 172

Sponge, 96, 98-99, 103

Thaw, 272

Toning, 172

Turbulence, 272

Twirl, 272

Warp, 272

Zoom, 162, 164, 272

Transform command, 72

transform options, 76-77

Transform, Flip Horizontal command (Edit menu), 205

Transformations, 71-72, 74-77

applying multiple, 76

reapplying, 74

translucent masks, painting, 61

Turbulence tool (Liquify filter), 272

Turbulent Jitter option (Liquify filter), 272

Twirl effect, 235, 238

Twirl tool (Liquify filter), 272

U-V

Undo command, shortcuts, 89

Unsharp Mark filter, 96, 98

Unsharp Mask dialog box, 99, 101

Use All Layers option (Clone Stamp tool), 185

values

Amplitude, 240-241

blend values, 194

displacement maps, 244

Wavelength, 240-241

Variations dialog box, 129

Variations variable (component controls), 124-125

Viewing Liquify tool options, 273

Vivid Light category (blending modes), 199

W-Z

warp effects, 235, 238

Warp tool (Liquify filter), 272

Wave dialog box, 240, 247

Wave effect, 235

Wave filter, 240

wave generators, 240

Wavelength value, 240-241

Web Color, 91

Wet Splatter effect (brushes), 223

White Matte option, 51

White points, 87

setting, 88-89

Window menu commands

Brushes, 212

Info, 126, 136

windows, Preview, 284

wrap effects, 234

wrapping, 242

Wrap Around check box, 239

Yellows command (Edit menu), 139

ZigZag effect, 238

Zoom tool, 162, 164, 272

For more images and information, log on to the official Web site:

www.artofphotoshop.com

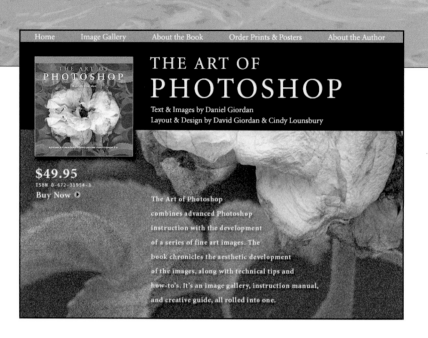

Learn More About *The Art of Photoshop*, Buy Limited Edition Prints from the Book, and Check Out Other Books and Images from Daniel Giordan

Learn About *The Art of Photoshop*

The official Web site for *The Art of Photoshop* provides full details on the book itself, including an introduction, table of contents, and sample chapter. You can also purchase additional copies of the book online, and email Daniel Giordan with questions or comments.

Purchase Limited Edition Prints

All of the images featured in *The Art of Photoshop* are available at the Web site in a series of limited edition prints. These images are printed using the Glicee process, are 100% archival, and come with a full certificate of authenticity. Each print is signed and numbered by the artist, and will not be reprinted once the edition has expired. View all available prints and learn more about the process at www.artofphotoshop.com/order/.

Author Interviews and Insights

Daniel Giordan shares his views and insights on Photoshop and digital imaging; you can access the Wacom.com Web site interview, as part of Giordan's inclusion in the Top Guns of Photoshop series. The site also features Giordan's favorite Photoshop tips and tricks for digital imaging and Web design.

See Exclusive Images and Designs

Many images developed during the course of *The Art of Photoshop* series never made it into the final book. All images that were auditioned for the book are included at the Web site, including variations, revisions, and new designs.

www.artofphotoshop.com

How to Use Photoshop CS

Daniel Giordan
ISBN: 0-7897-3039-1
$29.99 US • $45.99 CAN

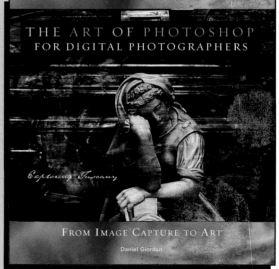

Special Edition Using Adobe Creative Suite 2

ISBN: 0-7897-3367-6
$49.99 US • $71.99 CAN

Art of Photoshop For Digital Photographers

Daniel Giordan
ISBN: 0-672-32713-9
$49.99 US • $71.99 CAN

What's on the CD-ROM

The CD-ROM included with *The Art of Photoshop* includes all of the author's source and final files, and the following third-party software for your use or evaluation:

- Adobe Photoshop CS tryout (Mac/Windows)
- Adobe Illustrator CS tryout (Mac/Windows)